50 World's Greatest Speeches

CLASSICS

Reprint 2022

FINGERPRINT! CLASSICS
An imprint of Prakash Books India Pvt. Ltd.

113/A, Darya Ganj,
New Delhi-110 002
Tel: (011) 2324 7062 – 65, Fax: (011) 2324 6975
Email: info@prakashbooks.com/sales@prakashbooks.com

facebook www.facebook.com/fingerprintpublishing
twitter www.twitter.com/FingerprintP
www.fingerprintpublishing.com

ISBN: 978 93 8814 453 7

Processed & printed in India

The human history is filled with great speeches that have immortalized its speakers, their inspiring and enlightening words reverberating in our minds even today. There have been memorable speeches that gave hope, made us laugh, made us think . . . and then there were groundbreaking speeches that started wars, appealed for peace, and changed the course of history.

The public-speaking podium has been a stage to debate social and political issues for centuries. Be it Queen Elizabeth proclaiming that her gender was not going to be her weakness, Susan B. Anthony railing against a society that had seen fit to jail her for voting in the national election, or Martin Luther King Jr. dreaming of a world where racial bias becomes a thing of the past.

Although oratory addressed issues like gender inequality, suffrage rights, and racial discrimination, it was—and still is—dominantly political. Who can forget Bal Gangadhar Tilak emotionally expressing that freedom was his birthright? Or Subhash Chandra Bose? Who was convinced that if India was to gain freedom, blood would inevitably be spilled. A tremendous portion of the rhetoric history is filled with the words of freedom fighters speaking against totalitarianism and colonial domination, and fuelling the citizens' patriotism.

Indeed, oratory and politics go hand-in-hand. Addresses delivered by presidents at their inauguration, retirement, and, more importantly, at times of turmoil, have been widely studied and often-quoted, most notably *The Gettysburg Address* by Abraham Lincoln—a mere two-minute long speech, and Lincoln wasn't even the main speaker of the event.

Imbued with the timeless wisdom of renowned personalities who were remarkable orators, their oratory intended to persuade, to prove a point, or sometimes just reflect, is our edition of fifty of the greatest speeches ever delivered, filled with the power of words which enthralled their audience then and rivet their readers even today.

CONTENTS

1

SPEECH TO THE TROOPS AT TILBURY

Queen Elizabeth I

Essex, U.K.

19 August 1588 (New Style)

England's troops had assembled at Tilbury, waiting for the Spanish Armada to strike and initiate the battle. After Queen Elizabeth gave this rousing speech, England emerged victorious. England's victory over the Spanish Armada is hailed as one of England's greatest military achievements.

In this speech, the Queen of England set a precedent for all female monarchs. Addressing her soldiers, she proclaimed that though people considered her gender to be her weakness, she was unmatched in her spirit and bravery.

My loving people:

We have been persuaded by some that are careful of our safety, to take heed how we commit ourselves to armed multitudes, for fear of treachery; but I assure you, I do not desire to live to distrust my faithful and loving people. Let tyrants fear. I have always so behaved myself that, under God, I have placed my chiefest strength and safeguard in the loyal hearts and goodwill of my subjects. And therefore I am come amongst you at this time, not as for my recreation or sport, but being resolved, in the midst and heat of the battle, to live or die amongst you all; to lay down, for my God, and for my kingdom, and for my people, my honour and my blood, even the dust.

I know I have but the body of a weak and feeble woman; but I have the heart of a king, and of a king of England too, and think foul scorn that Parma or Spain, or any prince of Europe, should dare to invade the borders of my realms: to which, rather than any dishonour should grow by me, I myself will take up arms, I myself will be your general, judge, and rewarder of every one of your virtues in the field.

I know already, by your forwardness, that you have deserved rewards and crowns; and we do assure you, on the word of a prince, they shall be duly paid you. In the mean my lieutenant general shall be in my stead, than whom never prince commanded a more noble and worthy subject; not doubting by your obedience to my general, by your concord in the camp, and by your valour in the field, we shall shortly have a famous victory over the enemies of my God, of my kingdom, and of my people.

Note: The term 'new style' has been used with the date of this speech to indicate that calendar convention during the 1580s had changed. The Julian calendar was used for the old style, according to which the date this speech was delivered on was 9th August. This calendar was discarded in Great Britain in favour of the Gregorian calendar in 1582.

2

I GO FROM A CORRUPTIBLE TO AN INCORRUPTIBLE CROWN

King Charles I

London, U.K.

30 January 1649

Charles I was a king unpopular among his Protestant citizens due to his marriage to the Catholic princess, Henrietta Maria. His tussle with the parliament for power led to the outbreak of the first English Civil War. Convicted of treason, he was termed a 'tyrant, traitor, and murderer,' and sentenced to death. The following speech was given by him immediately before his execution.

I shall be very little heard of anybody here, I shall therefore speak a word unto you here.

Indeed I could hold my peace very well, if I did not think that holding my peace would make some men think that I did submit to the guilt as well as to the punishment. But I think it is my duty to God first and to my country for to clear myself both as an honest man and a good King, and a good Christian.

I shall begin first with my innocence.

In truth I think it not very needful for me to insist long upon this, for all the world knows that I never did begin a War with the two Houses of Parliament. And I call God to witness, to whom I must shortly make an account, that I never did intend for to encroach upon their privileges. They began upon me, it is the Militia they began upon, they confessed that the Militia was mine, but they thought it fit for to have it from me. And, to be short, if anybody will look to the dates of Commissions, of their commissions and mine, and likewise to the Declarations, will see clearly that they began these unhappy troubles, not I. So that as the guilt of these enormous crimes that are laid against me I hope in God that God will clear me of it.

I will not, I am in charity. God forbid that I should lay it upon the two Houses of Parliament. There is no necessity of either. I hope that they are free of this guilt, for I do believe that ill instruments between them and me has been the chief cause of all this bloodshed; so that by way of speaking, as I find myself clear of this, I hope and pray God that they may too; yet for all this, God forbid that I should be so ill a Christian as not to say that God's Judgments are just upon me.

Many times He does pay justice by an unjust sentence, that is ordinary. I will only say this, that an unjust sentence that I suffered to take effect, is punished now by an unjust sentence upon me. That is, so far as I have said, to show you that I am an innocent man.

Now to show you that I am a good Christian; I hope there is [pointing to D. Juxon] a good man that will bear me witness that I have forgiven all the world, and even those in particular that have been the chief causers of my death. Who they are, God knows, I do not desire to know, God forgive them. But this is not all, my charity must go further.

I wish that they may repent, for indeed they have committed a great sin in that particular. I pray God, with St. Stephen, that this be not laid to their charge. Nay, not only so, but that they may take the right way to the peace of the kingdom, for my charity commands me not only to forgive particular men, but my charity commands me to endeavour to the last gasp the peace of the kingdom.

So, sirs, I do wish with all my soul, and I do hope there is some here [turning to some gentlemen that wrote] that will carry it further, that they may endeavour the peace of the kingdom.

Now, sirs, I must show you both how you are out of the way and will put you in a way.

First, you are out of the way, for certainly all the way you have ever had yet, as I could find by anything, is by way of conquest. Certainly this is an ill way, for Conquest, sirs, in my opinion, is never just, except that there be a good just cause, either for matter of wrong or just title. And then if you go beyond it, the first quarrel that you have to it, that makes it unjust at the end that was just at the first. But if it be only matter of conquest, there is a great robbery, as a pirate said to Alexander the Great, that he was the great robber, he was just a petty robber. And so, sirs, I do think the way that you are in, is much out of the way.

Now, sirs, to put you in the way, believe it, you will never do right, nor God will never prosper you, until you give God his due, the King his due (that is, my successors) and the people their due. I am as much for them as any of you.

You must give God his due by regulating rightly His church according to the Scripture, which is now out of order. For to set you in a way particularly, now I cannot, but only this. A national synod freely called, freely debating among themselves, must settle this, when that every opinion is freely and clearly heard.

For the King, indeed I will not, [then turning to a gentlemen that touched the axe, said, Hurt not the Axe, that may hurt me.]

For the King: the Laws of the land will clearly instruct you for that; therefore, because it concerns my own particular, I only give you a touch of it.

For the people, and truly I desire their liberty and freedom as much as anybody whomsoever. But I must tell you that their liberty and freedom consists in having of government. Those Laws by which their life and their goods may be most their own. It is not for having share in government, sirs. That is nothing pertaining to them. A subject and a sovereign are clean different things, and therefore until they do that, I mean, that you do put the people in that liberty as I say, certainly they will never enjoy themselves.

Sirs, it was for this that now I am come here. If I would have given way to an arbitrary way, for to have all laws changed according to the power of the sword, I needed not to have come here. And therefore I tell you, and I pray God it be not laid to your charge, that I am the martyr of the people.

In truth, sirs, I shall not hold you much longer, for I will only say thus to you. That in truth I could have desired some little time longer, because I would have put then that I have said in a little more order, and a little better digested than I have done. And, therefore, I hope that you will excuse me.

I have delivered my conscience. I pray God, that you do take those courses that are best for the good of the kingdom and your own salvation.

I thank you very heartily, my Lord, for that. I had almost forgotten it.

In truth, sirs, my conscience in religion, I think, is very well known to all the world. And therefore, I declare before you all that I die a Christian, according to the profession of the Church of England, as I found it left me by my father.

And this honest man I think will witness it. Sirs, excuse me for this same. I have a good Cause, and I have a gracious God. I will say no more. Take care that they do not put me to pain. And sir, this, and it please you. Take heed of the axe, pray, take heed of the axe.

I shall say but very short prayers, and when I thrust out my hands. I have a good cause, and a gracious God on my side. There is but one stage more. This stage is turbulent and troublesome; it is a short one. But you may consider that it will soon carry you from earth to heaven; and there you shall find a great deal of cordial, joy, and comfort.

I go from a corruptible, to an incorruptible Crown, where no disturbance can be, no disturbance in the world.

3

IN THE NAME OF GOD, GO

Oliver Cromwell

London, U.K.

20 April 1653

Tension between the parliament and Cromwell had started in the early months of 1653. A day before this speech was given, Cromwell had addressed the parliamentarians, requesting them to suspend their activities temporarily while preparations for an election to decide the representative were put into place. They had agreed. However, the next day, Cromwell learned much to his displeasure that the members of the parliament had continued a discussion for a new representative regardless of what he had requested.

Infuriated, Cromwell delivered this speech to the MPs of the Rump Parliament, informing them that their sitting was at an end.

It is high time for me to put an end to your sitting in this place, which you have dishonoured by your contempt of all virtue, and defiled by your practice of every vice; ye are a factious crew, and enemies to all good government; ye are a pack of mercenary wretches, and would like Esau sell your country for a mess of pottage, and like Judas betray your God for a few pieces of money.

Is there a single virtue now remaining amongst you? Is there one vice you do not possess? Ye have no more religion than my horse; gold is your God; which of you have not barter'd your conscience for bribes? Is there a man amongst you that has the least care for the good of the Commonwealth?

Ye sordid prostitutes have you not defil'd this sacred place, and turn'd the Lord's temple into a den of thieves, by your immoral principles and wicked practices? Ye are grown intolerably odious to the whole nation; you were deputed here by the people to get grievances redress'd, are yourselves gone! So! Take away that shining bauble there, and lock up the doors.

In the name of God, go!

4

GIVE ME LIBERTY OR GIVE ME DEATH

Patrick Henry

Richmond, Virginia, U.S.A.

23 March 1775

Fighting for independence for the state of Virginia, Henry addressed the people at the Virginia House of Burgesses. He espoused in his speech that Britain had been treating Virginians not as equals but as subordinates. It was time to fight to overthrow the British to gain their freedom, or die trying.

A month after this speech, the Battle of Lexington and Concord had started. This was the first event that marked the start of the Revolutionary War from 1775 to 1783.

No man thinks more highly than I do of the patriotism, as well as abilities, of the very worthy gentlemen who have just addressed the House. But different men often see the same subject in different lights; and, therefore, I hope that it will not be thought disrespectful to those gentlemen, if, entertaining as I do opinions of a character very opposite to theirs, I shall speak forth my sentiments freely and without reserve. This is no time for ceremony. The question before the House is one of awful moment to this country. For my own part I consider it as nothing less than a question of freedom or slavery; and in proportion to the magnitude of the subject ought to be the freedom of the debate. It is only in this way that we can hope to arrive at truth, and fulfil the great responsibility which we hold to God and our country. Should I keep back my opinions at such a time, through fear of giving offense, I should consider myself as guilty of treason towards my country, and of an act of disloyalty towards the majesty of heaven, which I revere above all earthly kings.

Mr. President, it is natural to man to indulge in the illusions of hope. We are apt to shut our eyes against a painful truth, and listen to the song of that siren, till she transforms us into beasts. Is this the part of wise men, engaged in a great and arduous struggle for liberty? Are we disposed to be of the number of those who, having eyes, see not, and having ears, hear not, the things which so nearly concern their temporal salvation? For my part, whatever anguish of spirit it may cost, I am willing to know the whole truth—to know the worst and to provide for it.

I have but one lamp by which my feet are guided; and that is the lamp of experience. I know of no way of judging of the future but by the past. And judging by the past, I wish to know what there has been in the conduct of the British ministry for the last ten years, to justify those hopes with which gentlemen have been pleased to solace themselves and the House.

Is it that insidious smile with which our petition has been lately received? Trust it not, sir; it will prove a snare to your feet. Suffer not yourselves to be betrayed with a kiss. Ask yourselves how this gracious reception of our petition comports with these warlike preparations which cover our waters and darken our land. Are fleets and armies necessary to a work of love and reconciliation? Have we shown ourselves so unwilling to be reconciled that force must be called in to win back our love? Let us not deceive ourselves, sir. These are the implements of war and subjugation—the last arguments to which kings resort. I ask gentlemen, sir, what means this martial array, if its purpose be not to force us to submission? Can gentlemen assign any other possible motives for it? Has Great Britain any enemy, in this quarter of the world, to call for all this accumulation of navies and armies?

No, sir, she has none. They are meant for us; they can be meant for no other. They are sent over to bind and rivet upon us those chains which the British ministry have been so long forging. And what have we to oppose to them? Shall we try argument? Sir, we have been trying that for the last ten years. Have we anything new to offer on the subject? Nothing.

We have held the subject up in every light of which it is capable; but it has been all in vain. Shall we resort to entreaty and humble supplication? What terms shall we find which have not been already exhausted? Let us not, I beseech you, sir, deceive ourselves longer.

Sir, we have done everything that could be done to avert the storm which is now coming on. We have petitioned; we have remonstrated; we have supplicated; we have prostrated ourselves before the throne, and have implored its interposition to arrest the tyrannical hands of the ministry and parliament.

Our petitions have been slighted; our remonstrances have produced additional violence and insult; our supplications have been disregarded; and we have been spurned, with contempt, from the foot of the throne. In vain, after these things, may we indulge the fond hope of peace and reconciliation. There is no longer any room for hope.

If we wish to be free—if we mean to preserve inviolate those inestimable privileges for which we have been so long contending—if we mean not basely to abandon the noble struggle in which we have been so long engaged, and which we have pledged ourselves never to abandon until the glorious object of our contest shall be obtained—we must fight! I repeat it, sir, we must fight! An appeal to arms and to the God of Hosts is all that is left us!

They tell us, sir, that we are weak; unable to cope with so formidable an adversary. But when shall we be stronger? Will it be the next week, or the next year? Will it be when we are totally disarmed, and when a British guard shall be stationed in every house? Shall we gather strength by irresolution and inaction? Shall we acquire the means of effectual resistance, by lying supinely on our backs, and hugging the delusive phantom of hope, until our enemies shall have bound us hand and foot?

Sir, we are not weak if we make a proper use of the means which the God of nature hath placed in our power. Three millions of people, armed in the holy cause of liberty, and in such a country as that which we possess, are invincible by any force which our enemy can send against us. Besides, sir, we shall not fight our battles alone. There is a just God who presides over the destinies of nations, and who will raise up friends to fight our battles for us.

The battle, sir, is not to the strong alone; it is to the vigilant, the active, the brave. Besides, sir, we have no election. If we were base enough to desire it, it is now too late to retire from the contest. There is no retreat but in submission and slavery! Our chains are forged! Their clanking may be heard on the plains of Boston! The war is inevitable—and let it come! I repeat it, sir, let it come!

It is in vain, sir, to extenuate the matter. Gentlemen may cry, Peace, Peace—but there is no peace. The war is actually begun! The next gale that sweeps from the north will bring to our ears the clash of resounding arms! Our brethren are already in the field! Why stand we here idle? What is it that gentlemen wish? What would they have? Is life so dear, or peace so sweet, as to be purchased at the price of chains and slavery? Forbid it, Almighty God! I know not what course others may take; but as for me, give me liberty or give me death!

Note: There is no written record of this speech. Henry's biographer, William Wirt, reconstructed the speech many years later from reminiscences of men who were present when it was delivered.

5

RESIGNATION SPEECH

George Washington
Annapolis, Maryland, U.S.A.
23 December 1783

The Continental Army had been formed in 1775, after the outbreak of the American Revolution. Washington was chosen to lead the army since he had prior military experience and had proved to be an able leader.

After the Treaty of Paris had been signed, George Washington addressed the congress and relinquished his post of commander-in-chief of the Continental Army, giving the military authority over to the civilians.

The great events on which my resignation depended having at length taken place; I have now the honour of offering my sincere Congratulations to Congress and of presenting myself before them to surrender into their hands the trust committed to me, and to claim the indulgence of retiring from the service of my country.

Happy in the confirmation of our Independence and Sovereignty, and pleased with the opportunity afforded the United

States of becoming a respectable Nation, I resign with satisfaction the Appointment I accepted with diffidence. A diffidence in my abilities to accomplish so arduous a task, which however was superseded by a confidence in the rectitude of our Cause, the support of the Supreme Power of the Union, and the patronage of Heaven.

The successful termination of the War has verified the most sanguine expectations, and my gratitude for the interposition of Providence, and the assistance I have received from my countrymen, increases with every review of the momentous contest.

While I repeat my obligations to the Army in general, I should do injustice to my own feelings not to acknowledge in this place the peculiar services and distinguished merits of the gentlemen who have been attached to my person during the war. It was impossible the choice of confidential officers to compose my family should have been more fortunate. Permit me, sir, to recommend in particular those, who have continued in service to the present moment, as worthy of the favourable notice and patronage of Congress.

I consider it an indispensable duty to close this last solemn act of my official life, by commending the interests of our dearest country to the protection of Almighty God, and those who have the superintendence of them, to his holy keeping.

Having now finished the work assigned me, I retire from the great theatre of action; and bidding an affectionate farewell to this August body under whose orders I have so long acted, I here offer my commission, and take my leave of all the employments of public life.

6

FIRST INAUGURAL SPEECH

George Washington

New York, U.S.A.

30 April 1789

George Washington delivered the very first inaugural address to a joint session of Congress at the Federal Hall on Wall Street. From then, it became a tradition and all the presidents after him have followed it.

This address garnered a favourable response from the Senate and the House, both of which promised to consider the president's recommendations.

Fellow citizens of the Senate and of the House of Representatives:

Among the vicissitudes incident to life no event could have filled me with greater anxieties than that of which the notification was transmitted by your order, and received on the fourteenth day of the present month. On the one hand, I was summoned by my Country, whose voice I can never hear but with veneration and love, from a retreat which I had chosen with the fondest predilection, and, in my flattering hopes, with an immutable decision, as the asylum of my declining years—a retreat which was rendered every day more necessary as well as more dear to me by the addition of habit to inclination, and of frequent interruptions in my health to the gradual waste committed on it by time. On the other hand, the magnitude and difficulty of the trust to which the voice of my country called me, being sufficient to awaken in the wisest and most experienced of her citizens a distrustful scrutiny into his qualifications, could not but overwhelm with despondence one who (inheriting inferior endowments from nature and unpractised in the duties of civil administration) ought to be peculiarly conscious of his own deficiencies. In this conflict of emotions all I dare aver is that it has been my faithful study to collect my duty from a just appreciation of every circumstance by which it might be affected. All I dare hope is that if, in executing this task, I have been too much swayed by a grateful remembrance of former instances, or by an affectionate sensibility to this transcendent proof of the confidence of my fellow citizens, and have thence too little consulted my incapacity as well as disinclination for the weighty and untried cares before me, my error will be palliated by the motives which mislead me, and its consequences be judged by my country with some share of the partiality in which they originated.

Such being the impressions under which I have, in obedience to the public summons, repaired to the present station, it would be peculiarly improper to omit in this first official act my fervent supplications to that Almighty Being who rules over the universe, who presides in the councils of nations, and whose providential aids can supply every human defect, that His benediction may consecrate to the liberties and happiness of the people of the United States a government instituted by themselves for these essential purposes, and may enable every instrument employed in its administration to execute with success the functions allotted to his charge. In tendering this homage to the Great Author of every public and private good, I assure myself that it expresses your sentiments not less than my own, nor those of my fellow citizens at large less than either. No people can be bound to acknowledge and adore the Invisible Hand which conducts the affairs of men more than those of the United States. Every step by which they have advanced to the character of an independent nation seems to have been distinguished by some token of providential agency; and in the important revolution just accomplished in the system of their united government the tranquil deliberations and voluntary consent of so many distinct communities from which the event has resulted cannot be compared with the means by which most governments have been established without some return of pious gratitude, along with an humble anticipation of the future blessings which the past seem to presage. These reflections, arising out of the present crisis, have forced themselves too strongly on my mind to be suppressed. You will join with me, I trust, in thinking that there are none under the influence of which the proceedings of a new and free government can more auspiciously commence.

By the article establishing the executive department it is made the duty of the president 'to recommend to your consideration such measures as he shall judge necessary and expedient.' The circumstances under which I now meet you will acquit me from entering into that subject further than to refer to the great constitutional charter under which you are assembled, and which, in defining your powers, designates the objects to which your attention is to be given. It will be more consistent with those circumstances, and far more congenial with the feelings which actuate me, to substitute, in place of a recommendation of particular measures, the tribute that is due to the talents, the rectitude, and the patriotism which adorn the characters selected to devise and adopt them. In these honourable qualifications I behold the surest pledges that as on one side no local prejudices or attachments, no separate views nor party animosities, will misdirect the comprehensive and equal eye which ought to watch over this great assemblage of communities and interests, so, on another, that the foundation of our national policy will be laid in the pure and immutable principles of private morality, and the pre-eminence of free government be exemplified by all the attributes which can win the affections of its citizens and command the respect of the world. I dwell on this prospect with every satisfaction which an ardent love for my country can inspire, since there is no truth more thoroughly established than that there exists in the economy and course of nature an indissoluble union between virtue and happiness; between duty and advantage; between the genuine maxims of an honest and magnanimous policy and the solid rewards of public prosperity and felicity; since we ought to be no less persuaded that the propitious smiles of Heaven can never be expected on a nation that disregards the eternal rules of order and right which Heaven itself has ordained; and since the preservation of the sacred fire of liberty and the destiny of the republican model of government are justly considered, perhaps, as deeply, as finally, staked on the experiment entrusted to the hands of the American people.

Besides the ordinary objects submitted to your care, it will remain with your judgment to decide how far an exercise of the occasional power delegated by the fifth article of the Constitution is rendered expedient at the present juncture by the nature of objections which have been urged against the system, or by the degree of in quietude which has given birth to them. Instead of undertaking particular recommendations on this subject, in which I could be guided by no lights derived from official opportunities, I shall again give way to my entire confidence in your discernment and pursuit of the public good; for I assure myself that whilst you carefully avoid every alteration which might endanger the benefits of an united and effective government, or which ought to await the future lessons of experience, a reverence for the characteristic rights of freemen and a regard for the public harmony will sufficiently influence your deliberations on the question how far the former can be impregnably fortified or the latter be safely and advantageously promoted. To the foregoing observations I have one to add, which will be most properly addressed to the House of Representatives. It concerns myself, and will therefore be as brief as possible. When I was first honoured with a call into the service of my country, then on the eve of an arduous struggle for its liberties, the light in which I contemplated my duty required that I should renounce every pecuniary compensation. From this resolution I have in no instance departed; and being still under the impressions which produced it, I must decline as inapplicable to myself any share in the personal emoluments which may be indispensably included in a permanent provision for the executive department, and must accordingly pray that the pecuniary estimates for the station in which I am placed may during my continuance in it be limited to such actual expenditures as the public good may be thought to require.

Having thus imparted to you my sentiments as they have been awakened by the occasion which brings us together, I shall take my present leave; but not without resorting once more to the benign Parent of the Human Race in humble supplication that, since He has been pleased to favour the American people with opportunities for deliberating in perfect tranquillity, and dispositions for deciding with unparalleled unanimity on a form of government for the security of their union and the advancement of their happiness, so His divine blessing may be equally conspicuous in the enlarged views, the temperate consultations, and the wise measures on which the success of this government must depend.

7

ON THE DEATH OF MARIE ANTOINETTE

Edmund Burke

France

16 October 1793

During Marie Antoinette's trial, she was charged with crimes ranging from incest to attempted genocide. Her response to these was: 'I was a queen, and you took away my crown; a wife, and you killed my husband; a mother, and you deprived me of my children. My blood alone remains: take it, but do not make me suffer long.'

The Queen of France was found guilty and executed on 16th October 1793.

In this speech, Burke lamented her passing and criticized the violence and inhumanity of the French Revolution.

It is now sixteen or seventeen years since I saw the Queen of France, then the Dauphiness, at Versailles; and surely never lighted on this orb, which she hardly seemed to touch, a more delightful vision. I saw her just above the horizon, decorating and cheering the elevated sphere she had just begun to move in, glittering like the morning star full of life and splendour and joy.

Oh, what a revolution! And what a heart must I have, to contemplate without emotion that elevation and that fall! Little did I dream, when she added titles of veneration to those of enthusiastic, distant, respectful love, that she should ever be obliged to carry the sharp antidote against disgrace concealed in that bosom; little did I dream that I should have lived to see such disasters fallen upon her, in a nation of gallant men, in a nation of men of honour, and of cavaliers! I thought ten thousand swords must have leaped from their scabbards, to avenge even a look that threatened her with insult.

But the age of chivalry is gone; that of sophisters, economists, and calculators has succeeded, and the glory of Europe is extinguished forever. Never, never more, shall we behold that generous loyalty to rank and sex, that proud submission, that dignified obedience, that subordination of the heart, which kept alive, even in servitude itself, the spirit of an exalted freedom! The unbought grace of life, the cheap defence of nations, the nurse of manly sentiment and heroic enterprise is gone. It is gone, that sensibility of principle, that chastity of honour, which felt a stain like a wound, which inspired courage whilst it mitigated ferocity, which ennobled whatever it touched, and under which vice itself lost half its evil, by losing all its grossness.

8

FAREWELL TO THE OLD GUARD

Napoleon Bonaparte

Fontainebleu, France

20 April 1814

Napoleon was an officer in the French Army who had then risen in his rank to become the Emperor of France. In 1812, he made a decision which triggered his downfall—he invaded Russia. With his army of 500,000 soldiers decimated to a mere 20,000, he was forced to acknowledge his defeat and retreat. Britain, Austria, Prussia, with Russia, then formed an alliance against Napoleon and captured him on 30th March 1814. Soon, he lost the support of his generals and was forced to abdicate the throne.

Napoleon delivered this speech to his remaining few soldiers of the Old Guard.

Soldiers of my Old Guard:

I bid you farewell. For twenty years I have constantly accompanied you on the road to honour and glory. In these latter times, as in the days of our prosperity, you have invariably been models of courage and fidelity. With men such as you our cause could not be lost; but the war would have been interminable; it would have been civil war, and that would have entailed deeper misfortunes on France.

I have sacrificed all of my interests to those of the country.

I go, but you, my friends, will continue to serve France. Her happiness was my only thought. It will still be the object of my wishes. Do not regret my fate; if I have consented to survive, it is to serve your glory. I intend to write the history of the great achievements we have performed together. Adieu, my friends. Would I could press you all to my heart.

9

JUSTICE FOR IRELAND

Daniel O'Connell

London, U.K.

4 February 1836

One of the most prominent Irish politicians, Daniel O'Connell was called the Liberator of Ireland by his supporters and King of Beggars by his enemies.

The nineteenth century was witnessing the might of the ever-expanding British empire. In 1801, Ireland was also engulfed by it, merging with Britain's other colonies.

O'Connell delivered the following speech before the House of Commons calling for just representation for the Irish, though he was never successful in re-establishing the Irish Parliament.

It appears to me impossible to suppose that the House will consider me presumptuous in wishing to be heard for a short time on this question, especially after the distinct manner in which I have been alluded to in the course of the debate. If I had no other excuse, that would be sufficient; but I do not want it; I have another and a better—the question is one in the highest degree interesting to the people of Ireland. It is, whether we mean to do justice to that country—whether we mean to continue the injustice which has been already done to it, or to hold out the hope that it will be treated in the same manner as England and Scotland. That is the question. We know what 'lip service' is; we do not want that. There are some men who will even declare that they are willing to refuse justice to Ireland; while there are others who, though they are ashamed to say so, are ready to consummate the iniquity, and they do so.

England never did do justice to Ireland—she never did. What we have got of it we have extorted from men opposed to us on principle—against which principle they have made us such concessions as we have obtained from them. The right honourable baronet opposite [Sir Robert Peel] says he does not distinctly understand what is meant by a principle. I believe him. He advocated religious exclusion on religious motives; he yielded that point at length, when we were strong enough to make it prudent for him to do so.

Here am I calling for justice to Ireland; but there is a coalition tonight—not a base unprincipled one—God forbid!—it is an extremely natural one; I mean that between the right honourable baronet and the noble lord the member for North Lancashire [Lord Stanley]. It is a natural coalition, and it is impromptu; for the noble lord informs us he had not even a notion of taking the part he has until the moment at which he seated himself where he now is. I know his candour; he told us it was a sudden inspiration which induced him to take part against Ireland. I believe it with the most potent faith, because I know that he requires no preparation for voting against the interests of the Irish people. [*Groans.*] I thank you for that groan—it is just of a piece with the rest. I regret much that I have been thrown upon arguing this particular question, because I should have liked to have dwelt upon the speech which has been so graciously delivered from the throne today—to have gone into its details, and to have pointed out the many great and beneficial alterations and amendments in our existing institutions which it hints at and recommends to the House. The speech of last year was full of reforms in words, and in words only; but this speech contains the great leading features of all the salutary reforms the country wants; and if they are worked out fairly and honestly in detail, I am convinced the country will require no further amelioration of its institutions, and that it will become the envy and admiration of the world. I, therefore, hail the speech with great satisfaction.

It has been observed that the object of a king's speech is to say as little in as many words as possible; but this speech contains more things than words—it contains those great principles which, adopted in practice, will be most salutary not only to the British Empire, but to the world. When speaking of our foreign policy, it rejoices in the cooperation between France and this country; but it abstains from conveying any ministerial approbation of alterations in the domestic laws of that country which aim at the suppression of public liberty, and the checking of public discussion, such as call for individual reprobation, and which I reprobate as much as anyone. I should like to know whether there is a statesman in the country who will get up in this House and avow his approval of such proceedings on the part of the French Government. I know it may be done out of the House amid the cheers of an assembly of friends; but the government have, in my opinion, wisely abstained from reprobating such measures in the speech, while they have properly exulted in such a union of the two countries as will contribute to the national independence and the public liberty of Europe.

Years are coming over me, but my heart is as young and as ready as ever in the service of my country, of which I glory in being the pensionary and the hired advocate. I stand in a situation in which no man ever stood yet—the faithful friend of my country—

its servant—its stave, if you will—I speak its sentiments by turns to you and to itself. I require no £20,000,000 on behalf of Ireland—I ask you only for justice: will you—can you—I will not say dare you refuse, because that would make you turn the other way. I implore you, as English gentlemen, to take this matter into consideration now, because you never had such an opportunity of conciliating. Experience makes fools wise; you are not fools, but you have yet to be convinced. I cannot forget the year 1825. We begged then as we would for a beggar's boon; we asked for emancipation by all that is sacred amongst us, and I remember how my speech and person were treated on the Treasury Bench, when I had no opportunity of reply. The other place turned us out and sent us back again, but we showed that justice was with us. The noble lord says the other place has declared the same sentiments with himself; but he could not use a worse argument. It is the very reason why we should acquiesce in the measure of reform, for we have no hope from that House—all our hopes are centred in this; and I am the living representative of those hopes. I have no other reason for adhering to the ministry than because they, the chosen representatives of the people of England, are anxiously determined to give the same measure of reform to Ireland as that which England has received. I have not fatigued myself, but the House, in coming forward upon this occasion. I may be laughed and sneered at by those who talk of my power; but what has created it but the injustice that has been done in Ireland? That is the end and the means of the magic, if you please—the groundwork of my influence in Ireland. If you refuse justice to that country, it is a melancholy consideration to me to think that you are adding substantially to that power and influence, while you are wounding my country to its very heart's core; weakening that throne, the monarch who sits upon which, you say you respect; severing that union which, you say, is bound together by the tightest links, and withholding that justice from

Ireland which she will not cease to seek till it is obtained; every man must admit that the course I am taking is the legitimate and proper course—I defy any man to say it is not. Condemn me elsewhere as much as you please, but this you must admit. You may taunt the ministry with having coalesced me, you may raise the vulgar cry of 'Irishman and Papist' against me, you may send out men called ministers of God to slander and calumniate me; they may assume whatever garb they please, but the question comes into this narrow compass. I demand, I respectfully insist: on equal justice for Ireland, on the same principle by which it has been administered to Scotland and England. I will not take less. Refuse me that if you can.

10

DECLARATION OF SENTIMENTS

Elizabeth Cady Stanton

Seneca Falls, New York, U.S.A.

19 July 1848

Stanton mostly drafted the Declaration of Sentiments and presented it at the Seneca Falls Women's Convention. This document advocates women's civil and suffrage rights.

As the name suggests, this document has been based on the Declaration of Independence. It was even presented in the same month that the Declaration of Independence had been adopted by the Congress.

Along with sixty-eight women, thirty-two men had also signed the Declaration of Sentiments. The men were mostly husbands or family members of the women present.

When, in the course of human events, it becomes necessary for one portion of the family of man to assume among the people of the earth a position different from that which they have hitherto occupied, but one to which the laws of nature and of nature's God entitle them, a decent respect to the opinions of mankind requires that they should declare the causes that impel them to such a course.

We hold these truths to be self-evident; that all men and women are created equal; that they are endowed by their Creator with certain inalienable rights; that among these are life, liberty, and the pursuit of happiness; that to secure these rights governments are instituted, deriving their just powers from the consent of the governed. Whenever any form of government becomes destructive of these ends, it is the right of those who suffer from it to refuse allegiance to it, and to insist upon the institution of a new government, laying its foundation on such principles, and organizing its powers in such form, as to them shall seem most likely to effect their safety and happiness. Prudence, indeed, will dictate that governments long established should not be changed for light and transient causes; and, accordingly, all experience hath shown that mankind are more disposed to suffer, while evils are sufferable, than to right themselves by abolishing the forms to which they were accustomed. But when a long train of abuses and usurpations, pursuing invariably the same object, evinces a design to reduce them under absolute despotism, it is their duty to throw off such government, and to provide new guards for their future security. Such has been the patient sufferance of the women under this government, and such is now the necessity which constrains them to demand the equal station to which they are entitled.

The history of mankind is a history of repeated injuries and usurpations on the part of man toward woman, having in direct object the establishment of an absolute tyranny over her. To prove this, let facts be submitted to a candid world. He has never permitted her to exercise her inalienable right to the elective franchise.

He has compelled her to submit to laws, in the formation of which she had no voice. He has withheld from her rights which are given to the most ignorant and degraded men—both natives and foreigners.

Having deprived her of this first right as a citizen, the elective franchise, thereby leaving her without representation in the halls of legislation, he has oppressed her on all sides.

He has made her, if married, in the eye of the law, civilly dead. He has taken from her all right in property, even to the wages she earns. He has made her morally, an irresponsible being, as she can commit many crimes with impunity, provided they be done in the presence of her husband. In the covenant of marriage, she is compelled to promise obedience to her husband, he becoming, to all intents and purposes, her master—the law giving him power to deprive her of her liberty, and to administer chastisement. He has so framed the laws of divorce, as to what shall be the proper causes of divorce, in case of separation, to whom the guardianship of the children shall be given; as to be wholly regardless of the happiness of the women—the law, in all cases, going upon a false supposition of the supremacy of man, and giving all power into his hands.

After depriving her of all rights as a married woman, if single and the owner of property, he has taxed her to support a government which recognizes her only when her property can be made profitable to it.

He has monopolized nearly all the profitable employments, and from those she is permitted to follow, she receives but a scanty remuneration. He closes against her all the avenues to wealth and distinction, which he considers most honourable to himself. As a teacher of theology, medicine, or law, she is not known. He has denied her the facilities for obtaining a thorough education—all colleges being closed against her.

He allows her in church, as well as State, but a subordinate position, claiming apostolic authority for her exclusion from the ministry, and, with some exceptions, from any public participation in the affairs of the church.

He has created a false public sentiment by giving to the world a different code of morals for men and women, by which moral delinquencies which exclude women from society, are not only tolerated but deemed of little account in man.

He has usurped the prerogative of Jehovah himself, claiming it as his right to assign for her a sphere of action, when that belongs to her conscience and her god. He has endeavoured, in every way that he could to destroy her confidence in her own powers, to lessen her self-respect, and to make her willing to lead a dependent and abject life.

Now, in view of this entire disfranchisement of one-half the people of this country, their social and religious degradation—in view of the unjust laws above mentioned, and because women do feel themselves aggrieved, oppressed, and fraudulently deprived of their most sacred rights, we insist that they have immediate admission to all the rights and privileges which belong to them as citizens of these United States.

In entering upon the great work before us, we anticipate no small amount of misconception, misrepresentation, and ridicule; but we shall use every instrumentality within our power to effect our object. We shall employ agents, circulate tracts, petition the state and national Legislatures, and endeavour to enlist the pulpit and the press in our behalf. We hope this Convention will be followed by a series of Conventions, embracing every part of the country.

Firmly relying upon the final triumph of the Right and the True, we do this day affix our signatures to this declaration.

11

THE HYPOCRISY OF AMERICAN SLAVERY

Frederick Douglass

Rochester, New York, U.S.A.

4 July 1852

Frederick Douglass had experienced the horrors of American slavery since he was a child. An illegitimate son of a white man and a black woman, he was separated from his mother and made to work on the southern plantations from a young age.

Douglass gave a speech denouncing slavery as the 'greatest sin and shame of America.' Right from the beginning of the speech, he voices the irony of calling a black man, a former slave, a man with virtually no freedom, to speak at the Fourth of July festivities.

Fellow citizens, pardon me, and allow me to ask, why am I called upon to speak here today? What have I or those I represent to do with your national independence? Are the great principles of political freedom and of natural justice, embodied in that Declaration of Independence, extended to us? And am I, therefore, called upon to bring our humble offering to the national altar, and to confess the benefits, and express devout gratitude for the blessings resulting from your independence to us?

Would to God, both for your sakes and ours, that an affirmative answer could be truthfully returned to these questions. Then would my task be light, and my burden easy and delightful. For who is there so cold that a nation's sympathy could not warm him? Who so obdurate and dead to the claims of gratitude, that would not thankfully acknowledge such priceless benefits? Who so stolid and selfish that would not give his voice to swell the hallelujahs of a nation's jubilee, when the chains of servitude had been torn from his limbs? I am not that man. In a case like that, the dumb might eloquently speak, and the 'lame man leap as an hart.'

But such is not the state of the case. I say it with a sad sense of disparity between us. I am not included within the pale of this glorious anniversary! Your high independence only reveals the immeasurable distance between us. The blessings in which you this day rejoice are not enjoyed in common. The rich inheritance of justice, liberty, prosperity, and independence bequeathed by your fathers is shared by you, not by me. The sunlight that brought life and healing to you has brought stripes and death to me. This Fourth of July is yours, not mine. You may rejoice, I must mourn. To drag a man in fetters into the grand illuminated temple of liberty, and call upon him to join you in joyous anthems, were inhuman mockery and sacrilegious irony. Do you mean, citizens, to mock me, by asking me to speak today? If so, there is a parallel to your conduct. And let me warn you, that it is dangerous to copy the example of a nation (Babylon) whose crimes, towering up to heaven, were thrown down by the breath of the Almighty, burying that nation in irrecoverable ruin.

Fellow citizens, above your national, tumultuous joy, I hear the mournful wail of millions, whose chains, heavy and grievous yesterday, are today rendered more intolerable by the jubilant shouts that reach them. If I do forget, if I do not remember those bleeding children of sorrow this day, 'may my right hand forget her cunning, and may my tongue cleave to the roof of my mouth!'

To forget them, to pass lightly over their wrongs and to chime in with the popular theme would be treason most scandalous and shocking, and would make me a reproach before God and the world.

My subject, then, fellow citizens, is 'American Slavery.' I shall see this day and its popular characteristics from the slave's point of view. Standing here, identified with the American bondman, making his wrongs mine, I do not hesitate to declare, with all my soul, that the character and conduct of this nation never looked blacker to me than on this Fourth of July.

Whether we turn to the declarations of the past, or to the professions of the present, the conduct of the nation seems equally hideous and revolting. America is false to the past, false to the present, and solemnly binds herself to be false to the future. Standing with God and the crushed and bleeding slave on this occasion, I will, in the name of humanity, which is outraged, in the name of liberty, which is fettered, in the name of the Constitution and the Bible, which are disregarded and trampled upon, dare to call in question and to denounce, with all the emphasis I can command, everything that serves to perpetuate slavery—the great sin and shame of America! 'I will not equivocate—I will not excuse.' I will use the severest language I can command, and yet not one word shall escape me that any man, whose judgment is not blinded by prejudice, or who is not at heart a slave-holder, shall not confess to be right and just.

But I fancy I hear some of my audience say it is just in this circumstance that you and your brother Abolitionists fail to make a favourable impression on the public mind. Would you argue more and denounce less, would you persuade more and rebuke less, your cause would be much more likely to succeed. But, I submit, where all is plain there is nothing to be argued. What point in the anti-slavery creed would you have me argue? On what branch of the subject do the people of this country need light? Must I undertake to prove that the slave is a man? That point is conceded already. Nobody doubts it. The slave-holders themselves acknowledge it in the enactment of laws for their government. They acknowledge it when they punish disobedience on the part of the slave. There are seventy-two crimes in the State of Virginia, which, if committed by a black man (no matter how ignorant he be), subject him to the punishment of death; while only two of these same crimes will subject a white man to like punishment.

What is this but the acknowledgment that the slave is a moral, intellectual, and responsible being? The manhood of the slave is conceded. It is admitted in the fact that Southern statute books are covered with enactments, forbidding, under severe fines and penalties, the teaching of the slave to read and write. When you can point to any such laws in reference to the beasts of the field, then I may consent to argue the manhood of the slave. When the dogs in your streets, when the fowls of the air, when the cattle on your hills, when the fish of the sea, and the reptiles that crawl, shall be unable to distinguish the slave from a brute, then I will argue with you that the slave is a man!

For the present it is enough to affirm the equal manhood of the Negro race. Is it not astonishing that, while we are plowing, planting, and reaping, using all kinds of mechanical tools, erecting houses, constructing bridges, building ships, working in metals of brass, iron, copper, silver, and gold; that while we are reading, writing, and ciphering, acting as clerks, merchants, and secretaries, having among us lawyers, doctors, ministers, poets, authors, editors, orators, and teachers; that we are engaged in all the enterprises common to other men—digging gold in California, capturing the whale in the Pacific, feeding sheep and cattle on the hillside, living, moving, acting, thinking, planning, living in families as husbands, wives, and children, and above all, confessing and worshipping the Christian God, and looking hopefully for life and immortality beyond the grave—we are called upon to prove that we are men?

Would you have me argue that man is entitled to liberty? That he is the rightful owner of his own body? You have already declared it. Must I argue the wrongfulness of slavery? Is that a question for republicans? Is it to be settled by the rules of logic and argumentation, as a matter beset with great difficulty, involving a doubtful application of the principle of justice, hard to understand? How should I look today in the presence of Americans, dividing and subdividing a discourse, to show that men have a natural right to freedom, speaking of it relatively and positively, negatively and affirmatively? To do so would be to make myself ridiculous, and to offer an insult to your understanding. There is not a man beneath the canopy of heaven who does not know that slavery is wrong for him.

What am I to argue that it is wrong to make men brutes, to rob them of their liberty, to work them without wages, to keep them ignorant of their relations to their fellow men, to beat them with sticks, to flay their flesh with the lash, to load their limbs with irons, to hunt them with dogs, to sell them at auction, to sunder their families, to knock out their teeth, to burn their flesh, to starve them into obedience and submission to their masters? Must I argue that a system thus marked with blood and stained with pollution is wrong? No—I will not. I have better employment for my time and strength than such arguments would imply.

What, then, remains to be argued? Is it that slavery is not divine; that God did not establish it; that our doctors of divinity are mistaken? There is blasphemy in the thought. That which is inhuman cannot be divine. Who can reason on such a proposition? They that can, may—I cannot. The time for such argument is past.

At a time like this, scorching irony, not convincing argument, is needed. Oh! had I the ability, and could I reach the nation's ear, I would today pour out a fiery stream of biting ridicule, blasting reproach, withering sarcasm, and stern rebuke. For it is not light that is needed, but fire; it is not the gentle shower, but thunder. We need the storm, the whirlwind, and the earthquake. The feeling of the nation must be quickened; the conscience of the nation must be roused; the propriety of the nation must be startled; the hypocrisy of the nation must be exposed; and its crimes against God and man must be denounced.

What to the American slave is your Fourth of July? I answer, a day that reveals to him more than all other days of the year, the gross injustice and cruelty to which he is the constant victim. To him your celebration is a sham; your boasted liberty an unholy license; your national greatness, swelling vanity; your sounds of rejoicing are empty and heartless; your shouts of liberty and equality, hollow mock; your prayers and hymns, your sermons and thanksgivings, with all your religious parade and solemnity, are to him mere bombast, fraud, deception, impiety, and hypocrisy—a thin veil to cover up crimes which would disgrace a nation of savages. There is not a nation of the earth guilty of practices more shocking and bloody than are the people of these United States at this very hour.

Go search where you will, roam through all the monarchies and despotisms of the Old World, travel through South America, search out every abuse and when you have found the last, lay your facts by the side of the everyday practices of this nation, and you will say with me that, for revolting barbarity and shameless hypocrisy, America reigns without a rival.

12

THE GETTYSBURG ADDRESS

Abraham Lincoln

Gettysburg, Pennsylvania, U.S.A.

19 November 1863

Lincoln delivered this speech to the American public four months after the Battle of Gettysburg during the Civil War. This battle had been a turning point for America as the Union army had emerged victorious over the Confederate forces.

This speech honours the soldiers slain in the battle at Gettysburg and addresses the importance of national unity to better combat the ongoing Civil War.

Four score and seven years ago our fathers brought forth on this continent, a new nation, conceived in liberty, and dedicated to the proposition that all men are created equal.

Now we are engaged in a great civil war, testing whether that nation, or any nation so conceived and so dedicated, can long endure. We are met on a great battlefield of that war. We have come to dedicate a portion of that field, as a final resting place for those who here gave their lives that that nation might live. It is altogether fitting and proper that we should do this.

But in a larger sense, we cannot dedicate—we cannot consecrate—we cannot hallow—this ground. The brave men, living and dead, who struggled here, have consecrated it, far above our poor power to add or detract. The world will little note, nor long remember, what we say here, but it can never forget what they did here. It is for us the living, rather, to be dedicated here to the unfinished work which they who fought here have thus far so nobly advanced. It is rather for us to be here dedicated to the great task remaining before us—that from these honoured dead we take increased devotion to that cause for which they gave the last full measure of devotion—that we here highly resolve that these dead shall not have died in vain—that this nation, under God, shall have a new birth of freedom—and that government of the people, by the people, for the people, shall not perish from the earth.

Note: The main speaker of the day had been Edward Everett, not Lincoln. Everett delivered his two-hour-long speech but Lincoln's two-minute speech is more famous than his.

13

TRIBUTE TO THE DOG

George Graham Vest

Missouri, U.S.A.

18 October 1869

It is often said that a dog is a man's best friend. This is one of the statements George Graham Vest made in the court while arguing the case for his client who had sued a man for killing his dog.

George Graham Vest was a lawyer before he entered politics. He was known for his debating skills, and he utilized them and won the case, concluding with the following summation.

Gentlemen of the Jury:

The best friend a man has in the world may turn against him and become his enemy. His son or daughter that he has reared with loving care may prove ungrateful. Those who are nearest and dearest to us, those whom we trust with our happiness and our good name may become traitors to their faith. The money that a man has, he may lose. It flies away from him, perhaps when he needs it most. A man's reputation may be sacrificed in a moment of ill-considered action. The people who are prone to fall on their knees to do us honour when success is with us, may be the first to throw the stone of malice when failure settles its cloud upon our heads.

The one absolutely unselfish friend that man can have in this selfish world, the one that never deserts him, the one that never proves ungrateful or treacherous is his dog. A man's dog stands by him in prosperity and in poverty, in health and in sickness. He will sleep on the cold ground, where the wintry winds blow and the snow drives fiercely, if only he may be near his master's side. He will kiss the hand that has no food to offer. He will lick the wounds and sores that come in encounters with the roughness of the world. He guards the sleep of his pauper master as if he were a prince. When all other friends desert, he remains. When riches take wings, and reputation falls to pieces, he is as constant in his love as the sun in its journey through the heavens.

If fortune drives the master forth, an outcast in the world, friendless and homeless, the faithful dog asks no higher privilege than that of accompanying him, to guard him against danger, to fight against his enemies. And when the last scene of all comes, and death takes his master in its embrace and his body is laid away in the cold ground, no matter if all other friends pursue their way, there by the graveside will the noble dog be found, his head between his paws, his eyes sad, but open in alert watchfulness, faithful and true even in death.

14

ARE WOMEN PERSONS

Susan B. Anthony

Monroe County, New York, U.S.A.

1873

In the election of 1872, Susan B. Anthony decided to vote. She did this along with fifteen other women but was the only one on trial. In the court, she declared to her audience that all she had done was exercise her right to vote, and that was no offense. She quotes the American Constitution, emphasizing the equality inherent in its words.

This speech was delivered close to the passing of the Fourteenth Amendment, giving black men the right to vote.

Friends and fellow citizens:

I stand before you tonight under indictment for the alleged crime of having voted at the last presidential election, without having a lawful right to vote. It shall be my work this evening to prove to you that in thus voting, I not only committed no crime, but, instead, simply exercised my citizen's rights, guaranteed to me and all United States citizens by the National Constitution, beyond the power of any state to deny.

The preamble of the Federal Constitution says:

'We, the people of the United States, in order to form a more perfect union, establish justice, insure domestic tranquillity, provide for the common defence, promote the general welfare, and secure the blessings of liberty to ourselves and our posterity, do ordain and establish this Constitution for the United States of America.'

It was we, the people; not we, the white male citizens; nor yet we, the male citizens; but we, the whole people, who formed the Union. And we formed it, not to give the blessings of liberty, but to secure them; not to the half of ourselves and the half of our posterity, but to the whole people—women as well as men. And it is a downright mockery to talk to women of their enjoyment of the blessings of liberty while they are denied the use of the only means of securing them provided by this democratic-republican government—the ballot.

For any state to make sex a qualification that must ever result in the disfranchisement of one entire half of the people, is to pass a bill of attainder, or, an ex post facto law, and is therefore a violation of the supreme law of the land. By it the blessings of liberty are forever withheld from women and their female posterity.

To them this government has no just powers derived from the consent of the governed. To them this government is not a democracy. It is not a republic. It is an odious aristocracy; a hateful oligarchy of sex; the most hateful aristocracy ever established on the face of the globe; an oligarchy of wealth, where the rich govern the poor. An oligarchy of learning, where the educated govern the ignorant, or even an oligarchy of race, where the Saxon rules the African, might be endured; but this oligarchy of sex, which makes father, brothers, husband, sons, the oligarchs over the mother and sisters, the wife and daughters, of every household which ordains all men sovereigns, all women subjects, carries dissension, discord, and rebellion into every home of the nation.

Webster, Worcester, and Bouvier all define a citizen to be a person in the United States, entitled to vote and hold office.

The only question left to be settled now is: Are women persons? And I hardly believe any of our opponents will have the hardihood to say they are not. Being persons, then, women are citizens; and no state has a right to make any law, or to enforce any old law, that shall abridge their privileges or immunities. Hence, every discrimination against women in the constitutions and laws of the several states is today null and void, precisely as is every one against Negroes.

Note: Susan B. Anthony had prepared another speech to discuss women's suffrage but the judge had not let her testify, claiming that she was an incompetent witness.

15

TONIC FOR THE HINDU MIND

Swami Vivekananda

Chicago, U.S.A.

11 September 1893

The Parliament of Religions was held from 11th to 27th September 1893. It was conducted to have a dialogue with people from diverse religious backgrounds.

Swami Vivekananda played an important role in introducing the philosophy of Hinduism to the world—which he did through his enthralling speech at the Parliament of Religions. He spoke on Hinduism being a harmonious and tolerant religion.

An article in The New York Herald *claimed Swami Vivekananda to be the greatest speaker in the Parliament of Religions, even though it was the first time that he had given a speech in public.*

Sisters and brothers of America, it fills my heart with joy unspeakable to respond to the warm and cordial welcome which you have given us. I thank you in the name of the most ancient order of monks in the world; I thank you in the name of the mother of religions;

and I thank you in the name of the millions and millions of Hindu people of all classes and sects. My thanks, also, to some of the speakers on this platform who, referring to the delegates from the Orient, have told you that these men from far-off nations may well claim the honour of bearing to the different lands, the idea of toleration but we accept all religions a true. I am proud to belong to a religion which has taught the world both tolerance and universal acceptance. We believe not only in universal toleration, but we accept all religions as true. I belong to a religion into whose sacred language, the Sanskrit, the word exclusion is untranslatable. I am proud to belong to a nation which has sheltered the persecuted and the refugees of all religions and all nations of the earth. I am proud to tell you that we have gathered in our bosom the purest remnant of the Israelites, a remnant who came to southern India and took refuge with us in the very year in which their holy temple was shattered to pieces by Roman tyranny. I am proud to belong to the religion which has sheltered and is still fostering the remains of the grand Zoroastrian nation. I will quote to you, brethren, a few lines from a hymn which I have recited from my earliest boyhood and which is repeated every day by millions of human beings: As the different, streams have their sources in different places and mingle their waters in the sea, Lord, so the different paths which men take through different tendencies, various though they appear, crooked or straight, all load to Thee.

The present convention, which is one of the most august assemblies ever held, is in itself a vindication, a declaration to the world, of the wonderful doctrine preached in the Bhagvad Gita: 'Whosoever comes to Me, through whatsoever form, I reach him; all men are struggling through paths which in the end lead to me.' Sectarianism, bigotry, and its horrible descendant, fanaticism, have long possessed this beautiful earth. They have filled the earth with violence, drenched it with human blood, destroyed civilizations, and sent whole nations to despair. Had it not been for these horrible demons, human society would be far more advanced than it is now. But now their time has come. I fervently hope that the bell that tolled this morning in honour of this convention may be the death-knell to all fanaticism, of all persecutions with the sword or the pen, and of all uncharitable feelings between persons wending their way to the same goal.

Note: On September 11, 2017, Prime Minister Narendra Modi marked this speech's 125th anniversary with the words: Just with a few words, a youngster from India won over the world and showed it the power of oneness.

16

THE MAN WITH THE MUCK RAKE

Theodore Roosevelt

Washington, D.C., U.S.A.

15 April 1906

In John Bunyan's Pilgrim's Progress, *the man with the muck rake had only focused on the filth on the floor, signifying that he only noticed the vile things in life. Roosevelt compared the journalists of his day with this man in the following speech. In his opinion, American writers, who were protesting about the problems in the country and solely criticizing the dishonest behaviour, crimes, and other misdeeds of individuals, needed to offer constructive criticism instead.*

This speech started a national debate about the role of the press in the nation. Some people agreed with Roosevelt, others thought that the press was doing much-needed work in exposing the corruption prevalent in the country.

Over a century ago Washington laid the corner stone of the Capitol in what was then little more than a tract of wooded wilderness here beside the Potomac. We now find it necessary to provide by great additional buildings for the business of the government.

This growth in the need for the housing of the government is but a proof and example of the way in which the nation has grown and the sphere of action of the national government has grown. We now administer the affairs of a nation in which the extraordinary growth of population has been outstripped by the growth of wealth in complex interests. The material problems that face us today are not such as they were in Washington's time, but the underlying facts of human nature are the same now as they were then. Under altered external form we war with the same tendencies toward evil that were evident in Washington's time, and are helped by the same tendencies for good. It is about some of these that I wish to say a word today.

In Bunyan's *Pilgrim's Progress*, you may recall the description of the Man with the Muck Rake, the man who could look no way but downward, with the muck rake in his hand; who was offered a celestial crown for his muck rake, but who would neither look up nor regard the crown he was offered, but continued to rake to himself the filth of the floor.

In *Pilgrim's Progress*, the man with the muck rake is set forth as the example of him whose vision is fixed on carnal instead of spiritual things. Yet he also typifies the man who in this life consistently refuses to see aught that is lofty, and fixes his eyes with solemn intentness only on that which is vile and debasing.

Now, it is very necessary that we should not flinch from seeing what is vile and debasing. There is filth on the floor, and it must be scraped up with the muck rake; and there are times and places where this service is the most needed of all the services that can be performed. But the man who never does anything else, who never thinks or speaks or writes, save of his feats with the muck rake, speedily becomes, not a help but one of the most potent forces for evil.

There are in the body politic, economic and social, many and grave evils, and there is urgent necessity for the sternest war upon them. There should be relentless exposure of and attack upon every evil man, whether politician or business man, every evil practice, whether in politics, business, or social life. I hail as a benefactor every writer or speaker, every man who, on the platform or in a book, magazine, or newspaper, with merciless severity makes such attack, provided always that he in his turn remembers that the attack is of use only if it is absolutely truthful.

The liar is no whit better than the thief, and if his mendacity takes the form of slander he may be worse than most thieves. It puts a premium upon knavery untruthfully to attack an honest man, or even with hysterical exaggeration to assail a bad man with untruth.

An epidemic of indiscriminate assault upon character does no good, but very great harm. The soul of every scoundrel is gladdened whenever an honest man is assailed, or even when a scoundrel is untruthfully assailed.

Now, it is easy to twist out of shape what I have just said, easy to affect to misunderstand it, and if it is slurred over in repetition not difficult really to misunderstand it. Some persons are sincerely incapable of understanding that to denounce mud slinging does not mean the endorsement of whitewashing; and both the interested individuals who need whitewashing and those others who practice mud slinging like to encourage such confusion of ideas.

One of the chief counts against those who make indiscriminate assault upon men in business or men in public life is that they invite a reaction which is sure to tell powerfully in favour of the unscrupulous scoundrel who really ought to be attacked, who ought to be exposed, who ought, if possible, to be put in the penitentiary. If Aristides is praised overmuch as just, people get tired of hearing it; and over-censure of the unjust finally and from similar reasons results in their favour.

Any excess is almost sure to invite a reaction; and, unfortunately, the reactions instead of taking the form of punishment of those guilty of the excess, is apt to take the form either of punishment of the unoffending or of giving immunity, and even strength, to offenders. The effort to make financial or political profit out of the destruction of character can only result in public calamity. Gross and reckless assaults on character, whether on the stump or in newspaper, magazine, or book, create a morbid and vicious public sentiment, and at the same time act as a profound deterrent to able men of normal sensitiveness and tend to prevent them from entering the public service at any price.

As an instance in point, I may mention that one serious difficulty encountered in getting the right type of men to dig the Panama canal is the certainty that they will be exposed, both without, and, I am sorry to say, sometimes within, Congress, to utterly reckless assaults on their character and capacity.

At the risk of repetition let me say again that my plea is not for immunity to, but for the most unsparing exposure of, the politician who betrays his trust, of the big business man who makes or spends his fortune in illegitimate or corrupt ways. There should be a resolute effort to hunt every such man out of the position he has disgraced. Expose the crime, and hunt down the criminal; but remember that even in the case of crime, if it is attacked in sensational, lurid, and untruthful fashion, the attack may do more damage to the public mind than the crime itself.

It is because I feel that there should be no rest in the endless war against the forces of evil that I ask the war be conducted with sanity as well as with resolution. The men with the muck rakes are often indispensable to the well-being of society; but only if they know when to stop raking the muck, and to look upward to the celestial crown above them, to the crown of worthy endeavour. There are beautiful things above and round about them; and if they gradually grow to feel that the whole world is nothing but muck, their power of usefulness is gone.

If the whole picture is painted black there remains no hue whereby to single out the rascals for distinction from their fellows. Such painting finally induces a kind of moral colour blindness; and people affected by it come to the conclusion that no man is really black, and no man really white, but they are all grey.

In other words, they neither believe in the truth of the attack, nor in the honesty of the man who is attacked; they grow as suspicious of the accusation as of the offense; it becomes well-nigh hopeless to stir them either to wrath against wrongdoing or to enthusiasm for what is right; and such a mental attitude in the public gives hope to every knave, and is the despair of honest men. To assail the great and admitted evils of our political and industrial life with such crude and sweeping generalizations as to include decent men in the general condemnation means the searing of the public conscience. There results a general attitude either of cynical belief in and indifference to public corruption or else of a distrustful inability to discriminate between the good and the bad. Either attitude is fraught with untold damage to the country as a whole.

The fool who has not sense to discriminate between what is good and what is bad is well-nigh as dangerous as the man who does discriminate and yet chooses the bad. There is nothing more distressing to every good patriot, to every good American, than the hard, scoffing spirit which treats the allegation of dishonesty in a public man as a cause for laughter. Such laughter is worse than the crackling of thorns under a pot, for it denotes not merely the vacant mind, but the heart in which high emotions have been choked before they could grow to fruition. There is any amount of good in the world, and there never was a time when loftier and more disinterested work for the betterment of mankind was being done than now. The forces that tend for evil are great and terrible, but the forces of truth and love and courage and honesty and generosity and sympathy are also stronger than ever before. It is a foolish and timid, no less than a wicked thing, to blink the fact that the forces of evil are strong, but it is even worse to fail to take into account the strength of the forces that tell for good.

Hysterical sensationalism is the poorest weapon wherewith to fight for lasting righteousness. The men who with stern sobriety and truth assail the many evils of our time, whether in the public press, or in magazines, or in books, are the leaders and allies of all engaged in the work for social and political betterment. But if they give good reason for distrust of what they say, if they chill the ardour of those who demand truth as a primary virtue, they thereby betray the good cause and play into the hands of the very men against whom they are nominally at war.

In his *Ecclesiastical Polity* that fine old Elizabethan divine, Bishop Hooker, wrote:

He that goeth about to persuade a multitude that they are not so well governed as they ought to be shall never want attentive and favourable hearers, because they know the manifold defects whereunto every kind of regimen is subject, but the secret lets and difficulties, which in public proceedings are innumerable and inevitable, they have not ordinarily the judgment to consider.

This truth should be kept constantly in mind by every free people desiring to preserve the sanity and poise indispensable to the permanent success of self-government. Yet, on the other hand, it is vital not to permit this spirit of sanity and self-command to degenerate into mere mental stagnation. Bad though a state of hysterical excitement is, and evil though the results are which come from the violent oscillations such excitement invariably produces, yet a sodden acquiescence in evil is even worse.

At this moment we are passing through a period of great

unrest—social, political, and industrial unrest. It is of the utmost importance for our future that this should prove to be not the unrest of mere rebelliousness against life, of mere dissatisfaction with the inevitable inequality of conditions, but the unrest of a resolute and eager ambition to secure the betterment of the individual and the nation.

So far as this movement of agitation throughout the country takes the form of a fierce discontent with evil, of a determination to punish the authors of evil, whether in industry or politics, the feeling is to be heartily welcomed as a sign of healthy life.

If, on the other hand, it turns into a mere crusade of appetite against appetite, of a contest between the brutal greed of the 'have-nots' and the brutal greed of the 'haves,' then it has no significance for good, but only for evil. If it seeks to establish a line of cleavage, not along the line which divides good men from bad, but along that other line, running at right angles thereto, which divides those who are well off from those who are less well off, then it will be fraught with immeasurable harm to the body politic.

We can no more and no less afford to condone evil in the man of capital than evil in the man of no capital. The wealthy man who exults because there is a failure of justice in the effort to bring some trust magnate to account for his misdeeds is as bad as, and no worse than, the so-called labour leader who clamorously strives to excite a foul class feeling on behalf of some other labour leader who is implicated in murder. One attitude is as bad as the other, and no worse; in each case the accused is entitled to exact justice; and in neither case is there need of action by others which can be construed into an expression of sympathy for crime.

It is a prime necessity that if the present unrest is to result in permanent good the emotion shall be translated into action, and that the action shall be marked by honesty, sanity, and self-restraint. There is mighty little good in a mere spasm of reform. The reform that counts is that which comes through steady, continuous growth; violent emotionalism leads to exhaustion.

It is important to this people to grapple with the problems connected with the amassing of enormous fortunes, and the use of those fortunes, both corporate and individual, in business. We should discriminate in the sharpest way between fortunes well won and fortunes ill won; between those gained as an incident to performing great services to the community as a whole and those gained in evil fashion by keeping just within the limits of mere law honesty. Of course, no amount of charity in spending such fortunes in any way compensates for misconduct in making them.

As a matter of personal conviction, and without pretending to discuss the details or formulate the system, I feel that we shall ultimately have to consider the adoption of some such scheme as that of a progressive tax on all fortunes, beyond a certain amount, either given in life or devised or bequeathed upon death to any individual—a tax so framed as to put it out of the power of the owner of one of these enormous fortunes to hand on more than a certain amount to any one individual; the tax of course, to be imposed by the national and not the state government. Such taxation should, of course, be aimed merely at the inheritance or transmission in their entirety of those fortunes swollen beyond all healthy limits. Again, the national government must in some form exercise supervision over corporations engaged in interstate business—and all large corporations engaged in interstate business—whether by license or otherwise, so as to permit us to deal with the far reaching evils of overcapitalization.

This year we are making a beginning in the direction of serious effort to settle some of these economic problems by the railway rate legislation. Such legislation, if so framed, as I am sure it will be, as to secure definite and tangible results, will amount to something of itself; and it will amount to a great deal more in so far as it is taken as a first step in the direction of a policy of superintendence and control over corporate wealth engaged in interstate commerce; this superintendence and control not to be exercised in a spirit of malevolence toward the men who have created the wealth, but with the firm purpose both to do justice to them and to see that they in their turn do justice to the public at large.

The first requisite in the public servants who are to deal in this shape with corporations, whether as legislators or as executives, is honesty. This honesty can be no respecter of persons. There can be no such thing as unilateral honesty. The danger is not really from corrupt corporations; it springs from the corruption itself, whether exercised for or against corporations.

The eighth commandment reads, 'Thou shalt not steal.' It does not read, 'Thou shalt not steal from the rich man.' It does not read, 'Thou shalt not steal from the poor man.' It reads simply and plainly, 'Thou shalt not steal.'

No good whatever will come from that warped and mock morality which denounces the misdeeds of men of wealth and forgets the misdeeds practiced at their expense; which denounces bribery, but blinds itself to blackmail; which foams with rage if a corporation secures favours by improper methods, and merely leers with hideous mirth if the corporation is itself wronged.

The only public servant who can be trusted honestly to protect the rights of the public against the misdeeds of a corporation is that public man who will just as surely protect the corporation itself from wrongful aggression.

If a public man is willing to yield to popular clamour and do wrong to the men of wealth or to rich corporations, it may be set down as certain that if the opportunity comes he will secretly and furtively do wrong to the public in the interest of a corporation.

But in addition to honesty, we need sanity. No honesty will make a public man useful if that man is timid or foolish, if he is a hot-headed zealot or an impracticable visionary. As we strive for reform we find that it is not at all merely the case of a long uphill pull. On the contrary, there is almost as much of breeching work as of collar work. To depend only on traces means that there will soon be a runaway and an upset.

The men of wealth who today are trying to prevent the regulation and control of their business in the interest of the public by the proper government authorities will not succeed, in my judgment, in checking the progress of the movement. But if they did succeed they would find that they had sown the wind and would surely reap the whirlwind, for they would ultimately provoke the violent excesses which accompany a reform coming by convulsion instead of by steady and natural growth.

On the other hand, the wild preachers of unrest and discontent, the wild agitators against the entire existing order, the men who act crookedly, whether because of sinister design or from mere puzzle headedness, the men who preach destruction without proposing any substitute for what they intend to destroy, or who propose a substitute which would be far worse than the existing evils—all these men are the most dangerous opponents of real reform. If they get their way they will lead the people into a deeper pit than any into which they could fall under the present system. If they fail to get their way they will still do incalculable harm by provoking the kind of reaction which in its revolt against the senseless evil of their teaching would enthrone more securely than ever the evils which their misguided followers believe they are attacking.

More important than aught else is the development of the broadest sympathy of man for man. The welfare of the wage worker, the welfare of the tiller of the soil, upon these depend the welfare of the entire country; their good is not to be sought in pulling down others; but their good must be the prime object of all our statesmanship.

Materially we must strive to secure a broader economic opportunity for all men, so that each shall have a better chance to show the stuff of which he is made. Spiritually and ethically we must strive to bring about clean living and right thinking. We appreciate that the things of the body are important; but we appreciate also that the things of the soul are immeasurably more important.

The foundation stone of national life is, and ever must be, the high individual character of the average citizen.

17

MAN IN THE ARENA

Theodore Roosevelt

Sorbonne, Paris, France

23 April 1910

Theodore Roosevelt had left office in 1909. He toured Europe in 1910, attending events and giving speeches.

This speech is also known as 'Citizenship in a Republic' but his audience didn't consist of citizens alone. According to Edmund Morris, Roosevelt delivered the following speech before 'ministers in court dress, army and navy officers in full uniform, nine hundred students, and an audience of two thousand ticket holders.'

Criticizing comes easily to people. The key point of the speech is to exalt the man who tries to make an effort for the cause he believes in, even though he might not succeed. For such a man is similar to a man fighting in the arena.

Strange and impressive associations rise in the mind of a man from the New World who speaks before this august body in this ancient institution of learning. Before his eyes pass the shadows of mighty kings and war-like nobles, of great masters of law and theology;

through the shining dust of the dead centuries he sees crowded figures that tell of the power and learning and splendour of times gone by; and he sees also the innumerable host of humble students to whom clerkship meant emancipation, to whom it was well-nigh the only outlet from the dark thraldom of the Middle Ages.

This was the most famous university of mediaeval Europe at a time when no one dreamed that there was a New World to discover. Its services to the cause of human knowledge already stretched far back into the remote past at a time when my forefathers, three centuries ago, were among the sparse bands of traders, ploughmen, wood-choppers, and fisher folk who, in hard struggle with the iron unfriendliness of the Indian-haunted land, were laying the foundations of what has now become the giant republic of the West. To conquer a continent, to tame the shaggy roughness of wild nature, means grim warfare; and the generations engaged in it cannot keep, still less add to, the stores of garnered wisdom which where once theirs, and which are still in the hands of their brethren who dwell in the old land. To conquer the wilderness means to wrest victory from the same hostile forces with which mankind struggled on the immemorial infancy of our race. The primeval conditions must be met by the primeval qualities which are incompatible with the retention of much that has been painfully acquired by humanity as through the ages it has striven upward toward civilization. In conditions so primitive there can be but a primitive culture. At first only the rudest school can be established, for no others would meet the needs of the hard-driven, sinewy folk who thrust forward the frontier in the teeth of savage men and savage nature; and many years elapse before any of these schools can develop into seats of higher learning and broader culture.

The pioneer days pass; the stump-dotted clearings expand into vast stretches of fertile farm land; the stockaded clusters of log cabins change into towns; the hunters of game, the fellers of trees, the rude frontier traders and tillers of the soil, the men who wander all their lives long through the wilderness as the heralds and harbingers of an oncoming civilization, themselves vanish before the civilization for which they have prepared the way. The children of their successors and supplanters, and then their children and their children and children's children, change and develop with extraordinary rapidity. The conditions accentuate vices and virtues, energy and ruthlessness, all the good qualities and all the defects of an intense individualism, self-reliant, self-centred, far more conscious of its rights than of its duties, and blind to its own shortcomings. To the hard materialism of the frontier days succeeds the hard materialism of an industrialism even more intense and absorbing than that of the older nations; although these themselves have likewise already entered on the age of a complex and predominantly industrial civilization.

As the country grows, its people, who have won success in so many lines, turn back to try to recover the possessions of the mind and the spirit, which perforce their fathers threw aside in order better to wage the first rough battles for the continent their children inherit. The leaders of thought and of action grope their way forward to a new life, realizing, sometimes dimly, sometimes clear-sightedly, that the life of material gain, whether for a nation or an individual, is of value only as a foundation, only as there is added to it the uplift that comes from devotion to loftier ideals. The new life thus sought can in part be developed afresh from what is roundabout in the New World; but it can be developed in full only by freely drawing upon the treasure-houses of the Old World, upon the treasures stored in the ancient abodes of wisdom and learning, such as this is where I speak today. It is a mistake for any nation to merely copy another; but it is even a greater mistake, it is a proof of weakness in any nation, not to be anxious to learn from one another and willing and able to adapt that learning to the new national conditions and make it fruitful and productive therein. It is for us of the New World to sit at the feet of Gamaliel of the Old; then, if we have the right stuff in us, we can show that Paul in his turn can become a teacher as well as a scholar.

Today I shall speak to you on the subject of individual citizenship, the one subject of vital importance to you, my hearers, and to me and my countrymen, because you and we a great citizens of great democratic republics. A democratic republic such as ours—an effort to realize its full sense government by, of, and for the people—represents the most gigantic of all possible social experiments, the one fraught with great responsibilities alike for good and evil. The success of republics like yours and like ours means the glory, and our failure of despair, of mankind; and for you and for us the question of the quality of the individual citizen is supreme. Under other forms of government, under the rule of one man or very few men, the quality of the leaders is all-important. If, under such governments, the quality of the rulers is high enough, then the nations for generations lead a brilliant career, and add substantially to the sum of world achievement, no matter how low the quality of average citizen; because the average citizen is an almost negligible quantity in working out the final results of that type of national greatness. But with you and us the case is different. With you here, and with us in my own home, in the long run, success or failure will be conditioned upon the way in which the average man, the average women, does his or her duty, first in the ordinary, everyday affairs of life, and next in those great occasional cries which call for heroic virtues. The average citizen must be a good citizen if our republics are to succeed. The stream will not permanently rise higher than the main source; and the main source of national power and national greatness is found in the average citizenship of the nation. Therefore it behoves us to do our best to see that the standard of the average citizen is kept high; and the average cannot be kept high unless the standard of the leaders is very much higher.

It is well if a large proportion of the leaders in any republic, in any democracy, are, as a matter of course, drawn from the classes represented in this audience today; but only provided that those classes possess the gifts of sympathy with plain people and of devotion to great ideals. You and those like you have received special advantages; you have all of you had the opportunity for mental training; many of you have had leisure; most of you have had a chance for enjoyment of life far greater than comes to the majority of your fellows. To you and your kind much has been given, and from you much should be expected. Yet there are certain failings against which it is especially incumbent that both men of trained and cultivated intellect, and men of inherited wealth and position should especially guard themselves, because to these failings they are especially liable; and if yielded to, their—your—chances of useful service are at an end. Let the man of learning, the man of lettered leisure, beware of that queer and cheap temptation to pose to himself and to others as a cynic, as the man who has outgrown emotions and beliefs, the man to whom good and evil are as one. The poorest way to face life is to face it with a sneer. There are many men who feel a kind of twister pride in cynicism; there are many who confine themselves to criticism of the way others do what they themselves dare not even attempt. There is no more unhealthy being, no man less worthy of respect, than he who either really holds, or feigns to hold, an attitude of sneering disbelief toward all that is great and lofty, whether in achievement or in that noble effort which, even if it fails, comes to second achievement. A cynical habit of thought and speech, a readiness to criticize work which the critic himself never tries to perform, an intellectual aloofness which will not accept contact with life's realities—all these are marks, not as the possessor would fain to think, of superiority but of weakness. They mark the men unfit to bear their part painfully in the stern strife of living, who seek, in the affection of contempt for the achievements of others, to hide from others and from themselves in their own weakness. The role is easy; there is none easier, save only the role of the man who sneers alike at both criticism and performance.

It is not the critic who counts; not the man who points out how the strong man stumbles, or where the doer of deeds could have done them better. The credit belongs to the man who is actually in the arena, whose face is marred by dust and sweat and blood; who strives valiantly; who errs, who comes short again and again, because there is no effort without error and shortcoming; but who does actually strive to do the deeds; who knows great enthusiasms, the great devotions; who spends himself in a worthy cause; who at the best knows in the end the triumph of high achievement, and who at the worst, if he fails, at least fails while daring greatly, so that his place shall never be with those cold and timid souls who neither know victory nor defeat. Shame on the man of cultivated taste who permits refinement to develop into fastidiousness that unfits him for doing the rough work of a workaday world. Among the free peoples who govern themselves there is but a small field of usefulness open for the men of cloistered life who shrink from contact with their fellows. Still less room is there for those who deride of slight what is done by those who actually bear the brunt of the day; nor yet for those others who always profess that they would like to take action, if only the conditions of life were not exactly what they actually are. The man who does nothing cuts the same sordid figure in the pages of history, whether he be a cynic, or fop, or voluptuary. There is little use for the being whose tepid soul knows nothing of great and generous emotion, of the high pride, the stern belief, the lofty enthusiasm, of the men who quell the storm and ride the thunder. Well for these men if they succeed;

well also, though not so well, if they fail, given only that they have nobly ventured, and have put forth all their heart and strength. It is war-worn Hotspur, spent with hard fighting, he of the many errors and valiant end, over whose memory we love to linger, not over the memory of the young lord who 'but for the vile guns would have been a valiant soldier.'

France has taught many lessons to other nations: surely one of the most important lesson is the lesson her whole history teaches, that a high artistic and literary development is compatible with notable leadership in arms and statecraft. The brilliant gallantry of the French soldier has for many centuries been proverbial; and during these same centuries at every court in Europe the freemasons of fashion: have treated the French tongue as their common speech; while every artist and man of letters, and every man of science able to appreciate that marvellous instrument of precision, French prose, had turned toward France for aid and inspiration. How long the leadership in arms and letters has lasted is curiously illustrated by the fact that the earliest masterpiece in a modern tongue is the splendid French epic which tells of Roland's doom and the vengeance of Charlemange when the lords of the Frankish hosts where stricken at Roncesvalles. Let those who have, keep, let those who have not, strive to attain, a high standard of cultivation and scholarship. Yet let us remember that these stand second to certain other things. There is need of a sound body, and even more of a sound mind. But above mind and above body stands character—the sum of those qualities which we mean when we speak of a man's force and courage, of his good faith and sense of honour. I believe in exercise for the body, always provided that we keep in mind that physical development is a means and not an end. I believe, of course, in giving to all the people a good education. But the education must contain much besides book-learning in order to be really good. We must ever remember that no keenness and subtleness of intellect, no polish, no cleverness, in any way make up for the lack of the great solid qualities. Self-restraint, self-mastery, common sense, the power of accepting individual responsibility and yet of acting in conjunction with others, courage and resolution—these are the qualities which mark a masterful people. Without them no people can control itself, or save itself from being controlled from the outside. I speak to brilliant assemblage; I speak in a great university which represents the flower of the highest intellectual development; I pay all homage to intellect and to elaborate and specialized training of the intellect; and yet I know I shall have the assent of all of you present when I add that more important still are the commonplace, everyday qualities and virtues.

Such ordinary, everyday qualities include the will and the power to work, to fight at need, and to have plenty of healthy children. The need that the average man shall work is so obvious as hardly to warrant insistence. There are a few people in every country so born that they can lead lives of leisure. These fill a useful function if they make it evident that leisure does not mean idleness; for some of the most valuable work needed by civilization is essentially non-remunerative in its character, and of course the people who do this work should in large part be drawn from those to whom remuneration is an object of indifference. But the average man must earn his own livelihood. He should be trained to do so, and he should be trained to feel that he occupies a contemptible position if he does not do so; that he is not an object of envy if he is idle, at whichever end of the social scale he stands, but an object of contempt, an object of derision. In the next place, the good man should be both a strong and a brave man; that is, he should be able to fight, he should be able to serve his country as a soldier, if the need arises. There are well-meaning philosophers who declaim against the unrighteousness of war. They are right only if they lay all their emphasis upon the unrighteousness. War is a dreadful thing, and unjust war is a crime against humanity. But it is such a crime because it is unjust, not because it is a war. The choice must ever be in favour of righteousness, and this is whether the alternative be peace or whether the alternative be war. The question must not be merely, Is there to be peace or war? The question must be, Is it right to prevail? Are the great laws of righteousness once more to be fulfilled? And the answer from a strong and virile people must be 'Yes,' whatever the cost. Every honourable effort should always be made to avoid war, just as every honourable effort should always be made by the individual in private life to keep out of a brawl, to keep out of trouble; but no self-respecting individual, no self-respecting nation, can or ought to submit to wrong.

Finally, even more important than ability to work, even more important than ability to fight at need, is it to remember that chief of blessings for any nations is that it shall leave its seed to inherit the land. It was the crown of blessings in Biblical times and it is the crown of blessings now. The greatest of all curses is the curse of sterility, and the severest of all condemnations should be that visited upon wilful sterility. The first essential in any civilization is that the man and women shall be father and mother of healthy children, so that the race shall increase and not decrease. If that is not so, if through no fault of the society there is failure to increase, it is a great misfortune. If the failure is due to the deliberate and wilful fault, then it is not merely a misfortune, it is one of those crimes of ease and self-indulgence, of shrinking from pain and effort and risk, which in the long run Nature punishes more heavily than any other. If we of the great republics, if we, the free people who claim to have emancipated ourselves from the thraldom of wrong and error, bring down on our heads the curse that comes upon the wilfully barren, then it will be an idle waste of breath to prattle of our achievements, to boast of all that we have done. No refinement of life, no delicacy of taste, no material progress, no sordid heaping up riches, no sensuous development of art and literature, can in any way compensate for the loss of the great fundamental virtues; and of these great fundamental virtues the greatest is the race's power to perpetuate the race. Character must show itself in the man's performance both of the duty he owes himself and of the duty he owes the state. The man's foremost duty is owed to himself and his family; and he can do this duty only by earning money, by providing what is essential to material well-being; it is only after this has been done that he can hope to build a higher superstructure on the solid material foundation; it is only after this has been done that he can help in movements for the general well-being. He must pull his own weight first, and only after this can his surplus strength be of use to the general public. It is not good to excite that bitter laughter which expresses contempt; and contempt is what we feel for the being whose enthusiasm to benefit mankind is such that he is a burden to those nearest him; who wishes to do great things for humanity in the abstract, but who cannot keep his wife in comfort or educate his children.

Nevertheless, while laying all stress on this point, while not merely acknowledging but insisting upon the fact that there must be a basis of material well-being for the individual as for the nation, let us with equal emphasis insist that this material well-being represents nothing but the foundation, and that the foundation, though indispensable, is worthless unless upon it is raised the superstructure of a higher life. That is why I decline to recognize the mere multimillionaire, the man of mere wealth, as an asset of value to any country; and especially as not an asset to my own country. If he has earned or uses his wealth in a way that makes him a real benefit, of real use—and such is often the case—why, then he does become an asset of real worth. But it is the way in which it has been earned or used, and not the mere fact of wealth, that entitles him to the credit. There is need in business, as in most other forms of human activity, of the great guiding intelligences. Their places cannot be supplied by any number of lesser intelligences. It is a good thing that they should have ample recognition, ample reward. But we must not transfer our admiration to the reward instead of to the deed rewarded; and if what should be the reward exists without the service having been rendered, then admiration will only come from those who are mean of soul. The truth is that, after a certain measure of tangible material success or reward has been achieved, the question of increasing it becomes of constantly less importance compared to the other things that can be done in life. It is a bad thing for a nation to raise and to admire a false standard of success; and there can be no falser standard than that set by the deification of material well-being in and for itself. But the man who, having far surpassed the limits of providing for the wants; both of the body and mind, of himself and of those depending upon him, then piles up a great fortune, for the acquisition or retention of which he returns no corresponding benefit to the nation as a whole, should himself be made to feel that, so far from being desirable, he is an unworthy, citizen of the community: that he is to be neither admired nor envied; that his right-thinking fellow countrymen put him low in the scale of citizenship, and leave him to be consoled by the admiration of those whose level of purpose is even lower than his own.

My position as regards the moneyed interests can be put in a few words. In every civilized society property rights must be carefully safeguarded; ordinarily, and in the great majority of cases, human rights and property rights are fundamentally and in the long run identical; but when it clearly appears that there is a real conflict between them, human rights must have the upper hand, for property belongs to man and not man to property. In fact, it is essential to good citizenship clearly to understand that there are certain qualities which we in a democracy are prone to admire in and of themselves, which ought, by rights, to be judged admirable or the reverse solely from the standpoint of the use made of them. Foremost among these I should include two very distinct gifts—the gift of money-making and the gift of oratory. Money-making, the money touch I have spoken of above. It is a quality which in a moderate degree is essential. It may be useful when developed to a very great degree, but only if accompanied and controlled by other qualities; and without such control the possessor tends to develop into one of the least attractive types produced by a modern industrial democracy. So it is with the orator. It is highly desirable that a leader of opinion in democracy should be able to state his views clearly and convincingly. But all that the oratory can do of value to the community is enable the man thus to explain himself; if it enables the orator to put false values on things, it merely makes him power for mischief. Some excellent public servants have not that gift at all, and must merely rely on their deeds to speak for them; and unless oratory does represent genuine conviction based on good common sense and able to be translated into efficient performance, then the better the oratory the greater the damage to the public it deceives. Indeed, it is a sign of marked political weakness in any commonwealth if the people tend to be carried away by mere oratory, if they tend to value words in and for themselves, as divorced from the deeds for which they are supposed to stand. The phrase-maker, the phrase-monger, the ready talker, however great his power, whose speech does not make for courage, sobriety, and right understanding, is simply a noxious element in the body politic, and it speaks ill for the public if he has influence over them. To admire the gift of oratory without regard to the moral quality behind the gift is to do wrong to the republic.

Of course all that I say of the orator applies with even greater force to the orator's latter-day and more influential brother, the journalist. The power of the journalist is great, but he is entitled neither to respect nor admiration because of that power unless it is used aright. He can do, and often does, great good. He can do, and he often does, infinite mischief. All journalists, all writers, for the very reason that they appreciate the vast possibilities of their profession, should bear testimony against those who deeply discredit it. Offenses against taste and morals, which are bad enough in a private citizen, are infinitely worse if made into instruments for debauching the community through a newspaper. Mendacity, slander, sensationalism, inanity, vapid triviality, all are potent factors for the debauchery of the public mind and conscience. The excuse advanced for vicious writing, that the public demands it and that demand must be supplied, can no more be admitted than if it were advanced by purveyors of food who sell poisonous adulterations. In short, the good citizen in a republic must realize that he ought to possess two sets of qualities, and that neither avails without the other. He must have those qualities which make for efficiency; and that he also must have those qualities which direct the efficiency into channels for the public good. He is useless if he is inefficient. There is nothing to be done with that type of citizen of whom all that can be said is that he is harmless. Virtue which is dependent upon a sluggish circulation is not impressive. There is little place in active life for the timid good man. The man who is saved by weakness from robust wickedness is likewise rendered immune from robuster virtues. The good citizen in a republic must first of all be able to hold his own. He is no good citizen unless he has the ability which will make him work hard and which at need will make him fight hard. The good citizen is not a good citizen unless he is an efficient citizen.

But if a man's efficiency is not guided and regulated by a moral sense, then the more efficient he is the worse he is, the more dangerous to the body politic. Courage, intellect, all the masterful qualities, serve but to make a man more evil if they are merely used for that man's own advancement, with brutal indifference to the rights of others. It speaks ill for the community if the community worships these qualities and treats their possessors as heroes regardless of whether the qualities are used rightly or wrongly. It makes no difference as to the precise way in which this sinister efficiency is shown. It makes no difference whether such a man's force and ability betray themselves in a career of money-maker or politician, soldier or orator, journalist or popular leader. If the man works for evil, then the more successful he is the more he should be despised and condemned by all upright and far-seeing men. To judge a man merely by success is an abhorrent wrong; and if the people at large habitually so judge men, if they grow to condone wickedness because the wicked man triumphs, they show their inability to understand that in the last analysis free institutions rest upon the character of citizenship, and that by such admiration of evil they prove themselves unfit for liberty. The homely virtues of the household, the ordinary workaday virtues which make the woman a good housewife and housemother, which make the man a hard worker, a good husband and father, a good soldier at need, stand at the bottom of character. But of course many other must be added thereto if a state is to be not only free but great. Good citizenship is not good citizenship if only exhibited in the home. There remains the duties of the individual in relation to the State, and these duties are none too easy under the conditions which exist where the effort is made to carry on the free government in a complex industrial civilization. Perhaps the most important thing the ordinary citizen, and, above all, the leader of ordinary citizens, has to remember in political life is that he must not be a sheer doctrinaire. The closet philosopher, the refined and cultured individual who from his library tells how men ought to be governed under ideal conditions, is of no use in actual governmental work;

and the one-sided fanatic, and still more the mob-leader, and the insincere man who to achieve power promises what by no possibility can be performed, are not merely useless but noxious.

The citizen must have high ideals, and yet he must be able to achieve them in practical fashion. No permanent good comes from aspirations so lofty that they have grown fantastic and have become impossible and indeed undesirable to realize. The impractical visionary is far less often the guide and precursor than he is the embittered foe of the real reformer, of the man who, with stumblings and shortcoming, yet does in some shape, in practical fashion, give effect to the hopes and desires of those who strive for better things. Woe to the empty phrase-maker, to the empty idealist, who, instead of making ready the ground for the man of action, turns against him when he appears and hampers him when he does work! Moreover, the preacher of ideals must remember how sorry and contemptible is the figure which he will cut, how great the damage that he will do, if he does not himself, in his own life, strive measurably to realize the ideals that he preaches for others. Let him remember also that the worth of the ideal must be largely determined by the success with which it can in practice be realized. We should abhor the so-called 'practical' men whose practicality assumes the shape of that peculiar baseness which finds its expression in disbelief in morality and decency, in disregard of high standards of living and conduct. Such a creature is the worst enemy of the body of politic. But only less desirable as a citizen is his nominal opponent and real ally, the man of fantastic vision who makes the impossible better forever the enemy of the possible good.

We can just as little afford to follow the doctrinaires of an extreme individualism as the doctrinaires of an extreme socialism. Individual initiative, so far from being discouraged, should be stimulated; and yet we should remember that, as society develops and grows more complex, we continually find that things which once it was desirable to leave to individual initiative can, under changed conditions, be performed with better results by common effort. It is quite impossible, and equally undesirable, to draw in theory a hard-and-fast line which shall always divide the two sets of cases. This everyone who is not cursed with the pride of the closest philosopher will see, if he will only take the trouble to think about some of our closet phenomena. For instance, when people live on isolated farms or in little hamlets, each house can be left to attend to its own drainage and water-supply; but the mere multiplication of families in a given area produces new problems which, because they differ in size, are found to differ not only in degree, but in kind from the old; and the questions of drainage and water-supply have to be considered from the common standpoint. It is not a matter for abstract dogmatizing to decide when this point is reached; it is a matter to be tested by practical experiment. Much of the discussion about socialism and individualism is entirely pointless, because of the failure to agree on terminology. It is not good to be a slave of names. I am a strong individualist by personal habit, inheritance, and conviction; but it is a mere matter of common sense to recognize that the State, the community, the citizens acting together, can do a number of things better than if they were left to individual action. The individualism which finds its expression in the abuse of physical force is checked very early in the growth of civilization, and we of today should in our turn strive to shackle or destroy that individualism which triumphs by greed and cunning, which exploits the weak by craft instead of ruling them by brutality. We ought to go with any man in the effort to bring about justice and the equality of opportunity, to turn the tool-user more and more into the tool-owner, to shift burdens so that they can be more equitably borne. The deadening effect on any race of the adoption of a logical and extreme socialistic system could not be overstated;

it would spell sheer destruction; it would produce grosser wrong and outrage, fouler immortality, than any existing system. But this does not mean that we may not with great advantage adopt certain of the principles professed by some given set of men who happen to call themselves Socialists; to be afraid to do so would be to make a mark of weakness on our part.

But we should not take part in acting a lie any more than in telling a lie. We should not say that men are equal where they are not equal, nor proceed upon the assumption that there is an equality where it does not exist; but we should strive to bring about a measurable equality, at least to the extent of preventing the inequality which is due to force or fraud. Abraham Lincoln, a man of the plain people, blood of their blood, and bone of their bone, who all his life toiled and wrought and suffered for them, at the end died for them, who always strove to represent them, who would never tell an untruth to or for them, spoke of the doctrine of equality with his usual mixture of idealism and sound common sense. He said (I omit what was of merely local significance):

'I think the authors of the Declaration of Independence intended to include all men, but they did not mean to declare all men equal in all respects. They did not mean to say all men were equal in colour, size, intellect, moral development or social capacity. They defined with tolerable distinctness in what they did consider all men created equal—equal in certain inalienable rights, among which are life, liberty and pursuit of happiness. This they said, and this they meant. They did not mean to assert the obvious untruth that all were actually enjoying that equality, or yet that they were about to confer it immediately upon them. They meant to set up a standard maxim for free society which should be familiar to all—constantly looked to, constantly laboured for, and, even though never perfectly attained, constantly approximated, and thereby constantly spreading and deepening its influence, and augmenting the happiness and value of life to all people, everywhere."

We are bound in honour to refuse to listen to those men who would make us desist from the effort to do away with the inequality which means injustice; the inequality of right, opportunity, of privilege. We are bound in honour to strive to bring ever nearer the day when, as far is humanly possible, we shall be able to realize the ideal that each man shall have an equal opportunity to show the stuff that is in him by the way in which he renders service. There should, so far as possible, be equal of opportunity to render service; but just so long as there is inequality of service there should and must be inequality of reward. We may be sorry for the general, the painter, the artists, the worker in any profession or of any kind, whose misfortune rather than whose fault it is that he does his work ill. But the reward must go to the man who does his work well; for any other course is to create a new kind of privilege, the privilege of folly and weakness; and special privilege is injustice, whatever form it takes.

To say that the thriftless, the lazy, the vicious, the incapable, ought to have reward given to those who are far-sighted, capable, and upright, is to say what is not true and cannot be true. Let us try to level up, but let us beware of the evil of levelling down. If a man stumbles, it is a good thing to help him to his feet. Every one of us needs a helping hand now and then. But if a man lies down, it is a waste of time to try and carry him; and it is a very bad thing for every one if we make men feel that the same reward will come to those who shirk their work and those who do it. Let us, then, take into account the actual facts of life, and not be misled into following any proposal for achieving the millennium, for recreating the golden age, until we have subjected it to hard-headed examination. On the other hand, it is foolish to reject a proposal merely because it is advanced by visionaries. If a given scheme is proposed, look at it on its merits, and, in considering it, disregard formulas. It does not matter in the least who proposes it, or why. If it seems good, try it. If it proves good, accept it; otherwise reject it. There are plenty of good men calling themselves Socialists with whom, up to a certain point, it is quite possible to work. If the next step is one which both we and they wish to take, why of course take it, without any regard to the fact that our views as to the tenth step may differ. But, on the other hand, keep clearly in mind that, though it has been worthwhile to take one step, this does not in the least mean that it may not be highly disadvantageous to take the next. It is just as foolish to refuse all progress because people demanding it desire at some points to go to absurd extremes, as it would be to go to these absurd extremes simply because some of the measures advocated by the extremists were wise.

The good citizen will demand liberty for himself, and as a matter of pride he will see to it that others receive liberty which he thus claims as his own. Probably the best test of true love of liberty in any country in the way in which minorities are treated in that country. Not only should there be complete liberty in matters of religion and opinion, but complete liberty for each man to lead his life as he desires, provided only that in so he does not wrong his neighbour. Persecution is bad because it is persecution, and without reference to which side happens at the most to be the persecutor and which the persecuted. Class hatred is bad in just the same way, and without regard to the individual who, at a given time, substitutes loyalty to a class for loyalty to a nation, or substitutes hatred of men because they happen to come in a certain social category, for judgement awarded them according to their conduct. Remember always that the same measure of condemnation should be extended to the arrogance which would look down upon or crush any man because he is poor and to envy and hatred which would destroy a man because he is wealthy. The overbearing brutality of the man of wealth or power, and the envious and hateful malice directed against wealth or power, are really at root merely different manifestations of the same quality, merely two sides of the same shield. The man who, if born to wealth and power, exploits and ruins his less fortunate brethren is at heart the same as the greedy and violent demagogue who excites those who have not property to plunder those who have. The gravest wrong upon his country is inflicted by that man, whatever his station, who seeks to make his countrymen divide primarily in the line that separates class from class, occupation from occupation, men of more wealth from men of less wealth, instead of remembering that the only safe standard is that which judges each man on his worth as a man, whether he be rich or whether he be poor, without regard to his profession or to his station in life. Such is the only true democratic test, the only test that can with propriety be applied in a republic. There have been many republics in the past, both in what we call antiquity and in what we call the Middle Ages. They fell, and the prime factor in their fall was the fact that the parties tended to divide along the wealth that separates wealth from poverty. It made no difference which side was successful; it made no difference whether the republic fell under the rule of oligarchy or the rule of a mob. In either case, when once loyalty to a class had been substituted for loyalty to the republic, the end of the republic was at hand. There is no greater need today than the need to keep ever in mind the fact that the cleavage between right and wrong, between good citizenship and bad citizenship, runs at right angles to, and not parallel with, the lines of cleavage between class and class, between occupation and occupation. Ruin looks us in the face if we judge a man by his position instead of judging him by his conduct in that position.

In a republic, to be successful we must learn to combine intensity of conviction with a broad tolerance of difference of conviction. Wide differences of opinion in matters of religious, political, and social belief must exist if conscience and intellect alike are not be stunted, if there is to be room for healthy growth. Bitter internecine hatreds, based on such differences, are signs, not of earnestness of belief, but of that fanaticism which, whether religious or antireligious, democratic or antidemocratic, it itself but a manifestation of the gloomy bigotry which has been the chief factor in the downfall of so many, many nations.

Of one man in especial, beyond anyone else, the citizens of a republic should beware, and that is of the man who appeals to them to support him on the ground that he is hostile to other citizens of the republic, that he will secure for those who elect him, in one shape or another, profit at the expense of other citizens of the republic. It makes no difference whether he appeals to class hatred or class interest, to religious or antireligious prejudice. The man who makes such an appeal should always be presumed to make it for the sake of furthering his own interest. The very last thing an intelligent and self-respecting member of a democratic community should do is to reward any public man because that public man says that he will get the private citizen something to which this private citizen is not entitled, or will gratify some emotion or animosity which this private citizen ought not to possess. Let me illustrate this by one anecdote from my own experience. A number of years ago I was engaged in cattle-ranching on the great plains of the western United States. There were no fences. The cattle wandered free, the ownership of each one was determined by the brand; the calves were branded with the brand of the cows they followed. If on a round-up an animal was passed by, the following year it would appear as an unbranded yearling, and was then called a maverick. By the custom of the country these mavericks were branded with the brand of the man on whose range they were found. One day I was riding the range with a newly hired cowboy, and we came upon a maverick. We roped and threw it; then we built a fire, took out a cinch-ring, heated it in the fire; and then the cowboy started to put on the brand. I said to him, 'It so-and-so's brand,' naming the man on whose range we happened to be. He answered: 'That's all right, boss; I know my business.' In another moment I said to him: 'Hold on, you are putting on my brand!' To which he answered: 'That's all right; I always put on the boss's brand.' I answered: 'Oh, very well. Now you go straight back to the ranch and get whatever is owing to you; I don't need you any longer.' He jumped up and said: 'Why, what's the matter? I was putting on your brand.' And I answered: 'Yes, my friend, and if you will steal for me then you will steal from me.'

Now, the same principle which applies in private life applies also in public life. If a public man tries to get your vote by saying that he will do something wrong in your interest, you can be absolutely certain that if ever it becomes worth his while he will do something wrong against your interest. So much for the citizenship to the individual in his relations to his family, to his neighbour, to the state. There remain duties of citizenship which the state, the aggregation of all the individuals, owes in connection with other States, with other nations. Let me say at once that I am no advocate of a foolish cosmopolitanism. I believe that a man must be a good patriot before he can be, and as the only possible way of being, a good citizen of the world. Experience teaches us that the average man who protests that his international feeling swamps his national feeling, that he does not care for his country because he cares so much for mankind, in actual practice proves himself the foe of mankind; that the man who says that he does not care to be a citizen of any one country, because he is the citizen of the world, is in fact usually and exceedingly undesirable citizen of whatever corner of the world he happens at the moment to be in. In the dim future all moral needs and moral standards may change; but at present, if a man can view his own country and all others countries from the same level with tepid indifference, it is wise to distrust him, just as it is wise to distrust the man who can take the same dispassionate view of his wife and mother. However broad and deep a man's sympathies, however intense his activities, he need have no fear that they will be cramped by love of his native land.

Now, this does not mean in the least that a man should not wish to good outside of his native land. On the contrary, just as I think that the man who loves his family is more apt to be a good neighbour than the man who does not, so I think that the most useful member of the family of nations is normally a strongly patriotic nation. So far from patriotism being inconsistent with a proper regard for the rights of other nations, I hold that the true patriot, who is as jealous of the national honour as a gentleman of his own honour, will be careful to see that the nations neither inflicts nor suffers wrong, just as a gentleman scorns equally to wrong others or to suffer others to wrong him. I do not for one moment admit that a man should act deceitfully as a public servant in his dealing with other nations, any more than he should act deceitfully in his dealings as a private citizen with other private citizens. I do not for one moment admit that a nation should treat other nations in a different spirit from that in which an honourable man would treat other men.

In practically applying this principle to the two sets of cases there is, of course, a great practical difference to be taken into account. We speak of international law; but international law is something wholly different from private or municipal law, and the capital difference is that there is a sanction for the one and no sanction for the other; that there is an outside force which compels individuals to obey the one, while there is no such outside force to compel obedience as regards to the other. International law will, I believe, as the generations pass, grow stronger and stronger until in some way or other there develops the power to make it respected.

But as yet it is only in the first formative period. As yet, as a rule, each nation is of necessity to judge for itself in matters of vital importance between it and its neighbours, and actions must be of necessity, where this is the case, be different from what they are where, as among private citizens, there is an outside force whose action is all-powerful and must be invoked in any crisis of importance. It is the duty of wise statesman, gifted with the power of looking ahead, to try to encourage and build up every movement which will substitute or tend to substitute some other agency for force in the settlement of international disputes. It is the duty of every honest statesman to try to guide the nation so that it shall not wrong any other nation. But as yet the great civilized peoples, if they are to be true to themselves and to the cause of humanity and civilization, must keep in mind that in the last resort they must possess both the will and the power to resent wrong-doings from others. The men who sanely believe in a lofty morality preach righteousness; but they do not preach weakness, whether among private citizens or among nations. We believe that our ideals should be so high, but not so high as to make it impossible measurably to realize them. We sincerely and earnestly believe in peace; but if peace and justice conflict, we scorn the man who would not stand for justice though the whole world came in arms against him.

And now, my hosts, a word in parting. You and I belong to the only two republics among the great powers of the world. The ancient friendship between France and the United States has been, on the whole, a sincere and disinterested friendship. A calamity to you would be a sorrow to us. But it would be more than that. In the seething turmoil of the history of humanity certain nations stand out as possessing a peculiar power or charm, some special gift of beauty or wisdom of strength, which puts them among the immortals, which makes them rank forever with the leaders of mankind. France is one of these nations. For her to sink would be a loss to all the world. There are certain lessons of brilliance and of generous gallantry that she can teach better than any of her sister nations. When the French peasantry sang of Malbrook, it was to tell how the soul of this warrior-foe took flight upward through the laurels he had won. Nearly seven centuries ago, Froisart, writing of the time of dire disaster, said that the realm of France was never so stricken that there were not left men who would valiantly fight for it. You have had a great past. I believe you will have a great future. Long may you carry yourselves proudly as citizens of a nation which bears a leading part in the teaching and uplifting of mankind.

18

FREEDOM OR DEATH

Emmeline Pankhurst

Hartford, Connecticut, U.S.A.

13 November 1913

Emmeline Pankhurst founded the Women's Social and Political Union in 1903 which aimed at obtaining voting rights for women in Britain. She had been imprisoned a few times for her propagation of gender equality, a fact she mentioned in the following speech.

Though Pankhurst was a woman rights activist but she starts her speech by announcing that she had not come to Hartford as an activist but as a soldier. The demand for women's suffrage was nothing short of a revolution. Hence, violence was inevitable.

However, anti-suffrage groups existed. Pankhurst, in her speech, promises them that she would, one day, achieve what she was campaigning for, or die trying.

I do not come here as an advocate, because whatever position the suffrage movement may occupy in the United States of America, in England it has passed beyond the realm of advocacy and it has entered into the sphere of practical politics. It has become the subject of revolution and civil war, and so tonight I am not here to advocate woman suffrage. American suffragists can do that very well for themselves.

I am here as a soldier who has temporarily left the field of battle in order to explain—it seems strange it should have to be explained—what civil war is like when civil war is waged by women. I am not only here as a soldier temporarily absent from the field at battle; I am here—and that, I think, is the strangest part of my coming—I am here as a person who, according to the law courts of my country, it has been decided, is of no value to the community at all: and I am adjudged because of my life to be a dangerous person, under sentence of penal servitude in a convict prison.

It is not at all difficult if revolutionaries come to you from Russia, if they come to you from China, or from any other part of the world, if they are men, to make you understand revolution in five minutes, every man and every woman to understand revolutionary methods when they are adopted by men. But since I am a woman it is necessary in the twentieth century to explain why women have adopted revolutionary methods in order to win the rights of citizenship. We women, in trying to make our case clear, always have to make as part of our argument, and urge upon men in our audience the fact—a very simple fact—that women are human beings.

Suppose the men of Hartford had a grievance, and they laid that grievance before their legislature, and the legislature obstinately refused to listen to them, or to remove their grievance, what would be the proper and the constitutional and the practical way of getting their grievance removed? Well, it is perfectly obvious at the next general election, when the legislature is elected, the men of Hartford in sufficient numbers would turn out that legislature and elect a new one.

But let the men of Hartford imagine that they were not in the position of being voters at all, that they were governed without their consent being obtained, that the legislature turned an absolutely deaf ear to their demands, what would the men of Hartford do then? They couldn't vote the legislature out. They would have to choose; they would have to make a choice of two evils: they would either have to submit indefinitely to an unjust state of affairs, or they would have to rise up and adopt some of the antiquated means by which men in the past got their grievances remedied.

Your forefathers decided that they must have representation for taxation, many, many years ago. When they felt they couldn't wait any longer, when they laid all the arguments before an obstinate British Government that they could think of, and when their arguments were absolutely disregarded, when every other means had failed, they began by the tea party at Boston, and they went on until they had won the independence of the United States of America. It is about eight years since the word militant was first used to describe what we were doing. It was not militant at all, except that it provoked militancy on the part of those who were opposed to it. When women asked questions in political meetings and failed to get answers, they were not doing anything militant. In Great Britain it is a custom, a time-honoured one, to ask questions of candidates for parliament and ask questions of members of the government. No man was ever put out of a public meeting for asking a question. The first people who were put out of a political meeting for asking questions, were women; they were brutally ill-used; they found themselves in jail before twenty-four hours had expired.

We were called militant, and we were quite willing to accept the name. We were determined to press this question of the enfranchisement of women to the point where we were no longer to be ignored by the politicians.

You have two babies very hungry and wanting to be fed. One

baby is a patient baby, and waits indefinitely until its mother is ready to feed it. The other baby is an impatient baby and cries lustily, screams and kicks and makes everybody unpleasant until it is fed. Well, we know perfectly well which baby is attended to first. That is the whole history of politics. You have to make more noise than anybody else, you have to make yourself more obtrusive than anybody else, you have to fill all the papers more than anybody else, in fact you have to be there all the time and see that they do not snow you under.

When you have warfare things happen; people suffer; the non-combatants suffer as well as the combatants. And so it happens in civil war. When your forefathers threw the tea into Boston harbour, a good many women had to go without their tea. It has always seemed to me an extraordinary thing that you did not follow it up by throwing the whiskey overboard; you sacrificed the women; and there is a good deal of warfare for which men take a great deal of glorification which has involved more practical sacrifice on women than it has on any man. It always has been so. The grievances of those who have got power, the influence of those who have got power commands a great deal of attention; but the wrongs and the grievances of those people who have no power at all are apt to be absolutely ignored. That is the history of humanity right from the beginning. Well, in our civil war people have suffered, but you cannot make omelettes without breaking eggs; you cannot have civil war without damage to something. The great thing is to see that no more damage is done than is absolutely necessary, that you do just as much as will arouse enough feeling to bring about peace, to bring about an honourable peace for the combatants, and that is what we have been doing.

We entirely prevented stock brokers in London from telegraphing to stock brokers in Glasgow and vice versa: for one whole day telegraphic and telephonic communication was entirely stopped. I am not going to tell you how it was done. I am not going to tell you how the women got to the mains and cut the wires; but it was done. It was done, and it was proved to the authorities that weak women, suffrage women, as we are supposed to be, had enough ingenuity to create a situation of that kind. Now, I ask you, if women can do that, is there any limit to what we can do except the limit we put upon ourselves?

If you are dealing with an industrial revolution, if you get the men and women of one class to rising up against the men and women of another class, you can locate the difficulty; if there is a great industrial strike, you know exactly where the violence is, and every man knows exactly how the warfare is going to be waged; but in our war against the government you can't locate it. We wear no mark; we belong to every class; we permeate every class of the community from the highest to the lowest; and so you see in the woman's civil war the dear men of my country are discovering it is absolutely impossible to deal with it: you cannot locate it, and you cannot stop it. 'Put them in prison,' they said, 'that will stop it.' But it didn't stop it: instead of the women giving it up, more women did it, and more and more and more women did it until there were three hundred women at a time, who had not broken a single law, only 'made a nuisance of themselves' as the politicians say. Then they began to legislate. The British Government has passed more stringent laws to deal with this agitation than it ever found it necessary during all the history of political agitation in my country. They were able to deal with the revolutionaries of the Chartists' time; they were able to deal with the trades union agitation; they were able to deal with the revolutionaries later on when the Reform Acts of 1867 and 1884 were passed: but the ordinary law has not sufficed to curb insurgent women. They had to dip back into the middle ages to find a means of repressing the women in revolt.

They have said to us, government rests upon force, the women haven't force so they must submit. Well, we are showing them that government does not rest upon force at all: it rests upon consent. As long as women consent to be unjustly governed, they can be, but directly women say: 'We withhold our consent, we will not be governed any longer so long as that government is unjust.' Not by the forces of civil war can you govern the very weakest woman. You can kill that woman, but she escapes you then; you cannot govern her. No power on earth can govern a human being, however feeble, who withholds his or her consent. When they put us in prison at first, simply for taking petitions, we submitted; we allowed them to dress us in prison clothes; we allowed them to put us in solitary confinement; we allowed them to put us amongst the most degraded of those criminals; we learned of some of the appalling evils of our so-called civilization that we could not have learned in any other way. It was valuable experience, and we were glad to get it.

I have seen men smile when they heard the words 'hunger strike,' and yet I think there are very few men today who would be prepared to adopt a 'hunger strike' for any cause. It is only people who feel an intolerable sense of oppression who would adopt a means of that kind. I know of no people who did it before us except revolutionaries in Russia—who adopted the hunger strike against intolerable prison conditions. Well, our women decided to terminate those unjust sentences at the earliest possible moment by the terrible means of the hunger strike. It means, you refuse food until you are at death's door, and then the authorities have to choose between letting you die, and letting you go; and then they let the women go.

Now, that went on so long that the government felt they had lost their power, and that they were unable to cope with the situation. Then it was that, to the shame of the British Government, they set the example to authorities all over the world of feeding sane, resisting human beings by force. There may be doctors in this meeting: if so, they know it is one thing to treat an insane person, to feed by force an insane person,; but it is quite another thing to feed a sane, resisting human being who resists with every nerve and with every fibre of her body the indignity and the outrage of forcible feeding. Now, that was done in England, and the government thought they had crushed us. But they found that it did not quell the agitation, that more and more women came in and even passed that terrible ordeal, and they were obliged to let them go. Then came the legislation which is known in England as the 'Cat and Mouse Act.' The home secretary said, 'Give me the power to let these women go when they are at death's door, and leave them at liberty under license until they have recovered their health again and then bring them back. It was passed to repress the agitation, to make the women yield—because that is what it has really come to, ladies and gentlemen. It has come to a battle between the women and the government as to who shall yield first, whether they will yield and give us the vote, or whether we will give up our agitation.

Well, they little know what women are. Women are very slow to rouse, but once they are aroused, once they are determined, nothing on earth and nothing in heaven will make women give way; it is impossible. And so this 'Cat and Mouse Act' which is being used against women today has failed: and the home secretary has taken advantage of the fact that parliament is not sitting, to revive and use alongside of it the forcible feeding. At the present time there are women lying at death's door, recovering enough strength to undergo operations, who have had both systems applied to them, and have not given in and won't give in, and who will be prepared, as soon as they get up from their sick beds, to go on as before. There are women who are being carried from their sick beds on stretchers into meetings. They are too weak to speak, but they go amongst their fellow workers just to show that their spirits are unquenched, and that their spirit is alive, and they mean to go on as long as life lasts.

Now, I want to say to you who think women cannot succeed, we have brought the Government of England to this position, that it has to face this alternative: either women are to be killed or women are to have the vote. I ask American men in this meeting, what would you say if in your state you were faced with that alternative, that you must either kill them or give them their citizenship. Well, there is only one answer to that alternative—you must give those women the vote.

You won your freedom in America when you had the revolution, by bloodshed, by sacrificing human life. You won the civil war by the sacrifice of human life when you decided to emancipate the negro. You have left it to women in your land, the men of all civilised countries have left it to women, to work out their own salvation. That is the way in which we women of England are doing. Human life for us is sacred, but we say if any life is to be sacrificed it shall be ours; we won't do it ourselves, but we will put the enemy in the position where they will have to choose between giving us freedom or giving us death.

So here am I. I come in the intervals of prison appearance. I come after having been four times imprisoned under the 'Cat and Mouse Act,' probably going back to be rearrested as soon as I set my foot on British soil. I come to ask you to help to win this fight. If we win it, this hardest of all fights, then, to be sure, in the future it is going to be made easier for women all over the world to win their fight when their time comes.

19

SPEECH AT BENARAS HINDU UNIVERSITY

Mahatma Gandhi

Benaras, India

4 February 1916

This speech marks the moment of Gandhi's arrival in Indian politics. He boldly charged at the patrons of the University. Watching the bedecked, bejewelled appearance of the patrons, he remembered the millions of poor Indians.

In this speech Gandhi concludes that the country could be salvaged only when the artisan had enough to feed and clothe himself and 'could be educated up to his sense of responsibility.'

I wish to tender my humble apology for the long delay that took place before I was able to reach this place. And you will readily accept the apology when I tell you that I am not responsible for the delay nor is any human agency responsible for it. The fact is that I am like an animal on show, and my keepers in their over kindness always manage to neglect a necessary chapter in this life, and, that is, pure accident. In this case, they did not provide for the series of accidents that happened to us—to me, keepers, and my carriers. Hence this delay.

Friends, under the influence of the matchless eloquence of Mrs. Besant who has just sat down, pray, do not believe that our University has become a finished product, and that all the young men who are to come to the University, that has yet to rise and come into existence, have also come and returned from it finished citizens of a great empire. Do not go away with any such impression, and if you, the student world to which my remarks are supposed to be addressed this evening, consider for one moment that the spiritual life, for which this country is noted and for which this country has no rival, can be transmitted through the lip, pray, believe me, you are wrong. You will never be able merely through the lip, to give the message that India, I hope, will one day deliver to the world. I myself have been fed up with speeches and lectures. I except the lectures that have been delivered here during the last two days from this category, because they are necessary. But I do venture to suggest to you that we have now reached almost the end of our resources in speech-making; it is not enough that our ears are feasted, that our eyes are feasted, but it is necessary that our hearts have got to be touched and that out hands and feet have got to be moved.

We have been told during the last two days how necessary it is, if we are to retain our hold upon the simplicity of Indian character, that our hands and feet should move in unison with our hearts. But this is only by way of preface. I wanted to say it is a matter of deep humiliation and shame for us that I am compelled this evening under the shadow of this great college, in this sacred city, to address my countrymen in a language that is foreign to me. I know that if I was appointed an examiner, to examine all those who have been attending during these two days this series of lectures, most of those who might be examined upon these lectures would fail. And why? Because they have not been touched.

I was present at the sessions of the great Congress in the month of December. There was a much vaster audience, and will you believe me when I tell you that the only speeches that touched the huge audience in Bombay were the speeches that were delivered in Hindustani? In Bombay, mind you, not in Benaras where everybody speaks Hindi. But between the vernaculars of the Bombay Presidency on the one hand and Hindi on the other, no such great dividing line exists as there does between English and the sister language of India; and the Congress audience was better able to follow the speakers in Hindi. I am hoping that this University will see to it that the youths who come to it will receive their instruction through the medium of their vernaculars. Our languages the reflection of ourselves, and if you tell me that our languages are too poor to express the best thought, then say that the sooner we are wiped out of existence the better for us. Is there a man who dreams that English can ever become the national language of India? Why this handicap on the nation? Just consider for one moment what an equal race our lads have to run with every English lad.

I had the privilege of a close conversation with some Poona professors. They assured me that every Indian youth, because he reached his knowledge through the English language, lost at least six precious years of life. Multiply that by the numbers of students turned out by our schools and colleges, and find out for yourselves how many thousand years have been lost to the nation. The charge against us is that we have no initiative. How can we have any, if we are to devote the precious years of our life to the mastery of a foreign tongue? We fail in this attempt also. Was it possible for any speaker yesterday and today to impress his audience as was possible for Mr. Higginbotham? It was not the fault of the previous speakers that they could not engage the audience. They had more than substance enough for us in their addresses. But their addresses could not go home to us. I have heard it said that after all it is English educated India which is leading and which is leading and which is doing all the things for the nation. It would be monstrous if it were otherwise. The only education we receive is English education. Surely we must show something for it. But suppose that we had been receiving during the past fifty years education through our vernaculars, what should we have today? We should have today a free India, we should have our educated men, not as if they were foreigners in their own land but speaking to the heart of the nation; they would be working amongst the poorest of the poor, and whatever they would have gained during these fifty years would be a heritage for the nation. Today even our wives are not the sharers in our best thought. Look at Professor Bose and Professor Ray and their brilliant researches. Is it not a shame that their researches are not the common property of the masses?

Let us now turn to another subject.

The Congress has passed a resolution about self-government, and I have no doubt that the All India Congress Committee and the Muslim League will do their duty and come forward with some tangible suggestions. But I, for one, must frankly confess that I am not so much interested in what they will be able to produce as I am interested in anything that the student world is going to produce or the masses are going to produce. No paper contribution will ever give us self-government. No amount of speeches will ever make us fit for self-government. It is only our conduct that will fit for us it. And how are we trying to govern ourselves?

I want to think audibly this evening. I do not want to make a speech and if you find me this evening speaking without reserve, pray, consider that you are only sharing the thoughts of a man who allows himself to think audibly, and if you think that I seem to transgress the limits that courtesy imposes upon me, pardon me for the liberty I may be taking. I visited the Vishwanath temple last evening, and ad I was walking through those lanes, these were the thoughts that touched me. If a stranger dropped from above on to this great temple, and he had to consider what we as Hindus were, would he not be justified in condemning us? Is not this great temple a reflection of our own character? I speak feelingly, as a Hindu. Is it right that the lanes of our sacred temple should be as dirty as they are? The houses round about are built anyhow. The lanes are tortuous and narrow. If even our temples are not models of roominess and cleanliness, what can our self-government be? Shall our temples be abodes of holiness, cleanliness and peace as soon as the English have retired from India, either of their own pleasure or by compulsion, bag and baggage?

I entirely agree with the President of the Congress that before we think of self-government, we shall have to do the necessary plodding. In every city there are two divisions, the cantonment and the city proper. The city mostly is a stinking den. But we are a people unused to city life. But if we want city life, we cannot reproduce the easy-going hamlet life. It is not comforting to think that people walk about the streets of Indian Bombay under the perpetual fear of dwellers in the storeyed building spitting upon them. I do a great deal of railway traveling. I observe the difficulty of third-class passengers. But the railway administration is by no means to blame for all their hard lot. We do not know the elementary laws of cleanliness. We spit anywhere on the carriage floor, irrespective of the thoughts that it is often used as sleeping space. We do not trouble ourselves as to how we use it; the result is indescribable filth in the compartment. The so-called better class passengers overawe their less fortunate brethren. Among them I have seen the student world also; sometimes they behave no better. They can speak English and they have worn Norfolk jackets and, therefore, claim the right to force their way in and command seating accommodation.

I have turned the searchlight all over, and as you have given me the privilege of speaking to you, I am laying my heart bare. Surely we must set these things right in our progress towards self-government. I now introduce you to another scene. His Highness the Maharaja who presided yesterday over our deliberations spoke about the poverty of India. Other speakers laid great stress upon it. But what did we witness in the great pandal in which the foundation ceremony was performed by the Viceroy? Certainly a most gorgeous show, an exhibition of jewellery, which made a splendid feast for the eyes of the greatest jeweller who chose to come from Paris. I compare with the richly bedecked noble men the millions of the poor. And I feel like saying to these noble men, 'There is no salvation for India unless you strip yourselves of this jewellery and hold it in trust for your countrymen in India.' I am sure it is not the desire of the King-Emperor or Lord Hardinge that in order to show the truest loyalty to our King-Emperor, it is necessary for us to ransack our jewellery boxes and to appear bedecked from top to toe. I would undertake, at the peril of my life, to bring to you a message from King George himself that he excepts nothing of the kind.

Sir, whenever I hear of a great palace rising in any great city of India, be it in British India or be it in India which is ruled by our great chiefs, I become jealous at once, and say, 'Oh, it is the money that has come from the agriculturists.' Over seventy-five per cent of the population are agriculturists and Mr. Higginbotham told us last night in his own felicitous language, that they are the men who grow two blades of grass in the place of one. But there cannot be much spirit of self-government about us, if we take away or allow others to take away from them almost the whole of the results of their labour. Our salvation can only come through the farmer. Neither the lawyers, nor the doctors, nor the rich landlords are going to secure it.

Now, last but not the least, it is my bounden duty to refer to what agitated our minds during these two or three days. All of us have had many anxious moments while the Viceroy was going through the streets of Banaras. There were detectives stationed in many places. We were horrified. We asked ourselves, 'Why this distrust?' Is it not better that even Lord Hardinge should die than live a living death? But a representative of a mighty sovereign may not. He might find it necessary to impose these detectives on us? We may foam, we may fret, we may resent, but let us not forget that India of today in her impatience has produced an army of anarchists. I myself am an anarchist, but of another type. But there is a class of anarchists amongst us, and if I was able to reach this class, I would say to them that their anarchism has no room in India, if India is to conqueror. It is a sign of fear. If we trust and fear God, we shall have to fear no one, not the Maharajas, not the Viceroys, not the detectives, not even King George.

I honour the anarchist for his love of the country. I honour him for his bravery in being willing to die for his country; but I ask him—is killing honourable? Is the dagger of an assassin a fit precursor of an honourable death? I deny it. There is no warrant for such methods in any scriptures. If I found it necessary for the salvation of India that the English should retire, that they should be driven out, I would not hesitate to declare that they would have to go, and I hope I would be prepared to die in defence of that belief. That would, in my opinion, be an honourable death. The bomb-thrower creates secret plots, is afraid to come out into the open, and when caught pays the penalty of misdirected zeal.

I have been told, 'Had we not done this, had some people not thrown bombs, we should never have gained what we have got with reference to the partition movement.' (Mrs. Besant: 'Please stop it.') This was what I said in Bengal when Mr. Lyon presided at the meeting. I think what I am saying is necessary. If I am told to stop I shall obey. (Turning to the Chairman) I await your orders. If you consider that by my speaking as I am, I am not serving the country and the empire I shall certainly stop. (Cries of 'Go on.') (The Chairman: 'Please, explain your object.') I am simply . . . (another interruption). My friends, please do not resent this interruption. If Mrs. Besant this evening suggests that I should stop, she does so because she loves India so well, and she considers that I am erring in thinking audibly before you young men. But even so, I simply say this, that I want to purge India of this atmosphere of suspicion on either side, if we are to reach our goal; we should have an empire which is to be based upon mutual love and mutual trust. Is it not better that we talk under the shadow of this college than that we should be talking irresponsibly in our homes? I consider that it is much better that we talk these things openly. I have done so with excellent results before now. I know that there is nothing that the students do not know. I am, therefore, turning the searchlight towards ourselves. I hold the name of my country so dear to me that I exchange these thoughts with you, and submit to you that there is no room for anarchism in India. Let us frankly and openly say whatever we want to say our rulers, and face the consequences if what we have to say does not please them. But let us not abuse.

I was talking the other day to a member of the much-abused Civil Service. I have not very much in common with the members of that Service, but I could not help admiring the manner in which he was speaking to mw. He said: 'Mr. Gandhi, do you for one moment suppose that all we, Civil Servants, are a bad lot, that we want to oppress the people whom we have come to govern?' 'No,' I said. 'Then if you get an opportunity put in a word for the much-abused Civil Service.' And I am here to put in that word. Yes, many members of the Indian Civil Service are most decidedly overbearing; they are tyrannical, at times thoughtless. Many other adjectives may be used. I grant all these things and I grant also that after having lived in India for a certain number of years some of them become somewhat degraded. But what does that signify? They were gentlemen before they came here, and if they have lost some of the moral fibre, it is a reflection upon ourselves.

Just think out for yourselves, if a man who was good yesterday has become bad after having come in contact with me, is he responsible that he has deteriorated or am I? The atmosphere of sycophancy and falsity that surrounds them on their coming to India demoralizes them, as it would many of us. It is well to take the blame sometimes. If we are to receive self-government, we shall have to take it. We shall never be granted self-government. Look at the history of the British Empire and the British nation; freedom loving as it is, it will not be a party to give freedom to a people who will not take it themselves. Learn your lesson if you wish to from the Boer War. Those who were enemies of that empire only a few years ago have now become friends.

20

POWER TO THE SOVIETS

Vladimir Ilyich Lenin

Russia

1917

The Bolshevik was a wing of the Russian Social Democratic Workers Party. Bolsheviks adopted the slogan, 'All power to the Soviets' during the 1917 revolution. It became one of the most popular slogans in revolutionary history. The party of Bolsheviks was founded by Lenin. It consisted of people from the working class.

Every revolution's objective is a shift in power. After the February Revolution, Lenin returned to Russia demanding that power be given to Soviets or workers' councils. The Soviets grasped this power in their hands and eventually defeated all their rival organizations.

'Drive nature out of the door and she will rush back through the window.' It seems that the Socialist-Revolutionary and Menshevik parties have to 'learn' this simple truth time and again by their own experience. They under took to be 'revolutionary democrats' and found themselves in the shoes of revolutionary democrats—they are now forced to draw the conclusions which every revolutionary democrat must draw.

Democracy is the rule of the majority. As long as the will of the majority was not clear, as long as it was possible to make it out to be unclear, at least with a grain of plausibility, the people were offered a counter-revolutionary bourgeois government disguised as 'democratic.' But this delay could not last long. During the several months that have passed since February 27th the will of the majority of the workers and peasants, of the overwhelming majority of the country's population, has become clear in more than a general sense. Their will has found expression in mass organisations—the Soviets of Workers', Soldiers' and Peasants' Deputies.

How, then, can anyone oppose the transfer of all power in the state to the Soviets? Such opposition means nothing but renouncing democracy! It means no more no less than imposing on the people a government which admittedly can neither come into being nor hold its ground democratically, i.e., as a result of truly free, truly popular elections.

It is a face, strange as it may seem at first sight, that the Socialist-revolutionaries and Mensheviks have forgotten this perfectly simple, perfectly obvious and palpable truth. Their position is so false, and they are so badly confused and bewildered, that they are unable to 'recover' this truth they have lost. Following the elections in Petrograd and in Moscow, the convocation of the All Russia Peasant Congress, and the Congress of Soviets, the classes and parties throughout Russia have shown what they stand for so clearly and specifically that people who have not gone mad or deliberately got themselves into a mess and simply cannot have any illusions on this score.

To tolerate the Cadet Ministers or the Cadet government or Cadet policies means challenging democrats and democracy. This is the source of the political crises since February 27th, and this also the source of the shakiness and vacillation of our government system. At every turn, daily and even hourly, appeals are being made to the people's revolutionary spirit and to their democracy on behalf of the most authoritative government institutions and congresses. Yet the government's policies in particular, are all departures from revolutionary principles, and breaches in democracy.

This sort of thing will not do.

It is inevitable that a situation like the present should show elements of instability now for one reason, now for another. And it is not exactly a clever policy of jib. Things are moving by fits and starts towards a point where power will be transferred to the Soviets, which is what our Party called for long ago.

21

WAR MESSAGE

Thomas Woodrow Wilson

Washington, D.C., U.S.A.

2 April 1917

The United States had proclaimed its neutrality from the beginning of World War I. However, in 1915, the Germans sunk 'Lusitania,' a British passenger ship, killing one hundred and twenty-eight Americans. America still maintained its neutrality in war, though Wilson sent a warning to Germany.

The year 1917 brought with it fresh offences committed by the Germans. Their unabated submarine warfare, sinking of the American cargo ship 'Housatonic' made Wilson break off his diplomatic ties with them.

Realizing that neutrality seemed impossible now, a month after his second inaugural address, Wilson addressed the Congress and asked for a declaration of war against Germany.

Two days after this speech, the U.S. Senate voted in favour of war by eighty-two votes to six.

Gentlemen of the Congress:

I have called the Congress into extraordinary session because there are serious, very serious, choices of policy to be made, and made immediately, which it was neither right nor constitutionally permissible that I should assume the responsibility of making.

On the third of February last I officially laid before you the extraordinary announcement of the Imperial German Government that on and after the first day of February it was its purpose to put aside all restraints of law or of humanity and use its submarines to sink every vessel that sought to approach either the ports of Great Britain and Ireland or the western coasts of Europe or any of the ports controlled by the enemies of Germany within the Mediterranean. That had seemed to be the object of the German submarine warfare earlier in the war, but since April of last year the Imperial Government had somewhat restrained the commanders of its undersea craft in conformity with its promise then given to us that passenger boats should not be sunk and that due warning would be given to all other vessels which its submarines might seek to destroy, when no resistance was offered or escape attempted, and care taken that their crews were given at least a fair chance to save their lives in their open boats. The precautions taken were meagre and haphazard enough, as was proved in distressing instance after instance in the progress of the cruel and unmanly business, but a certain degree of restraint was observed The new policy has swept every restriction aside. Vessels of every kind, whatever their flag, their character, their cargo, their destination, their errand, have been ruthlessly sent to the bottom without warning and without thought of help or mercy for those on board, the vessels of friendly neutrals along with those of belligerents. Even hospital ships and ships carrying relief to the sorely bereaved and stricken people of Belgium, though the latter were provided with safe conduct through the proscribed areas by the German Government itself and were distinguished by unmistakable marks of identity, have been sunk with the same reckless lack of compassion or of principle.

I was for a little while unable to believe that such things would in fact be done by any government that had hitherto subscribed to the humane practices of civilized nations. International law had its origin in the attempt to set up some law which would be respected and observed upon the seas, where no nation had right of dominion and where lay the free highways of the world. By painful stage after stage has that law been built up, with meagre enough results, indeed, after all was accomplished that could be accomplished, but always with a clear view, at least, of what the heart and conscience of mankind demanded. This minimum of right the German Government has swept aside under the plea of retaliation and necessity and because it had no weapons which it could use at sea except these which it is impossible to employ as it is employing them without throwing to the winds all scruples of humanity or of respect for the understandings that were supposed to underlie the intercourse of the world. I am not now thinking of the loss of property involved, immense and serious as that is, but only of the wanton and wholesale destruction of the lives of non-combatants, men, women, and children, engaged in pursuits which have always, even in the darkest periods of modern history, been deemed innocent and legitimate. Property can be paid for; the lives of peaceful and innocent people cannot be. The present German submarine warfare against commerce is a warfare against mankind.

It is a war against all nations. American ships have been sunk, American lives taken, in ways which it has stirred us very deeply to learn of, but the ships and people of other neutral and friendly nations have been sunk and overwhelmed in the waters in the same way. There has been no discrimination. The challenge is to all mankind. Each nation must decide for itself how it will meet it. The choice we make for ourselves must be made with a moderation of counsel and a temperateness of judgment befitting our character and our motives as a nation. We must put excited feeling away. Our motive will not be revenge or the victorious assertion of the physical might of the nation, but only the vindication of right, of human right, of which we are only a single champion.

When I addressed the Congress on the twenty-sixth of February last, I thought that it would suffice to assert our neutral rights with arms, our right to use the seas against unlawful interference, our right to keep our people safe against unlawful violence. But armed neutrality, it now appears, is impracticable. Because submarines are in effect outlaws when used as the German submarines have been used against merchant shipping, it is impossible to defend ships against their attacks as the law of nations has assumed that merchantmen would defend themselves against privateers or cruisers, visible craft giving chase upon the open sea. It is common prudence in such circumstances, grim necessity indeed, to endeavour to destroy them before they have shown their own intention. They must be dealt with upon sight, if dealt with at all. The German Government denies the right of neutrals to use arms at all within the areas of the sea which it has proscribed, even in the defence of rights which no modern publicist has ever before questioned their right to defend. The intimation is conveyed that the armed guards which we have placed on our merchant ships will be treated as beyond the pale of law and subject to be dealt with as pirates would be. Armed neutrality is ineffectual enough at best; in such circumstances and in the face of such pretensions it is worse than ineffectual; it is likely only to produce what it was meant to prevent; it is practically certain to draw us into the war without either the rights or the effectiveness of belligerents. There is one choice we cannot make, we are incapable of making: we will not choose the path of submission and suffer the most sacred rights of our nation and our people to be ignored or violated. The wrongs against which we now array ourselves are no common wrongs; they cut to the very roots of human life.

With a profound sense of the solemn and even tragical character of the step I am taking and of the grave responsibilities which it involves, but in unhesitating obedience to what I deem my constitutional duty, I advise that the Congress declare the recent course of the Imperial German Government to be in fact nothing less than war against the Government and people of the United States; that it formally accept the status of belligerent which has thus been thrust upon it, and that it take immediate steps not only to put the country in a more thorough state of defence but also to exert all its power and employ all its resources to bring the Government of the German Empire to terms and end the war.

What this will involve is clear. It will involve the utmost practicable cooperation in counsel and action with the governments now at war with Germany, and, as incident to that, the extension to those governments of the most liberal financial credits, in order that our resources may so far as possible be added to theirs. It will involve the organization and mobilization of all the material resources of the country to supply the materials of war and serve the incidental needs of the nation in the most abundant and yet the most economical and efficient way possible. It will involve the immediate full equipment of the Navy in all respects but particularly in supplying it with the best means of dealing with the enemy's submarines. It will involve the immediate addition to the armed forces of the United States already provided for by law in case of war at least 500,000 men, who should, in my opinion, be chosen upon the principle of universal liability to service, and also the authorization of subsequent additional increments of equal force so soon as they may be needed and can be handled in training. It will involve also, of course, the granting of adequate credits to the government, sustained, I hope, so far as they can equitably be sustained by the present generation, by well-conceived taxation.

While we do these things, these deeply momentous things, let us be very clear, and make very clear to all the world what our motives and our objects are. My own thought has not been driven from its habitual and normal course by the unhappy events of the last two months, and I do not believe that the thought of the nation has been altered or clouded by them I have exactly the same things in mind now that I had in mind when I addressed the Senate on the 22nd of January last; the same that I had in mind when I addressed the Congress on the 3rd of February and on the 26th of February. Our object now, as then, is to vindicate the principles of peace and justice in the life of the world as against selfish and autocratic power and to set up amongst the really free and self-governed peoples of the world such a concert of purpose and of action as will henceforth ensure the observance of those principles. Neutrality is no longer feasible or desirable where the peace of the world is involved and the freedom of its peoples, and the menace to that peace and freedom lies in the existence of autocratic governments backed by organized force which is controlled wholly by their will, not by the will of their people. We have seen the last of neutrality in such circumstances. We are at the beginning of an age in which it will be insisted that the same standards of conduct and of responsibility for wrong done shall be observed among nations and their governments that are observed among the individual citizens of civilized states.

We have no quarrel with the German people. We have no feeling towards them but one of sympathy and friendship. It was not upon their impulse that their government acted in entering this war. It was not with their previous knowledge or approval. It was a war determined upon as wars used to be determined upon in the old, unhappy days when peoples were nowhere consulted by their rulers and wars were provoked and waged in the interest of dynasties or of little groups of ambitious men who were accustomed to use their fellow men as pawns and tools. Self-governed nations do not fill their neighbour states with spies or set the course of intrigue to bring about some critical posture of affairs which will give them an opportunity to strike and make conquest. Such designs can be successfully worked out only under cover and where no one has the right to ask questions. Cunningly contrived plans of deception or aggression, carried, it may be, from generation to generation, can be worked out and kept from the light only within the privacy of courts or behind the carefully guarded confidences of a narrow and privileged class. They are happily impossible where public opinion commands and insists upon full information concerning all the nation's affairs.

A steadfast concert for peace can never be maintained except by a partnership of democratic nations. No autocratic government could be trusted to keep faith within it or observe its covenants. It must be a league of honour, a partnership of opinion. Intrigue would eat its vitals away; the plottings of inner circles who could plan what they would and render account to no one would be a corruption seated at its very heart. Only free peoples can hold their purpose and their honour steady to a common end and prefer the interests of mankind to any narrow interest of their own.

Does not every American feel that assurance has been added to our hope for the future peace of the world by the wonderful and heartening things that have been happening within the last few weeks in Russia? Russia was known by those who knew it best to have been always in fact democratic at heart, in all the vital habits of her thought, in all the intimate relationships of her people that spoke their natural instinct, their habitual attitude towards life. The autocracy that crowned the summit of her political structure, long as it had stood and terrible as was the reality of its power, was not in fact Russian in origin, character, or purpose; and now it has been shaken off and the great, generous Russian people have been added in all their naive majesty and might to the forces that are fighting for freedom in the world, for justice, and for peace. Here is a fit partner for a league of honour.

One of the things that has served to convince us that the Prussian autocracy was not and could never be our friend is that from the very outset of the present war it has filled our unsuspecting communities and even our offices of government with spies and set criminal intrigues everywhere afoot against our national unity of counsel, our peace within and without our industries and our commerce. Indeed it is now evident that its spies were here even before the war began; and it is unhappily not a matter of conjecture but a fact proved in our courts of justice that the intrigues which have more than once come perilously near to disturbing the peace and dislocating the industries of the country have been carried on at the instigation, with the support, and even under the personal direction of official agents of the Imperial Government accredited to the Government of the United States. Even in checking these things and trying to extirpate them we have sought to put the most generous interpretation possible upon them because we knew that their source lay, not in any hostile feeling or purpose of the German people towards us (who were, no doubt, as ignorant of them as we ourselves were), but only in the selfish designs of a government that did what it pleased and told its people nothing. But they have played their part in serving to convince us at last that that government entertains no real friendship for us and means to act against our peace and security at its convenience. That it means to stir up enemies against us at our very doors the intercepted note to the German Minister at Mexico City is eloquent evidence.

We are accepting this challenge of hostile purpose because we know that in such a government, following such methods, we can never have a friend; and that in the presence of its organized power, always lying in wait to accomplish we know not what purpose, there can be no assured security for the democratic governments of the world. We are now about to accept gage of battle with this natural foe to liberty and shall, if necessary, spend the whole force of the nation to check and nullify its pretensions and its power. We are glad, now that we see the facts with no veil of false pretence about them, to fight thus for the ultimate peace of the world and for the liberation of its peoples, the German peoples included: for the rights of nations great and small and the privilege of men everywhere to choose their way of life and of obedience. The world must be made safe for democracy. Its peace must be planted upon the tested foundations of political liberty. We have no selfish ends to serve. We desire no conquest, no dominion. We seek no indemnities for ourselves, no material compensation for the sacrifices we shall freely make. We are but one of the champions of the rights of mankind. We shall be satisfied when those rights have been made as secure as the faith and the freedom of nations can make them.

Just because we fight without rancour and without selfish object, seeking nothing for ourselves but what we shall wish to share with all free peoples, we shall, I feel confident, conduct our operations as belligerents without passion and ourselves observe with proud punctilio the principles of right and of fair play we profess to be fighting for.

I have said nothing of the governments allied with the Imperial Government of Germany because they have not made war upon us or challenged us to defend our right and our honour. The Austro-Hungarian Government has, indeed, avowed its unqualified endorsement and acceptance of the reckless and lawless submarine warfare adopted now without disguise by the Imperial German Government, and it has therefore not been possible for this government to receive Count Tarnowski, the Ambassador recently accredited to this government by the Imperial and Royal Government of Austria-Hungary; but that government has not actually engaged in warfare against citizens of the United States on the seas, and I take the liberty, for the present at least, of postponing a discussion of our relations with the authorities at Vienna. We enter this war only where we are clearly forced into it because there are no other means of defending our rights.

It will be all the easier for us to conduct ourselves as belligerents in a high spirit of right and fairness because we act without animus, not in enmity towards a people or with the desire to bring any injury or disadvantage upon them, but only in armed opposition to an irresponsible government which has thrown aside all considerations of humanity and of right and is running amuck. We are, let me say again, the sincere friends of the German people, and shall desire nothing so much as the early reestablishment of intimate relations of mutual advantage between us—however hard it may be for them, for the time being, to believe that this is spoken from our hearts. We have borne with their present government through all these bitter months because of that friendship—exercising a patience and forbearance which would otherwise have been impossible. We shall, happily, still have an opportunity to prove that friendship in our daily attitude and actions towards the millions of men and women of German birth and native sympathy, who live amongst us and share our life, and we shall be proud to prove it towards all who are in fact loyal to their neighbours and to the government in the hour of test. They are, most of them, as true and loyal Americans as if they had never known any other fealty or allegiance. They will be prompt to stand with us in rebuking and restraining the few who may be of a different mind and purpose. If there should be disloyalty, it will be dealt with, with a firm hand of stern repression; but, if it lifts its head at all, it will lift it only here and there and without countenance except from a lawless and malignant few.

It is a distressing and oppressive duty, gentlemen of the Congress, which I have performed in thus addressing you. There are, it may be, many months of fiery trial and sacrifice ahead of us. It is a fearful thing to lead this great peaceful people into war, into the most terrible and disastrous of all wars, civilization itself seeming to be in the balance. But the right is more precious than peace, and we shall fight for the things which we have always carried nearest our hearts—for democracy, for the right of those who submit to authority to have a voice in their own governments, for the rights and liberties of small nations, for a universal dominion of right by such a concert of free peoples as shall bring peace and safety to all nations and make the world itself at last free. To such a task we can dedicate our lives and our fortunes, everything that we are and everything that we have, with the pride of those who know that the day has come when America is privileged to spend her blood and her might for the principles that gave her birth and happiness and the peace which she has treasured. God helping her, she can do no other.

22

FREEDOM IS MY BIRTHRIGHT

Bal Gangadhar Tilak

Nasik, India

17 May 1917

Triggering a strong wave of patriotism, one of the most potent cries of the Indian freedom struggle was coined by Bal Gangadhar Tilak—'Freedom is my birthright.' He was the strongest advocate of Swaraj (self-rule). Swaraj for Tilak had to be complete self-rule, and he made no excuses about it.

The following speech was given at the first anniversary of the Home Rule League. Tilak founded the first league in April 1916. The organization's aim was to mobilize public opinion in favour of self-government in India.

Tilak's nationalism appealed to the Indian masses' sentiments with a spiritual approach. He refers to the Bhagvadgita and the Vedas in this speech in support of his arguments, proclaiming that Swaraj was their dharma.

I am young in spirit though old in body. I do not wish to lose this privilege of youth. To deny the growing capacity to my thinking power is to admit that I have no right to speak on this resolution. Whatever I am going to speak today is eternally young. The body might grow old, decrepit, and it might perish, but the soul is immortal. Similarly, if there might be an apparent lull in our home rule activities, the freedom of the spirit behind it is eternal and indestructible, and it will secure liberty for us. The Soul means Parameshwar and the mind will not get peace till it gets identified with him. If one body is worn out, the soul will take another: so assures the Gita. This philosophy is quite old. Freedom is my birthright. So long as it is awake within me, I am not old. No weapon can cut this spirit, no fire can burn it, no water can wet it, no wind can dry it. I say further that no C.I.D. can burn it. I declare the same principle to the Superintendent of Police who is sitting before me, to the Collector who had been invited to attend this meeting and to the government shorthand writer who is busy taking down notes of our speeches. This principle will not disappear even if it seems to be killed.

We ask for home rule and we must get it. The science which ends in home rule is the science of politics and not the one which ends in slavery. The science of politics is the 'veda' of the country. You have a soul and I only want to waken it up. I want to tear off the blind that has been let down by ignorant, conniving, and selfish people. The science of politics consists of two parts. The first is divine and the second is demonic. The slavery of a nation constitutes the latter part. There cannot be a moral justification for the demonic part of the science of politics. A nation which might justify this, is guilty of sin in the sight of God. Some people do and some do not have the courage to declare what is harmful to them. Political and religious teaching consists in giving the knowledge of this principle. Religious and political teachings are not separate, though they appear to be so on account of foreign rule. All philosophies are included in the science of politics.

Who does not know the meaning of home rule? Who does not want it? Would you like it if I enter your house and take possession of your kitchen? I must have the right to manage the affairs in my own house. It is only lunatics and children who do not know how to manage their own affairs. The cardinal creed of the conferences is that a member must be above twenty-one years of age. Do you not therefore think that you want your own rights? Not being lunatics or children you understand your own business, your own rights and therefore, you know home rule. We are told we are not fit for home rule. A century has passed away and the British Rule has not made us fit for home rule; now we will make our own efforts and make ourselves fit for it. To offer irrelevant excuses, to hold out any temptations, and to make other offers will be putting a stigma on the English policy. England is trying to protect the small state of Belgium with India's help; how can it then say that we should not have home rule? Those who find fault with us are avaricious people. But there are people who find fault even with the all-merciful God. We must work hard to save the soul of our nation without caring for anything.

The good of our country consists in guarding this birthright. The Congress has passed this home rule resolution. The provincial conference is only a child of the Congress, which submits to mandates of its father. We will follow Shri Ramachandra in obeying the order of our father the Congress. We are determined to make efforts to get this resolution enforced even if the effort leads us to the desert, compels us to live incognito, makes us suffer any hardships, and even if it finally brings us to death. Shri Ramachandra did it. Do not pass this resolution by merely clapping your hands, but by taking a solemn vow that you will work for it. We will work for it by every possible constitutional and law-abiding method to get home rule.

Through the grace of God, England has changed its mind

towards us. We feel our efforts will not be without success. England proudly thought that a tiny nation might be able to protect the Empire by itself. This pride has gone down. England has now begun to feel that it must make changes in the constitution of the Empire. Lloyd George has openly confessed that England cannot go on without the help of India. All notions about a nation of a thousand years old have to be changed. The English people have discovered that the wisdom of all their parties is not sufficient. The Indian soldiers have saved the lives of the British soldiers on the French battlefield and have showed their bravery. Those who once considered us as slaves have begun now to call us brothers. God has brought about all these changes. We must push our demands while the notion of this brotherhood is existing in the minds of the English. We must inform them that we, thirty crores of the Indian people, are ready to lay down our lives for the Empire; and that while we are with them, none shall dare cast an evil glance at the Empire.

The Karma Yoga which I preach is not a new theory; neither was the discovery of the Law of Karma made as recently as today. The knowledge of the law is so ancient that not even Shri Krishna was the great Teacher who first propounded it. It must be remembered that Karma Yoga has been our sacred heritage from time immemorial when we Indians were seated on the high pedestal of wealth and lore. Karma Yoga, or to put it in another way, the law of Duty, is the combination of all that is best in spiritual science, in actual action, and in an unselfish meditative life. Compliance with this universal law leads to the realization of the most cherished ideals of man. Swaraj is the natural consequence of diligent performance of duty. The Karma Yogin strives for Swaraj, and the Gnyanin or spiritualist yearns for it. What is then this Swaraj? It is a life centred in self and dependent upon elf. There is Swaraj in this world as well as in the world hereafter. The Rishis who laid down the law of duty betook themselves to forests, because the people were already enjoying Swaraj or People's Dominion, which was administered and defended in the first instance by the Kshatriya kings.

It is my conviction, it is my thesis, that Swaraj in the life to come cannot be the reward of a people who have not enjoyed it in this world. Such was the doctrine taught by our forefathers who never intended that the goal of life should be meditation alone. No one can expect the providence to protect one who sits with folded arms and throws his burden on others. God does not help the indolent. You must be doing all that you can to lift yourself up, and then only you may rely on the Almighty to help you. You should not, however, presume that you have to toil that you yourself might reap the fruit of your labours. That cannot always be the case.

Let us then try our utmost and leave the generations to come to enjoy that fruit. Remember, it is not you who had planted the mango trees the fruit whereof you have tasted. Let the advantage now go to our children and their descendants. It is only given to us to toil and work. And so, there ought to be no relaxation in our efforts, lest we incur the curse of those that come after us. Action alone must be our guiding principle, action disinterested and well thought out. It does not matter who the Sovereign is. It is enough if we have full liberty to elevate ourselves in the best possible manner. This is celled the immutable Dharma, and Karma Yoga is nothing but the method which leads to the attainment of Dharma or material and spiritual glory.

We demand Swaraj, as it is the foundation and not the height of our future prosperity. Swaraj does not at all imply a denial of British Sovereignty or British aegis. It means only that we Indians should be reckoned among the patriotic and self-respecting peoples of the Empire. We must refuse to be treated like the 'dumb cattle driven.' If poor Indians starve in famine days, it is other people who take care of them. This is not an enviable position. It is neither creditable nor beneficial if other people have to do everything for us. God has declared His will. He has willed that Self can be exalted only through its own efforts. Everything lies in your hands. Karma Yoga does not look upon this world as nothing; it requires only that our motives should be untainted by selfish interest and passion. This is the true view of practical Vedanta the key to which is apt to be lost in sophistry.

In practical politics some futile objections are raised to oppose our desire for Swaraj. Illiteracy of the bulk of our people is one of such objections but to my mind it ought not to be allowed to stand in our way. It would be sufficient for us even if the illiterate in our country have only a vague conception of Swaraj, just as it all goes well with them if they have simply a hazy idea about God. Those who can efficiently manage their own affairs may be illiterate; but they are not therefore idiots. They are as intelligent as any educated man and if they could understand their immediate concerns they should not find any difficulty in grasping the principle of Swaraj. If illiteracy is not a disqualification in civil law there is no reason why it should not be so in nature's law also. Even the illiterate are our brethren; they have the same rights and are actuated by the same aspirations. It is, therefore, out bounden duty to awaken the masses. Circumstances are changed, and are favourable. The voice has gone forth 'Now or never.' Rectitude and constitutional agitation is alone what is expected of you. Turn not back, and confidently leave the ultimate issue to the benevolence of the Almighty.

Note: The second home rule league was started by Annie Besant in September 1917.

23

THE FOURTEEN POINTS

Thomas Woodrow Wilson

Washington, D.C., U.S.A.

8 January 1918

President Wilson, addressing the Congress, lay down a blueprint for peace negotiations after World War I ended. The following speech was translated and distributed to the soldiers and citizens of Germany and Austria-Hungary.

Though the ideas presented in the speech were liberal and democratic, many leaders of other Allied nations disagreed with them. Some of them demanded stiff penalties for Germany at the Paris Peace Conference, held a year after this speech was delivered.

Gentlemen of the Congress:

Once more, as repeatedly before, the spokesmen of the Central Empires have indicated their desire to discuss the objects of the war and the possible basis of a general peace. Parleys have been in progress at Brest-Litovsk between Russian representatives and representatives of the Central Powers to which the attention of all the belligerents has been invited for the purpose of ascertaining whether it may be possible to extend these parleys into a general conference with regard to terms of peace and settlement.

The Russian representatives presented not only a perfectly definite statement of the principles upon which they would be willing to conclude peace, but also an equally definite program of the concrete application of those principles. The representatives of the Central Powers, on their part, presented an outline of settlement which, if much less definite, seemed susceptible of liberal interpretation until their specific program of practical terms was added. That program proposed no concessions at all, either to the sovereignty of Russia or to the preferences of the populations with whose fortunes it dealt, but meant, in a word, that the Central Empires were to keep every foot of territory their armed forces had occupied—every province, every city, every point of vantage as a permanent addition to their territories and their power.

It is a reasonable conjecture that the general principles of settlement which they at first suggested originated with the more liberal statesmen of Germany and Austria, the men who have begun to feel the force of their own peoples' thought and purpose, while the concrete terms of actual settlement came from the military leaders who have no thought but to keep what they have got. The negotiations have been broken off. The Russian representatives were sincere and in earnest. They cannot entertain such proposals of conquest and domination.

The whole incident is full of significance. It is also full of perplexity. With whom are the Russian representatives dealing? For whom are the representatives of the Central Empires speaking? Are they speaking for the majorities of their respective parliaments or for the minority parties, that military and imperialistic minority which has so far dominated their whole policy and controlled the affairs of Turkey and of the Balkan States which have felt obliged to become their associates in this war?

The Russian representatives have insisted, very justly, very wisely, and in the true spirit of modern democracy, that the conferences they have been holding with the Teutonic and Turkish statesmen should be held within open, not closed, doors, and all the world lies been audience, as was desired. To whom have we been listening, then? To those who speak the spirit and intention of the resolutions of the German Reichstag of the 9th of July last, the spirit and intention of the liberal leaders and parties of Germany, or to those who resist and defy that spirit and intention and insist upon conquest and subjugation? Or are we listening, in fact, to both, unreconciled and in open and hopeless contradiction? These are very serious and pregnant questions. Upon the answer to them depends the peace of the world.

But whatever the results of the parleys at Brest-Litovsk, whatever the confusions of counsel and of purpose in the utterances of the spokesmen of the Central Empires, they have again attempted to acquaint the world with their objects in the war and have again challenged their adversaries to say what their objects are and what sort of settlement they would deem just and satisfactory. There is no good reason why that challenge should not be responded to, and responded to with the utmost candour. We did not wait for it. Not once, but again and again we have laid our whole thought and purpose before the world, not in general terms only, but each time with sufficient definition to make it clear what sort of definite terms of settlement must necessarily spring out of them. Within the last week, Mr. Lloyd George has spoken with admirable candour and in admirable spirit for the people and Government of Great Britain.

There is no confusion of counsel among the adversaries of the Central Powers, no uncertainty of principle, no vagueness of detail. The only secrecy of counsel, the only lack of fearless frankness, the only failure to make definite statement of the objects of the war, lies with Germany and her allies. The issues of life and death hang upon these definitions. No statesman who has the least conception of his responsibility ought for a moment to permit himself to continue this tragical and appalling outpouring of blood and treasure unless he is sure beyond a peradventure that the objects of the vital sacrifice are part and parcel of the very life of society and that the people for whom he speaks think them right and imperative as he does.

There is, moreover, a voice calling for these definitions of principle and of purpose which is, it seems to me, more thrilling and more compelling than any of the many moving voices with which the troubled air of the world is filled. It is the voice of the Russian people. They are prostrate and all but helpless, it would seem, before the grim power of Germany, which has hitherto known no relenting and no pity. Their power, apparently, is shattered. And yet their soul is not subservient. They will not yield either in principle or in action. Their conception of what is right, of what is humane and honourable for them to accept, has been stated with a frankness, a largeness of view, a generosity of spirit, and a universal human sympathy which must challenge the admiration of every friend of mankind; and they have refused to compound their ideals or desert others that they themselves may be safe.

They call to us to say what it is that we desire, in what, if in anything, our purpose and our spirit differ from theirs; and I believe that the people of the United States would wish me to respond, with utter simplicity and frankness. Whether their present leaders believe it or not, it is our heartfelt desire and hope that some way may be opened whereby we may be privileged to assist the people of Russia to attain their utmost hope of liberty and ordered peace.

It will be our wish and purpose that the processes of peace, when they are begun, shall be absolutely open and that they shall involve and permit henceforth no secret understandings of any kind. The day of conquest and aggrandizement is gone by; so is also the day of secret covenants entered into in the interest of particular governments and likely at some unlooked-for moment to upset the peace of the world. It is this happy fact, now clear to the view of every public man whose thoughts do not still linger in an age that is dead and gone, which makes it possible for every nation whose purposes are consistent with justice and the peace of the world to avow now or at any other time the objects it has in view.

We entered this war because violations of right had occurred which touched us to the quick and made the life of our own people impossible unless they were corrected and the world secured once for all against their recurrence.

What we demand in this war, therefore, is nothing peculiar to ourselves. It is that the world be made fit and safe to live in; and particularly that it be made safe for every peace-loving nation which, like our own, wishes to live its own life, determine its own institutions, be assured of justice and fair dealing by the other peoples of the world, as against force and selfish aggression.

All the peoples of the world are in effect partners in this interest, and for our own part we see very clearly that unless justice be done to others it will not be done to us.

The program of the world's peace, therefore, is our programme; and that programme, the only possible programme, all we see it, is this:

1. Open covenants of peace must be arrived at, after which there will surely be no private international action or rulings of any kind, but diplomacy shall proceed always frankly and in the public view.
2. Absolute freedom of navigation upon the seas, outside territorial waters, alike in peace and in war, except as the

seas may be closed in whole or in part by international action for the enforcement of international covenants.

3. The removal, so far as possible, of all economic barriers and the establishment of an equality of trade conditions among all the nations consenting to the peace and associating themselves for its maintenance.
4. Adequate guarantees given and taken that national armaments will be reduced to the lowest points consistent with domestic safety.
5. A free, open-minded, and absolutely impartial adjustment of all colonial claims, based upon a strict observance of the principle that in determining all such questions of sovereignty the interests of the population concerned must have equal weight with the equitable claims of the government whose title is to be determined.
6. The evacuation of all Russian territory and such a settlement of all questions affecting Russia as will secure the best and freest cooperation of the other nations of the world in obtaining for her an unhampered and unembarrassed opportunity for the independent determination of her own political development and national policy, and assure her of a sincere welcome into the society of free nations under institutions of her own choosing; and, more than a welcome, assistance also of every kind that she may need and may herself desire. The treatment accorded Russia by her sister nations in the months to come will be the acid test of their goodwill, of their comprehension of her needs as distinguished from their own interests, and of their intelligent and unselfish sympathy.
7. Belgium, the whole world will agree, must be evacuated and restored, without any attempt to limit the sovereignty which she enjoys in common with all other free nations.

No other single act will serve as this will serve to restore confidence among the nations in the laws which they have themselves set and determined for the government of their relations with one another. Without this healing act the whole structure and validity of international law is forever impaired.

8. All French territory should be freed and the invaded portions restored, and the wrong done to France by Prussia in 1871 in the matter of Alsace-Lorraine, which has unsettled the peace of the world for nearly fifty years, should be righted, in order that peace may once more be made secure in the interest of all.
9. A readjustment of the frontiers of Italy should be effected along clearly recognizable lines of nationality.
10. The peoples of Austria-Hungary, whose place among the nations we wish to see safeguarded and assured, should be accorded the freest opportunity of autonomous development.
11. Romania, Serbia, and Montenegro should be evacuated; occupied territories restored; Serbia accorded free and secure access to the sea; and the relations of the several Balkan states to one another determined by friendly counsel along historically established lines of allegiance and nationality; and international guarantees of the political and economic independence and territorial integrity of the several Balkan states should be entered into.
12. The Turkish portion of the present Ottoman Empire should be assured a secure sovereignty, but the other nationalities which are now under Turkish rule should be assured an undoubted security of life and an absolutely unmolested opportunity of autonomous development, and the Dardanelles should be permanently opened as

a free passage to the ships and commerce of all nations under international guarantees.

13. An independent Polish state should be erected which should include the territories inhabited by indisputably Polish populations, which should be assured a free and secure access to the sea, and whose political and economic independence and territorial integrity should be guaranteed by international covenant.
14. A general association of nations must be formed under specific covenants for the purpose of affording mutual guarantees of political independence and territorial integrity to great and small states alike.

In regard to these essential rectifications of wrong and assertions of right, we feel ourselves to be intimate partners of all the governments and peoples associated together against the imperialists. We cannot be separated in interest or divided in purpose. We stand together until the end.

For such arrangements and covenants we are willing to fight and to continue to fight until they are achieved; but only because we wish the right to prevail and desire a just and stable peace such as can be secured only by removing the chief provocations to war, which this program does remove.

We have no jealousy of German greatness, and there is nothing in this program that impairs it. We grudge her no achievement or distinction of learning or of pacific enterprise such as have made her record very bright and very enviable. We do not wish to injure her or to block in any way her legitimate influence or power. We do not wish to fight her either with arms or with hostile arrangements of trade, if she is willing to associate herself with us and the other peace-loving nations of the world in covenants of justice and law and fair dealing.

We wish her only to accept a place of equality among the peoples of the world—the new world in which we now live—instead of a place of mastery.

Neither do we presume to suggest to her any alteration or modification of her institutions. But it is necessary, we must frankly say, and necessary as a preliminary to any intelligent dealings with her on our part, that we should know whom her spokesmen speak for when they speak to us, whether for the Reichstag majority or for the military party and the men whose creed is imperial domination.

We have spoken now, surely, in terms too concrete to admit of any further doubt or question. An evident principle runs through the whole program I have outlined. It is the principle of justice to all peoples and nationalities, and their right to live on equal terms of liberty and safety with one another, whether they be strong or weak.

Unless this principle be made its foundation, no part of the structure of international justice can stand. The people of the United States could act upon no other principle, and to the vindication of this principle they are ready to devote their lives, their honour, and everything that they possess. The moral climax of this, the culminating and final war for human liberty has come, and they are ready to put their own strength, their own highest purpose, their own integrity and devotion to the test.

24

BOYCOTT THE SIMON COMMISSION

Lala Lajpat Rai

New Delhi, India

16 February 1928

The Simon Commission consisted of Sir John Simon and six other members. It had been appointed in November 1927 to give a report on the working of the Indian Constitution. The fact that there were no Indians in the Commission was not received well.

Lala ji gave the following speech at the Legislative Assembly submitting a resolution for boycotting the Simon Commission. There were several Englishmen and government officers present in the Assembly, who voted against the resolution.

The day he died, Lala Lajpat Rai's cry 'Simon, go back!' reverberated in the air as he led a protest against the Simon Commission.

I rise to move the Resolution that stands in my name and I do so with the profoundest sense of responsibility that I have ever felt in the discharge of any public duty. I shall at the beginning give very briefly and categorically my reasons for the action that

I am taking. My first reason is that I have no faith in the bona fides of the government or of the people who have appointed this Commission. Why I have no faith in them, I shall state later on. My second reason is that I have no faith in the competency of the Commission that has been appointed. I acknowledge, sir, that Sir John Simon is one of the ablest members of the British nation and I give the members of the Commission the fullest possible credit for their good intentions and good motives. But the very fact which has been made a ground of their appointment, namely, their ignorance of India, Indian history and Indian politics, is, in my judgement, their greatest disqualification to enter upon the task which has been entrusted to them. The problem of India is so vast and so complicated that even if the gods were to descend from the heavens, they cannot master it in such a short time as is at the disposal or this Commission. Sir, the members of the Commission cannot in this short space of time make any intelligent recommendations which may be acceptable both to England and to India. My impression is that all that the Commission will do is practically recording, in a gramophone what they will be told by the bureaucracy here and eventually they will be recording in another gramophone their recommendations in consultation with some other people in England.

The very secretive methods which they are employing even now at the present moment in going about their business justify me in making this statement. They are very much afraid of going out in public and informing the people of their movements. They move from place to place in secrecy and a mystery is surrounding them. That in itself shows that the people who guide them will practically choose what they want to place before them. My third ground for the action which I am taking is that I have no faith in any Commission's ability to settle the Indian problem. I can understand commissions being appointed for inquiry into facts which are disputed or which are not clear but I question the competency of any commission to settle the fitness of nations to rule themselves and to settle constitutions for them which have to be worked by them in their own interests. In my judgment, the problem of India is not for Commissions, it must be tackled by representative men both from England and India in a spirit of conciliation and negotiations. It is only then that it may be possible to solve this problem by an agreement which, may eventually be ratified by parliament.

Sir, we on this side of the House, who have been taking that position, have been very much misrepresented about our attitude towards the parliament. It has been said that we do not realize the realities and that we ignore the fact that the parliament is the primary and ultimate arbiter of the destinies of India. Sir, their responsibility may be ultimate, but it is not primary. I do not concede that proposition. My own idea is that we have never, even on this side of the House, said that we propose to dictate to parliament. What we said was that the settlement of the question must be approached in a spirit of mutual conciliation, of mutual understanding of the interests of the two countries, and that only on that basis could we arrive at an agreement which may be acceptable to both parties and may be automatically sanctioned by parliament I use the word 'automatically,' because parliament never does anything except what the government for the time being wants it to do. Government represents the machinery of parliament, and therefore parliament is only in a way the machinery by which the government for the time being carries on its business and records its decisions. If the government for the time being enters into an agreement with the representatives of India, parliament will automatically ratify the agreement and give effect to it. That is what we mean by saying that we should be entrusted with the task of making a constitution and then parliament can sanction it.

Now, sir, having given these grounds briefly, I will come to the arguments that have been given by the Secretary of State for the appointment of such a commission. The Secretary of State has told us many things. One of the things he has told us is that it is the duty of parliament and parliament alone to consider and decide this question. He says that parliament took the government of the country from the East India Company, saved India from a welter of anarchy, and if today the British were to go out of India, India would again be thrown into a welter of anarchy. Unfortunately the Secretary of State's notions of anarchy and our notions of anarchy differ very much. He has spoken of the glorious and the great association of England with India. Yes, great and glorious from the British point of view, but inglorious and infamous from the Indian point of view. I do not admit the association of England with India has done us any substantial good. That is the chief point of difference between us and the Secretary of State for India.

Then he talks of a welter of anarchy. What anarchy can be greater than the anarchy of the law imposed at the point of the bayonet by a foreigner or body of foreigners? That is the greatest anarchy which can be inflicted on any self-respecting nation. What anarchy can be greater than the anarchy involved in the position that the people for whom governments are made, for whom governments are constituted, should have no voice in the determination of their fate? There can be no anarchy greater than that. All anarchies are followed at some time or the other by established and sound systems of government. Sir, no progress is made by threats. We're not scared by these threats of anarchy. I wish to say from my place in this House that I am not at all afraid of any anarchy that might follow the withdrawal of the British from this country. I am prepared for the worst. What can be worse than the conditions in which we are living now? There can be nothing worse. We have reached the lowest depths of misery and degradation imaginable. There can be nothing lower than that, and if the British Government think that by their withdrawal we shall be warring with each other, I shall welcome even that condition, because, after all, after a few years of warring and quarrelling, and even bloodshed, we shall be settling down and forming some kind of government, which will be our own handiwork, and which we can improve later on. (Laughter from the European non-official Benches.) The Members of the European group are indulging in a laugh at me. My reply is: 'You can have a hearty laugh, because you are like the painter who paints his own picture. If you were in our position you would not be laughing but weeping. Let us have a trial of ruling England for even two years and then we shall see who laughs and who weeps.'

25

ON THE EVE OF DANDI MARCH

Mahatma Gandhi

Ahemdabad, India

11 March 1930

Gandhi led the Salt March from Sabarmati Ashram to the coastal village of Dandi to produce salt from sea water. This started a non-violent protest against British salt tax, which was one of the ways for the British to generate revenue.

The British had introduced the Salt Act in 1882. According to this act, any person dealing with the illegal production of salt would be imprisoned up to six months. It is evident from the opening lines of the speech that Gandhi feared that the march would lead to his arrest.

In all probability this will be my last speech to you. Even if the government allow me to march tomorrow morning, this will be my last speech on the sacred banks of the Sabarmati. Possibly these may be the last words of my life here.

I have already told you yesterday what I had to say. Today I shall confine myself to what you should do after I and my companions are arrested. The programme of the march to Jalalpur must be fulfilled as originally settled. The enlistment of volunteers for this purpose should be confined to Gujarat. From what I have seen and heard during the last fortnight I am inclined to believe that the stream of civil resisters will flow unbroken.

But let there be not a semblance of breach of peace even after all of us have been arrested. We have resolved to utilize all our resources in the pursuit of an exclusively non-violent struggle. Let no one commit a wrong in anger. This is my hope and prayer. I wish these words of mine reached every nook and corner of the land. My task shall be done if I perish and so do my comrades. It will then be for the Working Committee of the Congress to show you the way and it will be up to you to follow its lead. That is the only meaning of the Working Committee's resolution. The reins of the movement will still remain in the hands of those of my associates who believe in non-violence as an article of faith. Of course, the Congress will be free to chalk out what course of action commends itself to it. So long as I have not reached Jalalpur, let nothing be done in contravention to the authority vested in me by the Congress. But once I am arrested, the whole general responsibility shifts to the Congress. No one who believes in non-violence, as a creed, need therefore sit still. My compact with the Congress ends as soon as I am arrested. In that case there should be no slackness in the enrolment of volunteers. Wherever possible, civil disobedience of salt laws should be started. These laws can be violated in three ways. It is an offence to manufacture salt wherever there are facilities for doing so. The possession and sale of contraband salt (which includes natural salt or salt earth) is also an offence. The purchasers of such salt will be equally guilty. To carry away the natural salt deposits on the seashore is likewise a violation of law. So is the hawking of such salt. In short, you may choose anyone or all of these devices to break the salt monopoly.

We are, however, not to be content with this alone. Wherever there are Congress Committees, wherever there is no ban by the Congress and wherever the local workers have self-confidence, other suitable measures may be adopted. I prescribe only one condition, viz., let our pledge of truth and non-violence as the only means for the attainment of swaraj be faithfully kept. For the rest, everyone has a free hand. But that does not give a license to all and sundry to carry on their individual responsibility. Wherever there are local leaders, their orders should be obeyed by the people. Where there are no leaders and only a handful of men have faith in the programme, they may do what they can, if they have enough self-confidence. They have a right, nay, it is their duty, to do so. The history of the world is full of instances of men who rose to leadership by sheer force of self-confidence, bravery and tenacity. We too, if we sincerely aspire to swaraj and are impatient to attain it, should have similar self-confidence. Our ranks will swell and our hearts strengthen as the number of our arrests by government increases.

Let nobody assume that after I am arrested there will be no one left to guide them. It is not I but Pandit Jawaharlal who is your guide. He has the capacity to lead. Though the fact is that those who have learnt the lesson of fearlessness and self-effacement need no leader, but if we lack these virtues, not even Jawaharlal will be able to produce them in us.

Much can be done in other ways besides these. Liquor and foreign-cloth shops can be picketed. We can refuse to pay taxes if we have the requisite strength. The lawyers can give up practice. The public can boycott the courts by refraining from litigation. Government servants can resign their posts. In the midst of the despair reigning all round people quake with fear of losing employment. Such men are unfit for swaraj. But why this despair? The number of government servants in the country does not exceed a few hundred thousand. What about the rest? Where are they to go? Even free India will not be able to accommodate a greater number of public servants. A collector then will not need the number of servants he has got today. He will be his own servant. How can a poor country like India afford to provide a collector with separate servants for performing the duties of carrying his papers, sweeping, cooking, latrine-cleaning and letter-carrying? Our starving millions can by no means afford this enormous expenditure. If, therefore, we are sensible enough, let us bid goodbye to government employment, no matter if it is the post of a judge or a peon. It may be difficult for a judge to leave his job, but where is the difficulty in the case of a peon? He can earn his bread everywhere by honest manual labour. This is the easiest solution of the problem of freedom. Let all who are cooperating with the government in one way or another, be it by paying taxes, keeping titles, or sending children to official schools, etc., withdraw their cooperation in all or as many ways as possible. One can devise other methods, too, of non-cooperating with the government. And then there are women who can stand shoulder to shoulder with men in this struggle.

You may take it as my will. It was the only message that I desired to impart to you before starting on the march or for the jail. I wish there to be no suspension or abandonment of the war that commences tomorrow morning, or earlier if I am arrested before that time. I shall eagerly await the news that ten batches are ready as soon as my batch is arrested. I believe there are men in India to complete the work begun by me today. I have faith in the righteousness of our cause and the purity of our weapons. And where the means are clean, there God is undoubtedly present with His blessings. And where these three combine, there defeat is an impossibility. A *satyagrahi*, whether free or incarcerated, is ever victorious. He is vanquished only when he forsakes truth and non-violence and turns a deaf ear to the inner voice. If, therefore, there is such a thing as defeat for even a satyagrahi, he alone is the cause of it. God bless you all and keep off all obstacles from the path in the struggle that begins tomorrow. Let this be our prayer.

Note: Dandi March ended on 6th April 1930. A month later, Gandhi was arrested.

26

SPEECH AT THE ROUND TABLE CONFERENCE

Mahatma Gandhi
London, U.K.
30 November 1931

To consider the future constitution of India, the British Government called for a series of meetings that came to be known as the Round Table Conferences.

An agreement had been reached through the Gandhi-Irwin Pact. Irwin promised to release the prisoners captured during the satyagraha campaign and Gandhi pledged to end the movement. Following his release from prison, Gandhi was appointed as the representative of Congress at the second session of the Round Table Conference, where he delivered the following speech.

It will be after all and at best a paper solution. But immediately you withdraw that wedge, the domestic ties, the domestic affection, the knowledge of common birth—do you suppose that all these will count for nothing?

Were Hindus and Mussalmans and Sikhs always at war with one another when there was no British rule, when there was no English face seen there? We have chapter and verse given to us by Hindu historians and by Mussalman historians to say that we were living in comparative peace even then. And Hindus and Mussalmans in the villages are not even today quarrelling. In those days they were not known to quarrel at all. The late Maulana Muhammad Ali often used to tell me, and he was himself a bit of an historian. He said: 'If God'—'Allah' as he called out—gives me life, I propose to write the history of Mussalman rule in India; and then I will show, through that documents that British people have preserved, that was not so vile as he has been painted by the British historian; that the Mogul rule was not so bad as it has been shown to us in British history; and so on. And so have Hindu historians written. This quarrel is not old; this quarrel is coeval with this acute shame. I dare to say, it is coeval with the British Advent, and immediately this relationship, the unfortunate, artificial, unnatural relationship between Great Britain and India is transformed into a natural relationship, when it becomes, if it does become, a voluntary partnership to be given up, to be dissolved at the will of either party, when it becomes that you will find that Hindus, Mussalmans, Sikhs, Europeans, Anglo-Indians, Christians, Untouchable, will all live together as one man.

I do not intend to say much tonight about the Princes, but I should be wronging them and should be wronging the Congress if I did not register my claim, not with the Round Table Conference but with the Princes. It is open to the Princes to give their terms on which they will join the Federation. I have appealed to them to make the path easy for those who inhabit the other part of India, and therefore, I can only make these suggestions for their favourable consideration, for their earnest consideration. I think that if they accepted, no matter what they are, but some fundamental rights as the common property of all India, and if they accepted that position and allowed those rights to be tested by the Court, which will be again of their own creation, and if they introduced elements—only elements—of representation on behalf of their subject, I think that they would have gone a long way to conciliate their subjects. They would have gone a long way to show to the world and to show to the whole of India that they are also fired with a democratic spirit, that they do not want to remain undiluted autocrats, but that they want to become constitutional monarch even as King George of Great Britain is.

An Autonomous Frontier Province: Let India get what she is entitled to and what she can really take, but whatever she gets, and whenever she gets it, let the Frontier Province get complete autonomy today. That Frontier will then be a standing demonstration to the whole of India, and therefore, the whole vote of the Congress will be given in favour of the Frontier Province getting provincial Autonomy tomorrow. Prime Minister, if you can possibly get your Cabinet to endorse the proposition that from tomorrow the Frontier Province becomes a full-fledged autonomous province, I shall then have a proper footing amongst the Frontier tribes and convince them to my assistance when those over the border cast an evil eye on India.

Thanks; last of all, my last is pleasant task for me. This is perhaps the last time that I shall be sitting with you at negotiations. It is not that I want that. I want to sit at the same table with you in your closets and to negotiate and to plead with you and to go down on bended knees before I take the final lead and final plunge.

But whether I have the good fortune to continue to tender my cooperation or not does not depend upon me. It largely depends upon you. It depends upon so many circumstances over which neither you nor we may have any control whatsoever. Then, let me perform this pleasant task of giving my thanks to all form Their Majesties down to the poorest men in the East End where I have taken up my habitation.

In that settlement, which represent the poor people of the East

End of London, I have become one of them. They have accepted me as a member, and as a favoured member of their family. It will be one of the richest treasures that I shall carry with me. Here, too, I have found nothing but courtesy and nothing but a genuine affection from all with whom I have come in touch. I have come in touch with so many Englishmen. It has been a priceless privilege to me, They have listened to what must have often appeared to them to be unpleasant, although it was true. Although I have often been obliged to say these things to them they have never shown the slightest impatience or irritation. It is impossible for me to forget these things. No matter what befalls me, no matter what the fortunes may be of this Round Table Conference, one thing I shall certainly carry with me, that is, that from high to low I have found nothing but the utmost courtesy and that utmost affection. I consider that it was well worth my paying this visit to England in order to find this human affection.

It has enhanced it has deepened my irrepressible faith in human nature that although English men and English women have been fed upon lies that I see so often disfiguring your Press, that although in Lancashire, the Lancashire people had perhaps some reason for becoming irritated against me, I found no irritation and no resentment even in the operatives. The operatives, men and women, hugged me. They treated me as one of their own. I shall never forget that.

I am carrying with me thousands upon thousands of English friendship. I do not know them but I read that affection in their eyes as early in the morning I walk through your streets. All this hospitality, all this kindness will never be effaced from my memory, no matter what befalls my unhappy land. I thank you for your forbearance.

27

THE ONLY THING WE HAVE TO FEAR IS FEAR ITSELF

Franklin Roosevelt

Washington, D.C., U.S.A.

4 March 1933

Franklin Delano Roosevelt led America through two of the greatest crisis of the twentieth century—the Great Depression and World War II. Between 1929 and 1933, the G.D.P. had declined by thirty per cent, farm prices went down by fifty-one per cent, and stocks had lost eighty-five per cent of their value.

At a time when the American economy was spiralling down, Roosevelt delivered his first inaugural address. He declared a 'war' against depression and appeased an anxious nation by reminding it that though the economy had fallen and the people were being plagued by unemployment, 'the only thing we have to fear is fear itself.'

President Hoover, Mr. Chief Justice, my friends:

This is a day of national consecration, and I am certain that my fellow Americans expect that on my induction into the Presidency I will address them with a candour and a decision which the present situation of our Nation impels. This is pre-eminently the time to speak the truth, the whole truth, frankly and boldly. Nor need we shrink from honestly facing conditions in our country today. This great Nation will endure as it has endured, will revive and will prosper. So, first of all, let me assert my firm belief that the only thing we have to fear is fear itself—nameless, unreasoning, unjustified terror which paralyzes needed efforts to convert retreat into advance. In every dark hour of our national life a leadership of frankness and vigour has met with that understanding and support of the people themselves which is essential to victory. I am convinced that you will again give that support to leadership in these critical days.

In such a spirit on my part and on yours we face our common difficulties. They concern, thank God, only material things. Values have shrunken to fantastic levels; taxes have risen; our ability to pay has fallen; government of all kinds is faced by serious curtailment of income; the means of exchange are frozen in the currents of trade; the withered leaves of industrial enterprise lie on every side; farmers find no markets for their produce; the savings of many years in thousands of families are gone.

More important, a host of unemployed citizens face the grim problem of existence, and an equally great number toil with little return. Only a foolish optimist can deny the dark realities of the moment.

Yet our distress comes from no failure of substance. We are stricken by no plague of locusts. Compared with the perils which our forefathers conquered because they believed and were not afraid, we have still much to be thankful for. Nature still offers her bounty and human efforts have multiplied it. Plenty is at our doorstep, but a generous use of it languishes in the very sight of the supply. Primarily this is because the rulers of the exchange of mankind's goods have failed, through their own stubbornness and their own incompetence, have admitted their failure, and abdicated. Practices of the unscrupulous money changers stand indicted in the court of public opinion, rejected by the hearts and minds of men.

True they have tried, but their efforts have been cast in the pattern of an outworn tradition. Faced by failure of credit they have proposed only the lending of more money. Stripped of the lure of profit by which to induce our people to follow their false leadership, they have resorted to exhortations, pleading tearfully for restored confidence. They know only the rules of a generation of self-seekers. They have no vision, and when there is no vision the people perish.

The money changers have fled from their high seats in the temple of our civilization. We may now restore that temple to the ancient truths. The measure of the restoration lies in the extent to which we apply social values more noble than mere monetary profit.

Happiness lies not in the mere possession of money; it lies in the joy of achievement, in the thrill of creative effort. The joy and moral stimulation of work no longer must be forgotten in the mad chase of evanescent profits. These dark days will be worth all they cost us if they teach us that our true destiny is not to be ministered unto but to minister to ourselves and to our fellow men.

Recognition of the falsity of material wealth as the standard of success goes hand in hand with the abandonment of the false belief that public office and high political position are to be valued only by the standards of pride of place and personal profit; and there must be an end to a conduct in banking and in business which too often has given to a sacred trust the likeness of callous and selfish wrongdoing. Small wonder that confidence languishes, for it thrives only on honesty, on honour, on the sacredness of obligations, on faithful protection, on unselfish performance; without them it cannot live.

Restoration calls, however, not for changes in ethics alone. This Nation asks for action, and action now.

Our greatest primary task is to put people to work. This is no unsolvable problem if we face it wisely and courageously. It can be accomplished in part by direct recruiting by the government itself, treating the task as we would treat the emergency of a war, but at the same time, through this employment, accomplishing greatly needed projects to stimulate and reorganize the use of our natural resources.

Hand in hand with this we must frankly recognize the overbalance of population in our industrial centres and, by engaging on a national scale in a redistribution, endeavour to provide a better use of the land for those best fitted for the land. The task can be helped by definite efforts to raise the values of agricultural products and with this the power to purchase the output of our cities. It can be helped by preventing realistically the tragedy of the growing loss through foreclosure of our small homes and our farms. It can be helped by insistence that the Federal, State, and local governments act forthwith on the demand that their cost be drastically reduced. It can be helped by the unifying of relief activities which today are often scattered, uneconomical, and unequal. It can be helped by national planning for and supervision of all forms of transportation and of communications and other utilities which have a definitely public character. There are many ways in which it can be helped, but it can never be helped merely by talking about it. We must act and act quickly.

Finally, in our progress toward a resumption of work we require two safeguards against a return of the evils of the old order; there must be a strict supervision of all banking and credits and investments; there must be an end to speculation with other people's money, and there must be provision for an adequate but sound currency.

There are the lines of attack. I shall presently urge upon a new Congress in special session detailed measures for their fulfilment, and I shall seek the immediate assistance of the several states.

Through this program of action we address ourselves to putting our own national house in order and making income balance outgo. Our international trade relations, though vastly important, are in point of time and necessity secondary to the establishment of a sound national economy. I favour as a practical policy the putting of first things first. I shall spare no effort to restore world trade by international economic readjustment, but the emergency at home cannot wait on that accomplishment.

The basic thought that guides these specific means of national recovery is not narrowly nationalistic. It is the insistence, as a first consideration, upon the interdependence of the various elements in all parts of the United States—a recognition of the old and permanently important manifestation of the American spirit of the pioneer. It is the way to recovery. It is the immediate way. It is the strongest assurance that the recovery will endure.

In the field of world policy I would dedicate this Nation to the policy of the good neighbour—the neighbour who resolutely respects himself and, because he does so, respects the rights of others—the neighbour who respects his obligations and respects the sanctity of his agreements in and with a world of neighbours.

If I read the temper of our people correctly, we now realize as we have never realized before our interdependence on each other; that we cannot merely take but we must give as well; that if we are to go forward, we must move as a trained and loyal army willing to sacrifice for the good of a common discipline, because without such discipline no progress is made, no leadership becomes effective. We are, I know, ready and willing to submit our lives and property to such discipline, because it makes possible a leadership which aims at a larger good. This I propose to offer, pledging that the larger purposes will bind upon us all as a sacred obligation with a unity of duty hitherto evoked only in time of armed strife.

With this pledge taken, I assume unhesitatingly the leadership of this great army of our people dedicated to a disciplined attack upon our common problems.

Action in this image and to this end is feasible under the form of government which we have inherited from our ancestors. Our Constitution is so simple and practical that it is possible always to meet extraordinary needs by changes in emphasis and arrangement without loss of essential form. That is why our constitutional system has proved itself the most superbly enduring political mechanism the modern world has produced. It has met every stress of vast expansion of territory, of foreign wars, of bitter internal strife, of world relations.

It is to be hoped that the normal balance of executive and legislative authority may be wholly adequate to meet the unprecedented task before us. But it may be that an unprecedented demand and need for undelayed action may call for temporary departure from that normal balance of public procedure.

I am prepared under my constitutional duty to recommend the measures that a stricken nation in the midst of a stricken world may require. These measures, or such other measures as the Congress may build out of its experience and wisdom, I shall seek, within my constitutional authority, to bring to speedy adoption.

But in the event that the Congress shall fail to take one of these two courses, and in the event that the national emergency is still critical, I shall not evade the clear course of duty that will then confront me. I shall ask the Congress for the one remaining instrument to meet the crisis—broad executive power to wage a war against the emergency, as great as the power that would be given to me if we were in fact invaded by a foreign foe.

For the trust reposed in me I will return the courage and the devotion that befit the time. I can do no less.

We face the arduous days that lie before us in the warm courage of the national unity; with the clear consciousness of seeking old and precious moral values; with the clean satisfaction that comes from the stern performance of duty by old and young alike. We aim at the assurance of a rounded and permanent national life.

We do not distrust the future of essential democracy. The people of the United States have not failed. In their need they have registered a mandate that they want direct, vigorous action. They have asked for discipline and direction under leadership. They have made me the present instrument of their wishes. In the spirit of the gift I take it.

In this dedication of a Nation we humbly ask the blessing of God. May He protect each and every one of us. May He guide me in the days to come.

28

ADDRESS TO THE REICHSTAG

Adolf Hitler

Berlin, Germany

1 September 1939

Germany's attack had begun on Poland the day Hitler delivered this speech before the Reichstag. He started by citing the problem Germany has with Poland over the city of Danzig. After World War I, Danzig had been declared a quasi-independent city. It was surrounded by Polish territory, so the port facilities were open to be used by the Polish. However, the Polish wanted Danzig to be within its boundaries.

Peace negotiations were made by the Fuhrer but all of them were rejected. It is believed that Hitler deliberately kept his demands a bit above the Polish tolerance. This enabled him to drag out the negotiations to buy time for Germany to go to war against Poland.

For months we have been suffering under the torture of a problem which the Versailles Diktat created—a problem which has deteriorated until it becomes intolerable for us. Danzig was and is a German city. The Corridor was and is German. Both these territories owe their cultural development exclusively to the German people. Danzig was separated from us, the Corridor was annexed by Poland. As in other German territories of the East, all German minorities living there have been ill-treated in the most distressing manner. More than 1,000,000 people of German blood had in the years 1919-1920 to leave their homeland.

As always, I attempted to bring about, by the peaceful method of making proposals for revision, an alteration of this intolerable position. It is a lie when the outside world says that we only tried to carry through our revisions by pressure. Fifteen years before the National Socialist Party came to power there was the opportunity of carrying out these revisions by peaceful settlements and understanding. On my own initiative I have, not once but several times, made proposals for the revision of intolerable conditions. All these proposals, as you know, have been rejected—proposals for limitation of armaments and even, if necessary, disarmament, proposals for limitation of war-making, proposals for the elimination of certain methods of modern warfare. You know the proposals that I have made to fulfil the necessity of restoring German sovereignty over German territories. You know the endless attempts I made for a peaceful clarification and understanding of the problem of Austria, and later of the problem of the Sudetenland, Bohemia, and Moravia. It was all in vain.

It is impossible to demand that an impossible position should be cleared up by peaceful revision and at the same time constantly reject peaceful revision. It is also impossible to say that he who undertakes to carry out these revisions for himself transgresses a law, since the Versailles Diktat is not law to us. A signature was forced out of us with pistols at our head and with the threat of hunger for millions of people. And then this document, with our signature, obtained by force, was proclaimed as a solemn law.

In the same way, I have also tried to solve the problem of Danzig, the Corridor, etc., by proposing a peaceful discussion. That the problems had to be solved was clear. It is quite understandable to us that the time when the problem was to be solved had little interest for the Western Powers. But that time is not a matter of indifference to us. Moreover, it was not and could not be a matter of indifference to those who suffer most.

In my talks with Polish statesmen I discussed the ideas which you recognize from my last speech to the Reichstag. No one could say that this was in any way an inadmissible procedure on undue pressure. I then naturally formulated at last the German proposals, and I must once more repeat that there is nothing more modest or loyal than these proposals. I should like to say this to the world. I alone was in the position to make such proposal, for I know very well that in doing so I brought myself into opposition to millions of Germans. These proposals have been refused. Not only were they answered first with mobilization, but with increased terror and pressure against our German compatriots and with a slow strangling of the Free City of Danzig—economically, politically, and in recent weeks by military and transport means.

Poland has directed its attacks against the Free City of Danzig. Moreover, Poland was not prepared to settle the Corridor question in a reasonable way which would be equitable to both parties, and she did not think of keeping her obligations to minorities.

I must here state something definitely; German has kept these obligations; the minorities who live in Germany are not persecuted. No Frenchman can stand up and say that any Frenchman living in the Saar territory is oppressed, tortured, or deprived of his rights. Nobody can say this.

For four months I have calmly watched developments, although I never ceased to give warnings. In the last few days I have increased these warnings. I informed the Polish Ambassador three weeks ago that if Poland continued to send to Danzig notes in the form of ultimata, and if on the Polish side an end was not put to Customs measures destined to ruin Danzig's trade, then the Reich could not remain inactive. I left no doubt that people who wanted to compare the Germany of today with the former Germany would be deceiving themselves.

An attempt was made to justify the oppression of the Germans by claiming that they had committed acts of provocation. I do not know in what these provocations on the part of women and children consist, if they themselves are maltreated, in some cases killed. One thing I do know—that no great Power can with honour long stand by passively and watch such events.

I made one more final effort to accept a proposal for mediation on the part of the British Government. They proposed, not that they themselves should carry on the negotiations, but rather that Poland and Germany should come into direct contact and once more pursue negotiations.

I must declare that I accepted this proposal, and I worked out a basis for these negotiations which are known to you. For two whole days I sat in my government and waited to see whether it was convenient for the Polish Government to send a plenipotentiary or not. Last night they did not send us a plenipotentiary, but instead informed us through their Ambassador that they were still considering whether and to what extent they were in a position to go into the British proposals. The Polish Government also said that they would inform Britain of their decision.

Deputies, if the German Government and its Leader patiently endured such treatment Germany would deserve only to disappear from the political stage. But I am wrongly judged if my love of peace and my patience are mistaken for weakness or even cowardice. I, therefore, decided last night and informed the British Government that in these circumstances I can no longer find any willingness on the part of the Polish Government to conduct serious negotiations with us.

These proposals for mediation have failed because in the meanwhile there, first of all, came as an answer the sudden Polish general mobilization, followed by more Polish atrocities. These were again repeated last night. Recently in one night there were as many as twenty-one frontier incidents: last night there were fourteen, of which three were quite serious. I have, therefore, resolved to speak to Poland in the same language that Poland for months past has used toward us. This attitude on the part of the Reich will not change.

The other European states understand in part our attitude. I should like here above all to thank Italy, which throughout has supported us, but you will understand that for the carrying on of this struggle we do not intend to appeal to foreign help. We will carry out this task ourselves. The neutral States have assured us of their neutrality, just as we had already guaranteed it to them.

When statesmen in the West declare that this affects their interests, I can only regret such a declaration. It cannot for a moment make me hesitate to fulfil my duty. What more is wanted? I have solemnly assured them, and I repeat it, that we ask nothing of those Western States and never will ask anything. I have declared that the frontier between France and Germany is a final one. I have repeatedly offered friendship and, if necessary, the closest cooperation to Britain, but this cannot be offered from one side only. It must find response on the other side. Germany has no interests in the West, and our western wall is for all time the frontier of the Reich on the west. Moreover, we have no aims of any kind there for the future. With this assurance we are in solemn earnest, and as long as others do not violate their neutrality we will likewise take every care to respect it.

I am happy particularly to be able to tell you of one event. You know that Russia and Germany are governed by two different doctrines. There was only one question that had to be cleared up. Germany has no intention of exporting its doctrine. Given the fact that Soviet Russia has no intention of exporting its doctrine to Germany. I no longer see any reason why we should still oppose one another. On both sides we are clear on that. Any struggle between our people would only be of advantage to others. We have, therefore, resolved to conclude a pact which rules out for ever any use of violence between us. It imposes the obligation on us to consult together in certain European questions. It makes possible for us economic cooperation, and above all it assures that the powers of both these powerful States are not wasted against one another. Every attempt of the West to bring about any change in this will fail.

At the same time I should like here to declare that this political decision means a tremendous departure for the future, and that it is a final one. Russia and Germany fought against one another in the World War. That shall and will not happen a second time. In Moscow, too, this pact was greeted exactly as you greet it. I can only endorse word for word the speech of Russian Foreign Commissar, Molotov.

I am determined to solve (1) the Danzig question; (2) the question of the Corridor; and (3) to see to it that a change is made in the relationship between Germany and Poland that shall ensure a peaceful co-existence. In this I am resolved to continue to fight until either the present Polish Government is willing to continue to bring about this change or until another Polish Government is ready to do so. I am resolved to remove from the German frontiers the element of uncertainty, the everlasting atmosphere of conditions resembling civil war. I will see to it that in the East there is, on the frontier, a peace precisely similar to that on our other frontiers.

In this I will take the necessary measures to see that they do not contradict the proposals I have already made known in the Reichstag itself to the rest of the world, that is to say, I will not war against women and children. I have ordered my air force to restrict itself to attacks on military objectives. If, however, the enemy thinks he can form that draw carte blanche on his side to fight by the other methods he will receive an answer that will deprive him of hearing and sight.

This night for the first time Polish regular soldiers fired on our territory. Since 5:45 a.m. we have been returning the fire, and from now on bombs will be met by bombs. Whoever fight with poison gas will be fought with poison gas. Whoever departs from the rules of humane warfare can only expect that we shall do the same. I will continue this struggle, no matter against whom, until the safety of the Reich and its rights are secured.

For six years now I have been working on the building up of the German defences. Over ninety million have in that time been spent on the building up of these defence forces. They are now the best equipped and are above all comparison with what they were in 1914. My trust in them is unshakable. When I called up these forces and when I now ask sacrifices of the German people and if necessary every sacrifice, then I have a right to do so, for I also am today absolutely ready, just as we were formerly, to make every possible sacrifice.

I am asking of no German man more than I myself was ready throughout four years at any time to do. There will be no hardships for Germans to which I myself will not submit. My whole life henceforth belongs more than ever to my people. I am from now on just first soldier of the German Reich. I have once more put on that coat that was the most sacred and dear to me. I will not take it off again until victory is secured, or I will not survive the outcome.

Should anything happen to me in the struggle then my first successor is Party Comrade Göring; should anything happen to Party Comrade Göring my next successor is Party Comrade Hess. You would then be under obligation to give to them as Führer the same blind loyalty and obedience as to myself. Should anything happen to Party Comrade Hess, then by law the Senate will be called, and will choose from its midst the most worthy—that is to say the bravest—successor.

As a National Socialist and as German soldier I enter upon this struggle with a stout heart. My whole life has been nothing but one long struggle for my people, for its restoration, and for Germany. There was only one watchword for that struggle: faith in this people. One word I have never learned: that is, surrender.

If, however, anyone thinks that we are facing a hard time, I should ask him to remember that once a Prussian King, with a ridiculously small State, opposed a stronger coalition, and in three wars finally came out successful because that State had that stout heart that we need in these times. I would, therefore, like to assure all the world that a November 1918 will never be repeated in German history. Just as I myself am ready at any time to stake my life—anyone can take it for my people and for Germany—so I ask the same of all others.

Whoever, however, thinks he can oppose this national command, whether directly or indirectly, shall fall. We have nothing to do with traitors. We are all faithful to our old principle. It is quite unimportant whether we ourselves live, but it is essential that our people shall live, that Germany shall live. The sacrifice that is demanded of us is not greater than the sacrifice that many generations have made. If we form a community closely bound together by vows, ready for anything, resolved never to surrender, then our will will master every hardship and difficulty. And I would like to close with the declaration that I once made when I began the struggle for power in the Reich. I then said: 'If our will is so strong that no hardship and suffering can subdue it, then our will and our German might shall prevail.'

Note: The British and French Governments had promptly demanded that Germany immediately stop all hostile actions and withdraw its troops from Polish territory by 3rd September, two days after this speech had been given.

29

BLOOD, TOIL, SWEAT, AND TEARS

Winston Churchill
London, U.K.
13 May 1940

Winston Churchill addressed the House of Commons and delivered his first speech while the Second World War was being waged. He had replaced Neville Chamberlain, who had been forced to resign since his non-aggression policy towards Germany had failed. Only three days before this speech, Hitler had defeated the Allied forces and conquered France.

Given amidst such times of turmoil, Churchill proclaimed that the war must fought with equal intensity and the country's sole aim was to win—'for without victory, there is no survival.'

Mister Speaker, on Friday evening last I received His Majesty's commission to form a new Administration. It was the evident wish and will of parliament and the nation that this should be conceived on the broadest possible basis and that it should include all parties, both those who supported the late government and also the parties of the Opposition. I have completed the most important part of this task. A War Cabinet has been formed of five Members, representing, with the Liberal Opposition, the unity of the nation. The three party Leaders have agreed to serve, either in the War Cabinet or in high executive office. The three Fighting Services have been filled. It was necessary that this should be done in one single day, on account of the extreme urgency and rigor of events. A number of other key positions were filled yesterday, and I am submitting a further list to His Majesty tonight. I hope to complete the appointment of the principal Ministers during tomorrow. The appointment of the other Ministers usually takes a little longer, but I trust that when parliament meets again, this part of my task will be completed, and that the administration will be complete in all respects.

Sir, I considered it in the public interest to suggest that the House should be summoned to meet today. Mr. Speaker agreed, and took the necessary steps, in accordance with the powers conferred upon him by the Resolution of the House. At the end of the proceedings today, the Adjournment of the House will be proposed until Tuesday, the 21st of May, with, of course, provision for earlier meeting, if need be. The business to be considered during that week will be notified to Members at the earliest opportunity. I now invite the House, by the Resolution which stands in my name, to record its approval of the steps taken and to declare its confidence in the new government.

Sir, to form an Administration of this scale and complexity is a serious undertaking in itself, but it must be remembered that we are in the preliminary stage of one of the greatest battles in history, that we are in action at many points in Norway and in Holland, that we have to be prepared in the Mediterranean, that the air battle is continuous and that many preparations have to be made here at home. In this crisis I hope I may be pardoned if I do not address the House at any length today. I hope that any of my friends and colleagues, or former colleagues, who are affected by the political reconstruction, will make all allowances for any lack of ceremony with which it has been necessary to act. I would say to the House, as I said to those who have joined the government: 'I have nothing to offer but blood, toil, tears and sweat.'

We have before us an ordeal of the most grievous kind. We have before us many, many long months of struggle and of suffering. You ask, what is our policy? I will say: It is to wage war, by sea, land and air, with all our might and with all the strength that God can give us; to wage war against a monstrous tyranny, never surpassed in the dark and lamentable catalogue of human crime. That is our policy. You ask, what is our aim? I can answer in one word: victory; victory at all costs, victory in spite of all terror, victory, however long and hard the road may be; for without victory, there is no survival. Let that be realized; no survival for the British Empire, no survival for all that the British Empire has stood for, no survival for the urge and impulse of the ages, that mankind will move forward towards its goal. But I take up my task with buoyancy and hope. I feel sure that our cause will not be suffered to fail among men. At this time I feel entitled to claim the aid of all, and I say, 'Come then, let us go forward together with our united strength.'

30

WE SHALL FIGHT ON THE BEACHES

Winston Churchill

United Kingdom

4 June 1940

The Second World War was going on. The German forces had pushed England's armed forces back at Dunkirk. People were worried. To assuage their fear, Churchill dramatically announced in this speech that they would soon turn the tables on the Germans, taking the fight to them no matter what it takes.

Delivered at the House of Commons a month after Churchill was elected prime minister, this speech is considered his most inspiring speech.

From the moment that the French defences at Sedan and on the Meuse were broken at the end of the second week of May, only a rapid retreat to Amiens and the south could have saved the British and French Armies who had entered Belgium at the appeal of the Belgian King; but this strategic fact was not immediately realized. The French High Command hoped they would be able to close the gap, and the Armies of the north were under their orders. Moreover, a retirement of this kind would have involved almost certainly the destruction of the fine Belgian Army of over twenty divisions and the abandonment of the whole of Belgium. Therefore, when the force and scope of the German penetration were realized and when a new French Generalissimo, General Weygand, assumed command in place of General Gamelin, an effort was made by the French and British Armies in Belgium to keep on holding the right hand of the Belgians and to give their own right hand to a newly created French Army which was to have advanced across the Somme in great strength to grasp it.

However, the German eruption swept like a sharp scythe around the right and rear of the Armies of the north. Eight or nine armoured divisions, each of about four hundred armoured vehicles of different kinds, but carefully assorted to be complementary and divisible into small self-contained units, cut off all communications between us and the main French Armies. It severed our own communications for food and ammunition, which ran first to Amiens and afterwards through Abbeville, and it shore its way up the coast to Boulogne and Calais, and almost to Dunkirk. Behind this armoured and mechanized onslaught came a number of German divisions in lorries, and behind them again there plodded comparatively slowly the dull brute mass of the ordinary German Army and German people, always so ready to be led to the trampling down in other lands of liberties and comforts which they have never known in their own.

I have said this armoured scythe-stroke almost reached Dunkirk—almost but not quite. Boulogne and Calais were the scenes of desperate fighting. The Guards defended Boulogne for a while and were then withdrawn by orders from this country. The Rifle Brigade, the 60th Rifles, and the Queen Victoria's Rifles, with a battalion of British tanks and a thousand Frenchmen, in all about four thousand strong, defended Calais to the last. The

British Brigadier was given an hour to surrender. He spurned the offer, and four days of intense street fighting passed before silence reigned over Calais, which marked the end of a memorable resistance. Only thirty unwounded survivors were brought off by the Navy, and we do not know the fate of their comrades. Their sacrifice, however, was not in vain. At least two armoured divisions, which otherwise would have been turned against the British Expeditionary Force, had to be sent to overcome them. They have added another page to the glories of the light divisions, and the time gained enabled the Graveline water lines to be flooded and to be held by the French troops.

Thus it was that the port of Dunkirk was kept open. When it was found impossible for the Armies of the north to reopen their communications to Amiens with the main French Armies, only one choice remained. It seemed, indeed, forlorn. The Belgian, British and French Armies were almost surrounded. Their sole line of retreat was to a single port and to its neighboring beaches. They were pressed on every side by heavy attacks and far outnumbered in the air.

When, a week ago today, I asked the House to fix this afternoon as the occasion for a statement, I feared it would be my hard lot to announce the greatest military disaster in our long history. I thought—and some good judges agreed with me—that perhaps twenty thousand or thirty thousand men might be re-embarked. But it certainly seemed that the whole of the French First Army and the whole of the British Expeditionary Force north of the Amiens-Abbeville gap would be broken up in the open field or else would have to capitulate for lack of food and ammunition. These were the hard and heavy tidings for which I called upon the House and the nation to prepare themselves a week ago. The whole root and core and brain of the British Army, on which and around which we were to build, and are to build, the great British Armies in the later years of the war, seemed about to perish upon the field or to be led into an ignominious and starving captivity.

That was the prospect a week ago. But another blow which might well have proved final was yet to fall upon us. The King of the Belgians had called upon us to come to his aid. Had not this Ruler and his government severed themselves from the Allies, who rescued their country from extinction in the late war, and had they not sought refuge in what was proved to be a fatal neutrality, the French and British Armies might well at the outset have saved not only Belgium but perhaps even Poland. Yet at the last moment, when Belgium was already invaded, King Leopold called upon us to come to his aid, and even at the last moment we came. He and his brave, efficient Army, nearly half a million strong, guarded our left flank and thus kept open our only line of retreat to the sea. Suddenly, without prior consultation, with the least possible notice, without the advice of his Ministers and upon his own personal act, he sent a plenipotentiary to the German Command, surrendered his Army, and exposed our whole flank and means of retreat.

I asked the House a week ago to suspend its judgement because the facts were not clear, but I do not feel that any reason now exists why we should not form our own opinions upon this pitiful episode. The surrender of the Belgian Army compelled the British at the shortest notice to cover a flank to the sea more than thirty miles in length. Otherwise all would have been cut off, and all would have shared the fate to which King Leopold had condemned the finest Army his country had ever formed. So in doing this and in exposing this flank, as anyone who followed the operations on the map will see, contact was lost between the British and two out of the three corps forming the First French Army, who were still farther from the coast than we were, and it seemed impossible that any large number of Allied troops could reach the coast.

The enemy attacked on all sides with great strength and

fierceness, and their main power, the power of their far more numerous Air Force, was thrown into the battle or else concentrated upon Dunkirk and the beaches. Pressing in upon the narrow exit, both from the east and from the west, the enemy began to fire with cannon upon the beaches by which alone the shipping could approach or depart. They sowed magnetic mines in the channels and seas; they sent repeated waves of hostile aircraft, sometimes more than a hundred strong in one formation, to cast their bombs upon the single pier that remained, and upon the sand dunes upon which the troops had their eyes for shelter. Their U-boats, one of which was sunk, and their motor launches took their toll of the vast traffic which now began. For four or five days an intense struggle reigned. All their armoured divisions—or what was left of them—together with great masses of infantry and artillery, hurled themselves in vain upon the ever-narrowing, ever-contracting appendix within which the British and French Armies fought.

Meanwhile, the Royal Navy, with the willing help of countless merchant seamen, strained every nerve to embark the British and Allied troops; two hundred and twenty light warships and six hundred and fifty other vessels were engaged. They had to operate upon the difficult coast, often in adverse weather, under an almost ceaseless hail of bombs and an increasing concentration of artillery fire. Nor were the seas, as I have said, themselves free from mines and torpedoes. It was in conditions such as these that our men carried on, with little or no rest, for days and nights on end, making trip after trip across the dangerous waters, bringing with them always men whom they had rescued. The numbers they have brought back are the measure of their devotion and their courage. The hospital ships, which brought off many thousands of British and French wounded, being so plainly marked were a special target for Nazi bombs; but the men and women on board them never faltered in their duty.

Meanwhile, the Royal Air Force, which had already been intervening in the battle, so far as its range would allow, from home bases, now used part of its main metropolitan fighter strength, and struck at the German bombers and at the fighters which in large numbers protected them. This struggle was protracted and fierce. Suddenly the scene has cleared, the crash and thunder has for the moment—but only for the moment—died away. A miracle of deliverance, achieved by valour, by perseverance, by perfect discipline, by faultless service, by resource, by skill, by unconquerable fidelity, is manifest to us all. The enemy was hurled back by the retreating British and French troops. He was so roughly handled that he did not hurry their departure seriously. The Royal Air Force engaged the main strength of the German Air Force, and inflicted upon them losses of at least four to one; and the Navy, using nearly thousand ships of all kinds, carried over 335,000 men, French and British, out of the jaws of death and shame, to their native land and to the tasks which lie immediately ahead. We must be very careful not to assign to this deliverance the attributes of a victory. Wars are not won by evacuations. But there was a victory inside this deliverance, which should be noted. It was gained by the Air Force. Many of our soldiers coming back have not seen the Air Force at work; they saw only the bombers which escaped its protective attack. They underrate its achievements. I have heard much talk of this; that is why I go out of my way to say this. I will tell you about it.

This was a great trial of strength between the British and German Air Forces. Can you conceive a greater objective for the Germans in the air than to make evacuation from these beaches impossible, and to sink all these ships which were displayed, almost to the extent of thousands? Could there have been an objective of greater military importance and significance for the whole purpose of the war than this? They tried hard, and they were beaten back;

they were frustrated in their task. We got the Army away; and they have paid fourfold for any losses which they have inflicted. Very large formations of German aeroplanes—and we know that they are a very brave race—have turned on several occasions from the attack of one-quarter of their number of the Royal Air Force, and have dispersed in different directions. Twelve aeroplanes have been hunted by two. One aeroplane was driven into the water and cast away by the mere charge of a British aeroplane, which had no more ammunition. All of our types—the Hurricane, the Spitfire and the new Defiant—and all our pilots have been vindicated as superior to what they have at present to face.

When we consider how much greater would be our advantage in defending the air above this Island against an overseas attack, I must say that I find in these facts a sure basis upon which practical and reassuring thoughts may rest. I will pay my tribute to these young airmen. The great French Army was very largely, for the time being, cast back and disturbed by the onrush of a few thousands of armoured vehicles. May it not also be that the cause of civilization itself will be defended by the skill and devotion of a few thousand airmen? There never has been, I suppose, in all the world, in all the history of war, such an opportunity for youth. The Knights of the Round Table, the Crusaders, all fall back into the past—not only distant but prosaic; these young men, going forth every morn to guard their native land and all that we stand for, holding in their hands these instruments of colossal and shattering power, of whom it may be said that 'Every morn brought forth a noble chance/And every chance brought forth a noble knight,' deserve our gratitude, as do all the brave men who, in so many ways and on so many occasions, are ready, and continue ready to give life and all for their native land.

I return to the Army. In the long series of very fierce battles, now on this front, now on that, fighting on three fronts at once, battles fought by two or three divisions against an equal or somewhat larger number of the enemy, and fought fiercely on some of the old grounds that so many of us knew so well—in these battles our losses in men have exceeded thirty thousand killed, wounded and missing. I take occasion to express the sympathy of the House to all who have suffered bereavement or who are still anxious. The President of the Board of Trade [Sir Andrew Duncan] is not here today. His son has been killed, and many in the House have felt the pangs of affliction in the sharpest form. But I will say this about the missing: We have had a large number of wounded come home safely to this country, but I would say about the missing that there may be very many reported missing who will come back home, some day, in one way or another. In the confusion of this fight it is inevitable that many have been left in positions where honour required no further resistance from them.

Against this loss of over thirty thousand men, we can set a far heavier loss certainly inflicted upon the enemy. But our losses in material are enormous. We have perhaps lost one-third of the men we lost in the opening days of the battle of 21st March 1918, but we have lost nearly as many guns—nearly one thousand—and all our transport, all the armoured vehicles that were with the Army in the north. This loss will impose a further delay on the expansion of our military strength. That expansion had not been proceeding as far as we had hoped. The best of all we had to give had gone to the British Expeditionary Force, and although they had not the numbers of tanks and some articles of equipment which were desirable, they were a very well and finely equipped Army. They had the first-fruits of all that our industry had to give, and that is gone. And now here is this further delay. How long it will be, how long it will last, depends upon the exertions which we make in this Island. An effort the like of which has never been seen in our records is now being made. Work is proceeding everywhere, night and day, Sundays and week days. Capital and Labour have cast aside their interests, rights, and customs and put them into the common stock. Already the flow of munitions has leaped forward. There is no reason why we should not in a few months overtake the sudden and serious loss that has come upon us, without retarding the development of our general program.

Nevertheless, our thankfulness at the escape of our Army and so many men, whose loved ones have passed through an agonizing week, must not blind us to the fact that what has happened in France and Belgium is a colossal military disaster. The French Army has been weakened, the Belgian Army has been lost, a large part of those fortified lines upon which so much faith had been reposed is gone, many valuable mining districts and factories have passed into the enemy's possession, the whole of the Channel ports are in his hands, with all the tragic consequences that follow from that, and we must expect another blow to be struck almost immediately at us or at France. We are told that Herr Hitler has a plan for invading the British Isles. This has often been thought of before. When Napoleon lay at Boulogne for a year with his flat-bottomed boats and his Grand Army, he was told by someone, 'There are bitter weeds in England.' There are certainly a great many more of them since the British Expeditionary Force returned.

The whole question of home defence against invasion is, of course, powerfully affected by the fact that we have for the time being in this Island incomparably more powerful military forces than we have ever had at any moment in this war or the last. But this will not continue. We shall not be content with a defensive war. We have our duty to our Ally. We have to reconstitute and build up the British Expeditionary Force once again, under its gallant Commander-in-Chief, Lord Gort. All this is in train; but in the interval we must put our defences in this Island into such a high state of organization that the fewest possible numbers will be required to give effective security and that the largest possible potential of offensive effort may be realized. On this we are now engaged. It will be very convenient, if it be the desire of the House, to enter upon this subject in a secret Session. Not that the government would necessarily be able to reveal in very great detail military secrets, but we like to have our discussions free, without the restraint imposed by the fact that they will be read the next day by the enemy; and the government would benefit by views freely expressed in all parts of the House by Members with their knowledge of so many different parts of the country. I understand that some request is to be made upon this subject, which will be readily acceded to by His Majesty's Government.

We have found it necessary to take measures of increasing stringency, not only against enemy aliens and suspicious characters of other nationalities, but also against British subjects who may become a danger or a nuisance should the war be transported to the United Kingdom. I know there are a great many people affected by the orders which we have made who are the passionate enemies of Nazi Germany. I am very sorry for them, but we cannot, at the present time and under the present stress, draw all the distinctions which we should like to do. If parachute landings were attempted and fierce fighting attendant upon them followed, these unfortunate people would be far better out of the way, for their own sakes as well as for ours. There is, however, another class, for which I feel not the slightest sympathy. Parliament has given us the powers to put down Fifth Column activities with a strong hand, and we shall use those powers subject to the supervision and correction of the House, without the slightest hesitation until we are satisfied, and more than satisfied, that this malignancy in our midst has been effectively stamped out.

Turning once again, and this time more generally, to the question of invasion, I would observe that there has never been a period in all these long centuries of which we boast when an absolute guarantee against invasion, still less against serious raids, could have been given to our people. In the days of Napoleon, the same wind which would have carried his transports across the Channel might have driven away the blockading fleet. There was always the chance, and it is that chance which has excited and befooled the imaginations of many Continental tyrants. Many are the tales that are told. We are assured that novel methods will be adopted, and when we see the originality of malice, the ingenuity of aggression, which our enemy displays, we may certainly prepare ourselves for every kind of novel stratagem and every kind of brutal and treacherous maneuver. I think that no idea is so outlandish that it should not be considered and viewed with a searching, but at the same time, I hope, with a steady eye. We must never forget the solid assurances of sea power and those which belong to air power if it can be locally exercised.

I have, myself, full confidence that if all do their duty, if nothing is neglected, and if the best arrangements are made, as they are being made, we shall prove ourselves once again able to defend our Island home, to ride out the storm of war, and to outlive the menace of tyranny, if necessary for years, if necessary alone.

At any rate, that is what we are going to try to do. That is the resolve of His Majesty's Government—every man of them. That is the will of parliament and the nation.

The British Empire and the French Republic, linked together in their cause and in their need, will defend to the death their native soil, aiding each other like good comrades to the utmost of their strength.

Even though large tracts of Europe and many old and famous States have fallen or may fall into the grip of the Gestapo and all the odious apparatus of Nazi rule, we shall not flag or fail.

We shall go on to the end, we shall fight in France, we shall fight on the seas and oceans, we shall fight with growing confidence and growing strength in the air, we shall defend our Island, whatever the cost may be, we shall fight on the beaches, we shall fight on the landing grounds, we shall fight in the fields and in the streets, we shall fight in the hills; we shall never surrender, and even if, which I do not for a moment believe, this Island or a large part of it were subjugated and starving, then our Empire beyond the seas, armed and guarded by the British Fleet, would carry on the struggle, until, in God's good time, the New World, with all its power and might, steps forth to the rescue and the liberation of the old.

31

THEIR FINEST HOUR

Winston Churchill

Westminster, London, U.K.

18 June 1940

It was a year into World War II. All of Europe now belonged to the Germans. They had just captured France, and they were coming for the only country left—the United Kingdom. At such a bleak hour, Churchill addressed the people at the House of Commons, inspiring them by stating that when the dreaded battle begins, that will be their finest hour.

I spoke the other day of the colossal military disaster which occurred when the French High Command failed to withdraw the northern Armies from Belgium at the moment when they knew that the French front was decisively broken at Sedan and on the Meuse. This delay entailed the loss of fifteen or sixteen French divisions and threw out of action for the critical period the whole of the British Expeditionary Force. Our Army and 120,000 French troops were indeed rescued by the British Navy from Dunkirk but only with the loss of their cannon, vehicles and modern equipment.

This loss inevitably took some weeks to repair, and in the first two of those weeks the battle in France has been lost. When we consider the heroic resistance made by the French Army against heavy odds in this battle, the enormous losses inflicted upon the enemy and the evident exhaustion of the enemy, it may well be the thought that these twenty-five divisions of the best-trained and best-equipped troops might have turned the scale. However, General Weygand had to fight without them. Only three British divisions or their equivalent were able to stand in the line with their French comrades. They have suffered severely, but they have fought well. We sent every man we could to France as fast as we could re-equip and transport their formations.

I am not reciting these facts for the purpose of recrimination. That I judge to be utterly futile and even harmful. We cannot afford it. I recite them in order to explain why it was we did not have, as we could have had, between twelve and fourteen British divisions fighting in the line in this great battle instead of only three. Now I put all this aside. I put it on the shelf, from which the historians, when they have time, will select their documents to tell their stories. We have to think of the future and not of the past. This also applies in a small way to our own affairs at home. There are many who would hold an inquest in the House of Commons on the conduct of the governments—and of parliaments, for they are in it, too—during the years which led up to this catastrophe. They seek to indict those who were responsible for the guidance of our affairs. This also would be a foolish and pernicious process. There are too many in it. Let each man search his conscience and search his speeches. I frequently search mine.

Of this I am quite sure, that if we open a quarrel between the past and the present, we shall find that we have lost the future. Therefore, I cannot accept the drawing of any distinctions between members of the present government. It was formed at a moment of crisis in order to unite all the Parties and all sections of opinion. It has received the almost unanimous support of both Houses of Parliament. Its members are going to stand together, and, subject to the authority of the House of Commons, we are going to govern the country and fight the war. It is absolutely necessary at a time like this that every Minister who tries each day to do his duty shall be respected; and their subordinates must know that their chiefs are not threatened men, men who are here today and gone tomorrow, but that their directions must be punctually and faithfully obeyed. Without this concentrated power we cannot face what lies before us. I should not think it would be very advantageous for the House to prolong this debate this afternoon under conditions of public stress. Many facts are not clear that will be clear in a short time. We are to have a secret session on Thursday, and I should think that would be a better opportunity for the many earnest expressions of opinion which members will desire to make and for the House to discuss vital matters without having everything read the next morning by our dangerous foes.

The disastrous military events which have happened during the past fortnight have not come to me with any sense of surprise. Indeed, I indicated a fortnight ago as clearly as I could to the House that the worst possibilities were open; and I made it perfectly clear that whatever happened in France would make no difference to the resolve of Britain and the British Empire to fight on, if necessary for years, if necessary alone.

During the last few days we have successfully brought off the great majority of the troops we had on the line of communication in France; and seven-eighths of the troops we have sent to France since the beginning of the war—that is to say, about 350,000 out of 400,000 men—are safely back in this country. Others are still fighting with the French, and fighting with considerable success in their local encounters against the enemy. We have also brought back a great mass of stores, rifles and munitions of all kinds which had been accumulated in France during the last nine months.

We have, therefore, in this Island today a very large and powerful military force. This force comprises all our best-trained and our finest troops, including scores of thousands of those who have already measured their quality against the Germans and found themselves at no disadvantage. We have under arms at the present time in this Island over a million and a quarter men. Behind these we have the Local Defense Volunteers, numbering half a million, only a portion of whom, however, are yet armed with rifles or other firearms. We have incorporated into our Defense Forces every man for whom we have a weapon. We expect very large additions to our weapons in the near future, and in preparation for this we intend forthwith to call up, drill and train further large numbers. Those who are not called up, or else are employed during the vast business of munitions production in all its branches—and their ramifications are innumerable—will serve their country best by remaining at their ordinary work until they receive their summons. We have also over here Dominions armies. The Canadians had actually landed in France, but have now been safely withdrawn, much disappointed, but in perfect order, with all their artillery and equipment. And these very high-class forces from the Dominions will now take part in the defense of the Mother Country.

Lest the account which I have given of these large forces should raise the question: Why did they not take part in the great battle in France? I must make it clear that, apart from the divisions training and organizing at home, only twelve divisions were equipped to fight upon a scale which justified their being sent abroad. And this was fully up to the number which the French had been led to expect would be available in France at the ninth month of the war. The rest of our forces at home have a fighting value for home defense which will, of course, steadily increase every week that passes. Thus, the invasion of Great Britain would at this time require the transportation across the sea of hostile armies on a very large scale, and after they had been so transported they would have to be continually maintained with all the masses of munitions and supplies which are required for continuous battle—as continuous battle it will surely be.

Here is where we come to the Navy—and after all, we have a Navy. Some people seem to forget that we have a Navy. We must remind them. For the last thirty years I have been concerned in discussions about the possibilities of oversea invasion, and I took the responsibility on behalf of the Admiralty, at the beginning of the last war, of allowing all regular troops to be sent out of the country. That was a very serious step to take, because our Territorials had only just been called up and were quite untrained. Therefore, this Island was for several months particularly denuded of fighting troops. The Admiralty had confidence at that time in their ability to prevent a mass invasion even though at that time the Germans had a magnificent battle fleet in the proportion of ten to sixteen, even though they were capable of fighting a general engagement every day and any day, whereas now they have only a couple of heavy ships worth speaking of—the Scharnhorst and the Gneisenau. We are also told that the Italian Navy is to come out and gain sea superiority in these waters. If they seriously intend it, I shall only say that we shall be delighted to offer Signor Mussolini a free and safeguarded passage through the Strait of Gibraltar in order that he may play the part to which he aspires. There is a general curiosity in the British Fleet to find out whether the Italians are up to the level they were at in the last war or whether they have fallen off at all.

Therefore, it seems to me that as far as sea-borne invasion on a great scale is concerned, we are far more capable of meeting it today than we were at many periods in the last war and during the early months of this war, before our other troops were trained, and while the B.E.F. had proceeded abroad. Now, the Navy have never pretended to be able to prevent raids by bodies of five thousand or ten thousand men flung suddenly across and thrown ashore at several points on the coast some dark night or foggy morning. The efficacy of sea power, especially under modern conditions, depends upon the invading force being of large size; It has to be of large size, in view of our military strength, to be of any use. If it is of large size, then the Navy have something they can find and meet and, as it were, bite on. Now, we must remember that even five divisions, however lightly equipped, would require two hundred to two hundred and fifty ships, and with modern air reconnaissance and photography it would not be easy to collect such an armada, marshal it, and conduct it across the sea without any powerful naval forces to escort it; and there would be very great possibilities, to put it mildly, that this armada would be intercepted long before it reached the coast, and all the men drowned in the sea or, at the worst blown to pieces with their equipment while they were trying to land. We also have a great system of minefields, recently strongly reinforced, through which we alone know the channels. If the enemy tries to sweep passages through these minefields, it will be the task of the Navy to destroy the mine-sweepers and any other forces employed to protect them. There should be no difficulty in this, owing to our great superiority at sea.

Those are the regular, well-tested, well-proved arguments on which we have relied during many years in peace and war. But the question is whether there are any new methods by which those solid assurances can be circumvented. Odd as it may seem, some attention has been given to this by the Admiralty, whose prime duty and responsibility is to destroy any large sea-borne expedition before it reaches, or at the moment when it reaches, these shores. It would not be a good thing for me to go into details of this. It might suggest ideas to other people which they have not thought of, and they would not be likely to give us any of their ideas in exchange. All I will say is that untiring vigilance and mind-searching must be devoted to the subject, because the enemy is crafty and cunning and full of novel treacheries and stratagems. The House may be assured that the utmost ingenuity is being displayed and imagination is being evoked from large numbers of competent officers, well-trained in tactics and thoroughly up to date, to measure and counterwork novel possibilities. Untiring vigilance and untiring searching of the mind is being, and must be, devoted to the subject, because, remember, the enemy is crafty and there is no dirty trick he will not do.

Some people will ask why, then, was it that the British Navy was not able to prevent the movement of a large army from Germany into Norway across the Skagerrak? But the conditions in the Channel and in the North Sea are in no way like those which prevail in the Skagerrak. In the Skagerrak, because of the distance, we could give no air support to our surface ships, and consequently, lying as we did close to the enemy's main air power, we were compelled to use only our submarines. We could not enforce the decisive blockade or interruption which is possible from surface vessels. Our submarines took a heavy toll but could not, by themselves, prevent the invasion of Norway. In the Channel and in the North Sea, on the other hand, our superior naval surface forces, aided by our submarines, will operate with close and effective air assistance.

This brings me, naturally, to the great question of invasion from the air, and of the impending struggle between the British and German Air Forces. It seems quite clear that no invasion on a scale beyond the capacity of our land forces to crush speedily is likely to take place from the air until our Air Force has been definitely overpowered. In the meantime, there may be raids by parachute troops and attempted descents of airborne soldiers. We should be able to give those gentry a warm reception both in the air and on the ground, if they reach it in any condition to continue the dispute. But the great question is: Can we break Hitler's air weapon? Now, of course, it is a very great pity that we have not got an Air Force at least equal to that of the most powerful enemy within striking distance of these shores. But we have a very powerful Air Force which has proved itself far superior in quality, both in men and in many types of machine, to what we have met so far in the numerous and fierce air battles which have been fought with the Germans. In France, where we were at a considerable disadvantage and lost many machines on the ground when they were standing round the aerodromes, we were accustomed to inflict in the air losses of as much as two and two-and-a-half to one. In the fighting over Dunkirk, which was a sort of no-man's-land, we undoubtedly beat the German Air Force, and gained the mastery of the local air, inflicting here a loss of three or four to one day after day. Anyone who looks at the photographs which were published a week or so ago of the re-embarkation, showing the masses of troops assembled on the beach and forming an ideal target for hours at a time, must realize that this re-embarkation would not have been possible unless the enemy had resigned all hope of recovering air superiority at that time and at that place.

In the defense of this Island the advantages to the defenders will be much greater than they were in the fighting around Dunkirk. We hope to improve on the rate of three or four to one which was realized at Dunkirk; and in addition all our injured machines and their crews which get down safely—and, surprisingly, a very great many injured machines and men do get down safely in modern air fighting—all of these will fall, in an attack upon these Islands, on friendly soil and live to fight another day; whereas all the injured enemy machines and their complements will be total losses as far as the war is concerned.

During the great battle in France, we gave very powerful and continuous aid to the French Army, both by fighters and bombers; but in spite of every kind of pressure we never would allow the entire metropolitan fighter strength of the Air Force to be consumed. This decision was painful, but it was also right, because the fortunes of the battle in France could not have been decisively affected even if we had thrown in our entire fighter force. That battle was lost by the unfortunate strategical opening, by the extraordinary and unforseen power of the armored columns, and by the great preponderance of the German Army in numbers. Our fighter Air Force might easily have been exhausted as a mere accident in that great struggle, and then we should have found ourselves at the present time in a very serious plight. But as it is, I am happy to inform the House that our fighter strength is stronger at the present time relatively to the Germans, who have suffered terrible losses, than it has ever been; and consequently we believe ourselves possessed of the capacity to continue the war in the air under better conditions than we have ever experienced before. I look forward confidently to the exploits of our fighter pilots—these splendid men, this brilliant youth—who will have the glory of saving their native land, their island home, and all they love, from the most deadly of all attacks.

There remains, of course, the danger of bombing attacks, which will certainly be made very soon upon us by the bomber forces of the enemy. It is true that the German bomber force is superior in numbers to ours; but we have a very large bomber force also, which we shall use to strike at military targets in Germany without intermission. I do not at all underrate the severity of the ordeal which lies before us; but I believe our countrymen will show themselves capable of standing up to it, like the brave men of Barcelona, and will be able to stand up to it, and carry on in spite of it, at least as well as any other people in the world. Much will depend upon this; every man and every woman will have the chance to show the finest qualities of their race, and render the highest service to their cause. For all of us, at this time, whatever our sphere, our station, our occupation or our duties, it will be a help to remember the famous lines:

He nothing common did or mean, Upon that memorable scene.

I have thought it right upon this occasion to give the House and the country some indication of the solid, practical grounds upon which we base our inflexible resolve to continue the war. There are a good many people who say, 'Never mind. Win or lose, sink or swim, better die than submit to tyranny—and such a tyranny.' And I do not dissociate myself from them. But I can assure them that our professional advisers of the three Services unitedly advise that we should carry on the war, and that there are good and reasonable hopes of final victory. We have fully informed and consulted all the self-governing Dominions, these great communities far beyond the oceans who have been built up on our laws and on our civilization, and who are absolutely free to choose their course, but are absolutely devoted to the ancient Motherland, and who feel themselves inspired by the same emotions which lead me to stake our all upon duty and honor. We have fully consulted them, and I have received from their prime ministers, Mr. Mackenzie King of Canada, Mr. Menzies of Australia, Mr. Fraser of New Zealand, and General Smuts of South Africa—that wonderful man, with his immense profound mind, and his eye watching from a distance the whole panorama of European affairs—I have received from all these eminent men, who all have governments behind them elected on wide franchises, who are all there because they represent the will of their people, messages couched in the most moving terms in which they endorse our decision to fight on, and declare themselves ready to share our fortunes and to persevere to the end. That is what we are going to do.

We may now ask ourselves: In what way has our position worsened since the beginning of the war? It has worsened by the fact that the Germans have conquered a large part of the coast line of Western Europe, and many small countries have been overrun by them. This aggravates the possibilities of air attack and adds to our naval preoccupations. It in no way diminishes, but on the contrary definitely increases, the power of our long-distance blockade. Similarly, the entrance of Italy into the war increases the power of our long-distance blockade. We have stopped the worst leak by that. We do not know whether military resistance will come to an end in France or not, but should it do so, then of course the Germans will be able to concentrate their forces, both military and industrial, upon us. But for the reasons I have given to the House these will not be found so easy to apply. If invasion has become more imminent, as no doubt it has, we, being relieved from the task of maintaining a large army in France, have far larger and more efficient forces to meet it.

If Hitler can bring under his despotic control the industries of the countries he has conquered, this will add greatly to his already vast armament output. On the other hand, this will not happen immediately, and we are now assured of immense, continuous and increasing support in supplies and munitions of all kinds from the United States; and especially of aeroplanes and pilots from the Dominions and across the oceans coming from regions which are beyond the reach of enemy bombers.

I do not see how any of these factors can operate to our detriment on balance before the winter comes; and the winter will impose a strain upon the Nazi regime, with almost all Europe writhing and starving under its cruel heel, which, for all their ruthlessness, will run them very hard. We must not forget that from the moment when we declared war on the 3rd September it was always possible for Germany to turn all her Air Force upon this country, together with any other devices of invasion she might conceive, and that France could have done little or nothing to prevent her doing so. We have, therefore, lived under this danger, in principle and in a slightly modified form, during all these months. In the meanwhile, however, we have enormously improved our methods of defense, and we have learned what we had no right to assume at the beginning, namely, that the individual aircraft and the individual British pilot have a sure and definite superiority. Therefore, in casting up this dread balance sheet and contemplating our dangers with a disillusioned eye, I see great reason for intense vigilance and exertion, but none whatever for panic or despair.

During the first four years of the last war the Allies experienced nothing but disaster and disappointment. That was our constant fear: one blow after another, terrible losses, frightful dangers. Everything miscarried. And yet at the end of those four years the morale of the Allies was higher than that of the Germans, who had moved from one aggressive triumph to another, and who stood everywhere triumphant invaders of the lands into which they had broken. During that war we repeatedly asked ourselves the question: 'How are we going to win?' And no one was able ever to answer it with much precision, until at the end, quite suddenly, quite unexpectedly, our terrible foe collapsed before us, and we were so glutted with victory that in our folly we threw it away.

We do not yet know what will happen in France or whether the French resistance will be prolonged, both in France and in the French Empire overseas. The French Government will be throwing away great opportunities and casting adrift their future if they do not continue the war in accordance with their treaty obligations, from which we have not felt able to release them. The House will have read the historic declaration in which, at the desire of many Frenchmen—and of our own hearts—we have proclaimed our willingness at the darkest hour in French history to conclude a union of common citizenship in this struggle. However matters may go in France or with the French Government, or other French Governments, we in this Island and in the British Empire will never lose our sense of comradeship with the French people. If we are now called upon to endure what they have been suffering, we shall emulate their courage, and if final victory rewards our toils they shall share the gains, aye, and freedom shall be restored to all. We abate nothing of our just demands; not one jot or tittle do we recede. Czechs, Poles, Norwegians, Dutch, Belgians have joined their causes to our own. All these shall be restored.

What General Weygand called the Battle of France is over. I expect that the Battle of Britain is about to begin. Upon this battle depends the survival of Christian civilization. Upon it depends our own British life, and the long continuity of our institutions and our Empire. The whole fury and might of the enemy must very soon be turned on us.

Hitler knows that he will have to break us in this Island or lose the war. If we can stand up to him, all Europe may be free and the life of the world may move forward into broad, sunlit uplands. But if we fail, then the whole world, including the United States, including all that we have known and cared for, will sink into the abyss of a new Dark Age made more sinister, and perhaps more protracted, by the lights of perverted science.

Let us therefore brace ourselves to our duties, and so bear ourselves that if the British Empire and its Commonwealth last for a thousand years, men will still say, 'This was their finest hour.'

Note: Churchill gave this entire speech with a cigar in his mouth. Some people concluded that he might have been drunk at that time.

32

THE ARSENAL OF DEMOCRACY

Franklin Roosevelt

Washington, D.C., U.S.A.

29 December 1940

Roosevelt had declared that America would not go to war on the Axis powers unless it was attacked. During World War II, Britain struggled to fight off Germany and turned to the U.S. for the provision of weapons. Roosevelt offered to help them fight by giving them military supplies while America stayed out of the actual fighting. In this speech given on a radio broadcast, Roosevelt implored the American public to become an 'arsenal of democracy' as though their own country was at war.

My friends:

This is not a fireside chat on war. It is a talk on national security; because the nub of the whole purpose of your president is to keep you now, and your children later, and your grandchildren much later, out of a last-ditch war for the preservation of American independence and all the things that American independence means to you and to me and to ours.

Tonight, in the presence of a world crisis, my mind goes back eight years to a night in the midst of a domestic crisis. It was a time when the wheels of American industry were grinding to a full stop, when the whole banking system of our country had ceased to function. I well remember that while I sat in my study in the White House, preparing to talk with the people of the United States, I had before my eyes the picture of all those Americans with whom I was talking. I saw the workmen in the mills, the mines, the factories; the girl behind the counter; the small shopkeeper; the farmer doing his spring ploughing; the widows and the old men wondering about their life's savings. I tried to convey to the great mass of American people what the banking crisis meant to them in their daily lives.

Tonight, I want to do the same thing, with the same people, in this new crisis which faces America. We met the issue of 1933 with courage and realism. We face this new crisis—this new threat to the security of our nation—with the same courage and realism. Never before since Jamestown and Plymouth Rock has our American civilization been in such danger as now. For, on 27th September 1940—this year—by an agreement signed in Berlin, three powerful nations, two in Europe and one in Asia, joined themselves together in the threat that if the United States of America interfered with or blocked the expansion program of these three nations—a program aimed at world control—they would unite in ultimate action against the United States.

The Nazi masters of Germany have made it clear that they intend not only to dominate all life and thought in their own country, but also to enslave the whole of Europe, and then to use the resources of Europe to dominate the rest of the world. It was only three weeks ago that their leader stated this: 'There are two worlds that stand opposed to each other.' And then in defiant reply to his opponents, he said this: 'Others are correct when they say:

'With this world we cannot ever reconcile ourselves' I can beat any other power in the world.' So said the leader of the Nazis.

In other words, the Axis not merely admits but the Axis proclaims that there can be no ultimate peace between their philosophy—their philosophy of government—and our philosophy of government. In view of the nature of this undeniable threat, it can be asserted, properly and categorically, that the United States has no right or reason to encourage talk of peace, until the day shall come when there is a clear intention on the part of the aggressor nations to abandon all thought of dominating or conquering the world.

At this moment, the forces of the States that are leagued against all peoples who live in freedom, are being held away from our shores. The Germans and the Italians are being blocked on the other side of the Atlantic by the British, and by the Greeks, and by thousands of soldiers and sailors who were able to escape from subjugated countries. In Asia, the Japanese are being engaged by the Chinese nation in another great defence. In the Pacific Ocean is our fleet.

Some of our people like to believe that wars in Europe and in Asia are of no concern to us. But it is a matter of most vital concern to us that European and Asiatic war-makers should not gain control of the oceans which lead to this hemisphere. One hundred and seventeen years ago, the Monroe Doctrine was conceived by our government as a measure of defence in the face of a threat against this hemisphere by an alliance in Continental Europe. Thereafter, we stood guard in the Atlantic, with the British as neighbours. There was no treaty. There was no 'unwritten agreement.' And yet, there was the feeling, proven correct by history, that we as neighbours could settle any disputes in peaceful fashion. And the fact is that during the whole of this time the Western Hemisphere has remained free from aggression from Europe or from Asia.

Does anyone seriously believe that we need to fear attack anywhere in the Americas while a free Britain remains our most powerful naval neighbour in the Atlantic? Does anyone seriously believe, on the other hand, that we could rest easy if the Axis powers were our neighbours there? If Great Britain goes down, the Axis powers will control the continents of Europe, Asia, Africa, Austral-Asia, and the high seas. And they will be in a position to bring enormous military and naval resources against this hemisphere. It is no exaggeration to say that all of us, in all the Americas, would be living at the point of a gun—a gun loaded with explosive bullets, economic as well as military. We should enter upon a new and terrible era in which the whole world, our hemisphere included, would be run by threats of brute force. And to survive in such a world, we would have to convert ourselves permanently into a militaristic power on the basis of war economy.

Some of us like to believe that even if Britain falls, we are still safe, because of the broad expanse of the Atlantic and of the Pacific. But the width of those oceans is not what it was in the days of clipper ships. At one point between Africa and Brazil, the distance is less from Washington than it is from Washington to Denver, Colorado—five hours for the latest type of bomber. And at the north end of the Pacific Ocean, America and Asia almost touch each other. Why, even today we have planes that could fly from the British Isles to New England and back again without refuelling. And remember that the range of the modern bomber is ever being increased.

During the past week many people in all parts of the nation have told me what they wanted me to say tonight. Almost all of them expressed a courageous desire to hear the plain truth about the gravity of the situation. One telegram, however, expressed the attitude of the small minority who want to see no evil and hear no evil, even though they know in their hearts that evil exists. That telegram begged me not to tell again of the ease with which our American cities could be bombed by any hostile power which had gained bases in this Western Hemisphere. The gist of that telegram was: 'Please, Mr. President, don't frighten us by telling us the facts.' Frankly and definitely there is danger ahead—danger against which we must prepare. But we well know that we cannot escape danger, or the fear of danger, by crawling into bed and pulling the covers over our heads.

Some nations of Europe were bound by solemn non-intervention pacts with Germany. Other nations were assured by Germany that they need never fear invasion. Non-intervention pact or not, the fact remains that they were attacked, overrun and thrown into modern slavery at an hour's notice, or even without any notice at all. As an exiled leader of one of these nations said to me the other day—'The notice was a minus quantity. It was given to my government two hours after German troops had poured into my country in a hundred places.' The fate of these nations tells us what it means to live at the point of a Nazi gun.

The Nazis have justified such actions by various pious frauds. One of these frauds is the claim that they are occupying a nation for the purpose of 'restoring order.' Another is that they are occupying or controlling a nation on the excuse that they are 'protecting it' against the aggression of somebody else.

For example, Germany has said that she was occupying Belgium to save the Belgians from the British. Would she then hesitate to say to any South American country, 'We are occupying you to protect you from aggression by the United States?' Belgium today is being used as an invasion base against Britain, now fighting for its life. Any South American country, in Nazi hands, would always constitute a jumping-off place for German attack on any one of the other Republics of this hemisphere.

Analyse for yourselves the future of two other places even

nearer to Germany if the Nazis won. Could Ireland hold out? Would Irish freedom be permitted as an amazing pet exception in an unfree world? Or the islands of the Azores which still fly the flag of Portugal after five centuries? You and I think of Hawaii as an outpost of defence in the Pacific. And yet, the Azores are closer to our shores in the Atlantic than Hawaii is on the other side.

There are those who say that the Axis powers would never have any desire to attack the Western Hemisphere. That is the same dangerous form of wishful thinking which has destroyed the powers of resistance of so many conquered peoples. The plain facts are that the Nazis have proclaimed, time and again, that all other races are their inferiors and therefore subject to their orders. And most important of all, the vast resources and wealth of this American Hemisphere constitute the most tempting loot in all the round world.

Let us no longer blind ourselves to the undeniable fact that the evil forces which have crushed and undermined and corrupted so many others are already within our own gates. Your government knows much about them and every day is ferreting them out. Their secret emissaries are active in our own and in neighbouring countries. They seek to stir up suspicion and dissension, to cause internal strife. They try to turn capital against labour, and vice versa. They try to reawaken long slumbering racial and religious enmities which should have no place in this country. They are active in every group that promotes intolerance. They exploit for their own ends our natural abhorrence of war. These trouble-breeders have but one purpose. It is to divide our people—to divide them into hostile groups and to destroy our unity and shatter our will to defend ourselves.

There are also American citizens, many of them in high places, who, unwittingly in most cases, are aiding and abetting the work of these agents. I do not charge these American citizens with being foreign agents. But I do charge them with doing exactly the kind of work that the dictators want done in the United States. These people not only believe that we can save our own skins by shutting our eyes to the fate of other nations. Some of them go much further than that. They say that we can and should become the friends and even the partners of the Axis powers. Some of them even suggest that we should imitate the methods of the dictatorships. Americans never can and never will do that.

The experience of the past two years has proven beyond doubt that no nation can appease the Nazis. No man can tame a tiger into a kitten by stroking it. There can be no appeasement with ruthlessness. There can be no reasoning with an incendiary bomb. We know now that a nation can have peace with the Nazis only at the price of total surrender. Even the people of Italy have been forced to become accomplices of the Nazis; but at this moment they do not know how soon they will be embraced to death by their allies.

The American appeasers ignore the warning to be found in the fate of Austria, Czechoslovakia, Poland, Norway, Belgium, the Netherlands, Denmark, and France. They tell you that the Axis powers are going to win anyway; that all of this bloodshed in the world could be saved; that the United States might just as well throw its influence into the scale of a dictated peace, and get the best out of it that we can. They call it a 'negotiated peace.' Nonsense! Is it a negotiated peace if a gang of outlaws surrounds your community and on threat of extermination makes you pay tribute to save your own skins? Such a dictated peace would be no peace at all. It would be only another armistice, leading to the most gigantic armament race and the most devastating trade wars in all history. And in these contests the Americas would offer the only real resistance to the Axis powers. With all their vaunted efficiency, with all their parade of pious purpose in this war, there are still in their background the concentration camp and the servants of God in chains.

The history of recent years proves that the shootings and the chains and the concentration camps are not simply the transient tools but the very altars of modern dictatorships. They may talk of a 'new order' in the world, but what they have in mind is only a revival of the oldest and the worst tyranny. In that there is no liberty, no religion, no hope. The proposed 'new order' is the very opposite of a United States of Europe or a United States of Asia. It is not a government based upon the consent of the governed. It is not a union of ordinary, self-respecting men and women to protect themselves and their freedom and their dignity from oppression. It is an unholy alliance of power and pelf to dominate and to enslave the human race.

The British people and their allies today are conducting an active war against this unholy alliance. Our own future security is greatly dependent on the outcome of that fight. Our ability to 'keep out of war' is going to be affected by that outcome. Thinking in terms of today and tomorrow, I make the direct statement to the American people that there is far less chance of the United States getting into war, if we do all we can now to support the nations defending themselves against attack by the Axis than if we acquiesce in their defeat, submit tamely to an Axis victory, and wait our turn to be the object of attack in another war later on.

If we are to be completely honest with ourselves, we must admit that there is risk in any course we may take. But I deeply believe that the great majority of our people agree that the course that I advocate involves the least risk now and the greatest hope for world peace in the future.

The people of Europe who are defending themselves do not ask us to do their fighting. They ask us for the implements of war, the planes, the tanks, the guns, the freighters which will enable them to fight for their liberty and for our security. Emphatically we must get these weapons to them, get them to them in sufficient volume and quickly enough, so that we and our children will be saved the agony and suffering of war which others have had to endure.

Let not the defeatists tell us that it is too late. It will never be earlier. Tomorrow will be later than today.

Certain facts are self-evident. In a military sense, Great Britain and the British Empire are today the spearhead of resistance to world conquest. And they are putting up a fight which will live forever in the story of human gallantry. There is no demand for sending an American Expeditionary Force outside our own borders. There is no intention by any member of your government to send such a force. You can, therefore, nail—nail any talk about sending armies to Europe as deliberate untruth.

Our national policy is not directed toward war. Its sole purpose is to keep war away from our country and our people. Democracy's fight against world conquest is being greatly aided, and must be more greatly aided, by the rearmament of the United States and by sending every ounce and every ton of munitions and supplies that we can possibly spare to help the defenders who are in the front lines. It is no more unneutral for us to do that than it is for Sweden, Russia and other nations near Germany, to send steel and ore and oil and other war materials into Germany every day in the week.

We are planning our own defence with the utmost urgency; and in its vast scale we must integrate the war needs of Britain and the other free nations which are resisting aggression. This is not a matter of sentiment or of controversial personal opinion. It is a matter of realistic, practical military policy, based on the advice of our military experts who are in close touch with existing warfare. These military and naval experts and the members of the Congress and the Administration have a single-minded purpose—the defence of the United States.

This nation is making a great effort to produce everything that is necessary in this emergency—and with all possible speed. This great effort requires great sacrifice. I would ask no one to defend a democracy which in turn would not defend everyone in the nation against want and privation. The strength of this nation shall not be diluted by the failure of the government to protect the economic well-being of its citizens. If our capacity to produce is limited by machines, it must ever be remembered that these machines are operated by the skill and the stamina of the workers.

As the government is determined to protect the rights of the workers, so the nation has a right to expect that the men who man the machines will discharge their full responsibilities to the urgent needs of defence. The worker possesses the same human dignity and is entitled to the same security of position as the engineer or the manager or the owner. For the workers provide the human power that turns out the destroyers, the airplanes and the tanks. The nation expects our defence industries to continue operation without interruption by strikes or lock-outs. It expects and insists that management and workers will reconcile their differences by voluntary or legal means, to continue to produce the supplies that are so sorely needed. And on the economic side of our great defence program, we are, as you know, bending every effort to maintain stability of prices and with that the stability of the cost of living.

Nine days ago I announced the setting up of a more effective organization to direct our gigantic efforts to increase the production of munitions. The appropriation of vast sums of money and a well-coordinated executive direction of our defence efforts are not in themselves enough. Guns, planes, ships and many other things have to be built in the factories and arsenals of America. They have to be produced by workers and managers and engineers with the aid of machines which in turn have to be built by hundreds of thousands of workers throughout the land. In this great work there has been splendid cooperation between the government and industry and labour; and I am very thankful.

American industrial genius, unmatched throughout the world in the solution of production problems, has been called upon to bring its resources and its talents into action. Manufacturers of watches, farm implements, linotypes, cash registers, automobiles, sewing machines, lawn mowers and locomotives are now making fuses, bomb packing crates, telescope mounts, shells, pistols, and tanks.

But all our present efforts are not enough. We must have more ships, more guns, more planes—more of everything. This can only be accomplished if we discard the notion of 'business as usual.' This job cannot be done merely by superimposing on the existing productive facilities the added requirements of the nation for defence. Our defence efforts must not be blocked by those who fear the future consequences of surplus plant capacity. The possible consequences of failure of our defence efforts now are much more to be feared. After the present needs of our defences are past, a proper handling of the country's peace-time needs will require all the new productive capacity—if not more. No pessimistic policy about the future of America shall delay the immediate expansion of those industries essential to defence. We need them.

I want to make it clear that it is the purpose of the nation to build now with all possible speed every machine, every arsenal, every factory that we need to manufacture our defence material. We have the men, the skill, the wealth, and above all, the will. I am confident that if and when production of consumer or luxury goods in certain industries requires the use of machines and raw materials that are essential for defence purposes, then such production must yield, and will gladly yield, to our primary and compelling purpose.

I appeal to the owners of plants, to the managers, to the workers, to our own government employees to put every ounce of effort into producing these munitions swiftly and without stint. With this appeal I give you the pledge that all of us who are officers of your government will devote ourselves to the same whole-hearted extent to the great task that lies ahead.

As planes and ships and guns and shells are produced, your government, with its defence experts, can then determine how best to use them to defend this hemisphere. The decision as to how much shall be sent abroad and how much shall remain at home must be made on the basis of our over-all military necessities.

We must be the great arsenal of democracy.

For us this is an emergency as serious as war itself. We must apply ourselves to our task with the same resolution, the same sense of urgency, the same spirit of patriotism and sacrifice as we would show were we at war.

We have furnished the British great material support and we will furnish far more in the future. There will be no 'bottlenecks' in our determination to aid Great Britain. No dictator, no combination of dictators, will weaken that determination by threats of how they will construe that determination. The British have received invaluable military support from the heroic Greek army, and from the forces of all the governments in exile. Their strength is growing. It is the strength of men and women who value their freedom more highly than they value their lives.

I believe that the Axis powers are not going to win this war. I base that belief on the latest and best information.

We have no excuse for defeatism. We have every good reason for hope—hope for peace, hope for the defence of our civilization and for the building of a better civilization in the future. I have the profound conviction that the American people are now determined to put forth a mightier effort than they have ever yet made to increase our production of all the implements of defence, to meet the threat to our democratic faith.

As President of the United States, I call for that national effort. I call for it in the name of this nation which we love and honour and which we are privileged and proud to serve. I call upon our people with absolute confidence that our common cause will greatly succeed.

Note: Roosevelt tried to keep America out of the war. But the country entered World War II less than a year after this speech was delivered, a day after the Pearl Harbor attack.

33

THE FOUR FREEDOMS

Franklin Roosevelt

Washington, D.C., U.S.A.

6 January 1941

Franklin Roosevelt addressed the Congress members and his countrymen in his effort to rally the public support to intervene and fight against Germany in the Second World War. The United States was not involved in the war yet, but Roosevelt warned that isolationism does not guarantee safety.

Every citizen in every nation has a right to freedom—freedom of speech and worship, and freedom from want and fear. The president conveyed in the following speech that he envisioned a world where every nation would be built on these essential four freedoms.

Mr. President, Mr. Speaker, Members of the Seventy-seventh Congress:

I address you, the Members of the members of this new Congress, at a moment unprecedented in the history of the Union. I use the word 'unprecedented,' because at no previous time has American security been as seriously threatened from without as it is today.

Since the permanent formation of our government under the Constitution, in 1789, most of the periods of crisis in our history have related to our domestic affairs. And fortunately, only one of these—the four-year War Between the States—ever threatened our national unity. Today, thank God, one hundred and thirty million Americans, in forty-eight States, have forgotten points of the compass in our national unity.

It is true that prior to 1914 the United States often had been disturbed by events in other Continents. We had even engaged in two wars with European nations and in a number of undeclared wars in the West Indies, in the Mediterranean and in the Pacific for the maintenance of American rights and for the principles of peaceful commerce. But in no case had a serious threat been raised against our national safety or our continued independence.

What I seek to convey is the historic truth that the United States as a nation has at all times maintained opposition, clear, definite opposition, to any attempt to lock us in behind an ancient Chinese wall while the procession of civilization went past. Today, thinking of our children and of their children, we oppose enforced isolation for ourselves or for any other part of the Americas.

That determination of ours, extending over all these years, was proved, for example, in the early days during the quarter century of wars following the French Revolution.

While the Napoleonic struggles did threaten interests of the United States because of the French foothold in the West Indies and in Louisiana, and while we engaged in the War of 1812 to vindicate our right to peaceful trade, it is nevertheless clear that neither France nor Great Britain, nor any other nation, was aiming at domination of the whole world.

And in like fashion from 1815 to 1914—ninety-nine years—no single war in Europe or in Asia constituted a real threat against our future or against the future of any other American nation.

Except in the Maximilian interlude in Mexico, no foreign power sought to establish itself in this Hemisphere; and the strength of the British fleet in the Atlantic has been a friendly strength. It is still a friendly strength.

Even when the World War broke out in 1914, it seemed to contain only small threat of danger to our own American future. But, as time went on, as we remember, the American people began to visualize what the downfall of democratic nations might mean to our own democracy.

We need not overemphasize imperfections in the Peace of Versailles. We need not harp on failure of the democracies to deal with problems of world reconstruction. We should remember that the Peace of 1919 was far less unjust than the kind of 'pacification' which began even before Munich, and which is being carried on under the new order of tyranny that seeks to spread over every continent today. The American people have unalterably set their faces against that tyranny.

I suppose that every realist knows that the democratic way of life is at this moment being directly assailed in every part of the world—assailed either by arms, or by secret spreading of poisonous propaganda by those who seek to destroy unity and promote discord in nations that are still at peace.

During sixteen long months this assault has blotted out the whole pattern of democratic life in an appalling number of independent nations, great and small. And the assailants are still on the march, threatening other nations, great and small.

Therefore, as your president, performing my constitutional duty to 'give to the Congress information of the state of the Union,' I find it, unhappily, necessary to report that the future and the safety of our country and of our democracy are overwhelmingly involved in events far beyond our borders.

Armed defence of democratic existence is now being gallantly waged in four continents. If that defence fails, all the population and all the resources of Europe, and Asia, and Africa and Australasia will be dominated by conquerors. And let us remember that the total of those populations in those four continents, the total of those populations and their resources greatly exceeds the sum total of the population and the resources of the whole of the Western Hemisphere—yes, many times over.

In times like these it is immature—and incidentally, untrue—for anybody to brag that an unprepared America, single-handed, and with one hand tied behind its back, can hold off the whole world.

No realistic American can expect from a dictator's peace international generosity, or return of true independence, or world disarmament, or freedom of expression, or freedom of religion—or even good business.

Such a peace would bring no security for us or for our neighbours. 'Those, who would give up essential liberty to purchase a little temporary safety, deserve neither liberty nor safety.'

As a nation, we may take pride in the fact that we are soft-hearted; but we cannot afford to be soft-headed.

We must always be wary of those who with sounding brass and a tinkling cymbal preach the 'ism' of appeasement.

We must especially beware of that small group of selfish men who would clip the wings of the American eagle in order to feather their own nests.

I have recently pointed out how quickly the tempo of modern warfare could bring into our very midst the physical attack which we must eventually expect if the dictator nations win this war.

There is much loose talk of our immunity from immediate and direct invasion from across the seas. Obviously, as long as the British Navy retains its power, no such danger exists. Even if there were no British Navy, it is not probable that any enemy would be stupid enough to attack us by landing troops in the United States from across thousands of miles of ocean, until it had acquired strategic bases from which to operate.

But we learn much from the lessons of the past years in Europe-particularly the lesson of Norway, whose essential seaports were captured by treachery and surprise built up over a series of years.

The first phase of the invasion of this Hemisphere would not be the landing of regular troops. The necessary strategic points would be occupied by secret agents and by their dupes—and great numbers of them are already here, and in Latin America.

As long as the aggressor nations maintain the offensive, they—not we—will choose the time and the place and the method of their attack.

And that is why the future of all the American Republics is today in serious danger.

That is why this Annual Message to the Congress is unique in our history.

That is why every member of the Executive Branch of the government and every member of the Congress face great responsibility and great accountability.

The need of the moment is that our actions and our policy should be devoted primarily—almost exclusively—to meeting this foreign peril. For all our domestic problems are now a part of the great emergency.

Just as our national policy in internal affairs has been based upon a decent respect for the rights and the dignity of all of our fellow men within our gates, so our national policy in foreign affairs has been based on a decent respect for the rights and the dignity of all nations, large and small. And the justice of morality must and will win in the end.

Our national policy is this:

First, by an impressive expression of the public will and

without regard to partisanship, we are committed to all-inclusive national defence.

Second, by an impressive expression of the public will and without regard to partisanship, we are committed to full support of all those resolute people everywhere who are resisting aggression and are thereby keeping war away from our Hemisphere. By this support, we express our determination that the democratic cause shall prevail; and we strengthen the defence and the security of our own nation.

Third, by an impressive expression of the public will and without regard to partisanship, we are committed to the proposition that principles of morality and considerations for our own security will never permit us to acquiesce in a peace dictated by aggressors and sponsored by appeasers. We know that enduring peace cannot be bought at the cost of other people's freedom.

In the recent national election there was no substantial difference between the two great parties in respect to that national policy. No issue was fought out on this line before the American electorate. And today it is abundantly evident that American citizens everywhere are demanding and supporting speedy and complete action in recognition of obvious danger.

Therefore, the immediate need is a swift and driving increase in our armament production.

Leaders of industry and labour have responded to our summons. Goals of speed have been set. In some cases these goals are being reached ahead of time; in some cases we are on schedule; in other cases there are slight but not serious delays; and in some cases—and I am sorry to say very important cases—we are all concerned by the slowness of the accomplishment of our plans.

The Army and Navy, however, have made substantial progress during the past year. Actual experience is improving and speeding up our methods of production with every passing day. And today's best is not good enough for tomorrow.

I am not satisfied with the progress thus far made. The men in charge of the program represent the best in training, in ability, and in patriotism. They are not satisfied with the progress thus far made. None of us will be satisfied until the job is done.

No matter whether the original goal was set too high or too low, our objective is quicker and better results.

We are behind schedule in turning out finished airplanes; we are working day and night to solve the innumerable problems and to catch up.

We are ahead of schedule in building warships but we are working to get even further ahead of that schedule.

To change a whole nation from a basis of peacetime production of implements of peace to a basis of wartime production of implements of war is no small task. And the greatest difficulty comes at the beginning of the program, when new tools, new plant facilities, new assembly lines, and new ship ways must first be constructed before the actual materiel begins to flow steadily and speedily from them.

The Congress, of course, must rightly keep itself informed at all times of the progress of the program. However, there is certain information, as the Congress itself will readily recognize, which, in the interests of our own security and those of the nations that we are supporting, must of needs be kept in confidence.

New circumstances are constantly begetting new needs for our safety. I shall ask this Congress for greatly increased new appropriations and authorizations to carry on what we have begun.

I also ask this Congress for authority and for funds sufficient to manufacture additional munitions and war supplies of many kinds, to be turned over to those nations which are now in actual war with aggressor nations.

Our most useful and immediate role is to act as an arsenal for them as well as for ourselves. They do not need man power, but they do need billions of dollars worth of the weapons of defence.

The time is near when they will not be able to pay for them all in ready cash. We cannot, and we will not, tell them that they must surrender, merely because of present inability to pay for the weapons which we know they must have.

I do not recommend that we make them a loan of dollars with which to pay for these weapons—a loan to be repaid in dollars.

I recommend that we make it possible for those nations to continue to obtain war materials in the United States, fitting their orders into our own program. And nearly all of their materiel would, if the time ever came, be useful in our own defence.

Taking counsel of expert military and naval authorities, considering what is best for our own security, we are free to decide how much should be kept here and how much should be sent abroad to our friends who by their determined and heroic resistance are giving us time in which to make ready our own defence.

For what we send abroad, we shall be repaid, repaid within a reasonable time following the close of hostilities, repaid in similar materials, or, at our option, in other goods of many kinds, which they can produce and which we need.

Let us say to the democracies: 'We Americans are vitally concerned in your defence of freedom. We are putting forth our energies, our resources and our organizing powers to give you the strength to regain and maintain a free world. We shall send you, in ever-increasing numbers, ships, planes, tanks, guns. This is our purpose and our pledge.'

In fulfilment of this purpose we will not be intimidated by the threats of dictators that they will regard as a breach of international law or as an act of war our aid to the democracies which dare to resist their aggression. Such aid . . . such aid is not an act of war, even if a dictator should unilaterally proclaim it so to be.

And when the dictators, if the dictators, are ready to make war upon us, they will not wait for an act of war on our part. They did not wait for Norway or Belgium or the Netherlands to commit an act of war.

Their only interest is in a new one-way international law, which lacks mutuality in its observance, and, therefore, becomes an instrument of oppression.

The happiness of future generations of Americans may well depend upon how effective and how immediate we can make our aid felt. No one can tell the exact character of the emergency situations that we may be called upon to meet. The Nation's hands must not be tied when the Nation's life is in danger.

Yes, and we must all prepare—all of us prepare—to make the sacrifices that the emergency—almost as serious as war itself—demands. Whatever stands in the way of speed and efficiency in defence—in defence preparations of any kind—must give way to the national need.

A free nation has the right to expect full cooperation from all groups. A free nation has the right to look to the leaders of business, of labour, and of agriculture to take the lead in stimulating effort, not among other groups but within their own groups.

The best way of dealing with the few slackers or trouble makers in our midst is, first, to shame them by patriotic example, and, if that fails, to use the sovereignty of government to save government.

As men do not live by bread alone, they do not fight by armaments alone. Those who man our defences, and those behind them who build our defences, must have the stamina and the courage which come from unshakable belief in the manner of life which they are defending. The mighty action that we are calling for cannot be based on a disregard of all things the worth fighting for.

The Nation takes great satisfaction and much strength from the things which have been done to make its people conscious of their individual stake in the preservation of democratic life in America. Those things have toughened the fibre of our people, have renewed their faith and strengthened their devotion to the institutions we make ready to protect.

Certainly this is no time for any of us to stop thinking about the social and economic problems which are the root cause of the social revolution which is today a supreme factor in the world.

For there is nothing mysterious about the foundations of a healthy and strong democracy. The basic things expected by our people of their political and economic systems are simple. They are:

Equality of opportunity for youth and for others.

Jobs for those who can work.

Security for those who need it.

The ending of special privilege for the few.

The preservation of civil liberties for all.

The enjoyment . . . the enjoyment of the fruits of scientific progress in a wider and constantly rising standard of living.

These are the simple, the basic things that must never be lost sight of in the turmoil and unbelievable complexity of our modern world. The inner and abiding strength of our economic and political systems is dependent upon the degree to which they fulfil these expectations.

Many subjects connected with our social economy call for immediate improvement.

As examples:

We should bring more citizens under the coverage of old-age pensions and unemployment insurance.

We should widen the opportunities for adequate medical care.

We should plan a better system by which persons deserving or needing gainful employment may obtain it.

I have called for personal sacrifice. And I am assured of the willingness of almost all Americans to respond to that call.

A part of the sacrifice means the payment of more money in taxes. In my Budget Message I will recommend that a greater portion of this great defence program be paid for from taxation than we are paying for today. No person should try, or be allowed, to get rich out of the program; and the principle of tax payments in accordance with ability to pay should be constantly before our eyes to guide our legislation.

If the Congress maintains these principles, the voters, putting patriotism ahead of pocketbooks, will give you their applause.

In the future days, which we seek to make secure, we look forward to a world founded upon four essential human freedoms.

The first is freedom of speech and expression—everywhere in the world.

The second is freedom of every person to worship God in his own way—everywhere in the world.

The third is freedom from want—which, translated into world terms, means economic understandings which will secure to every nation a healthy peacetime life for its inhabitants—everywhere in the world.

The fourth is freedom from fear—which, translated into world terms, means a world-wide reduction of armaments to such a point and in such a thorough fashion that no nation will be in a position to commit an act of physical aggression against any neighbor—anywhere in the world.

That is no vision of a distant millennium. It is a definite basis for a kind of world attainable in our own time and generation. That kind of world is the very antithesis of the so-called new order of tyranny which the dictators seek to create with the crash of a bomb.

To that new order we oppose the greater conception—the moral order. A good society is able to face schemes of world domination and foreign revolutions alike without fear.

Since the beginning of our American history, we have been engaged in change—in a perpetual peaceful revolution—a revolution which goes on steadily, quietly adjusting itself to changing conditions—without the concentration camp or the quick-lime in the ditch. The world order which we seek is the cooperation of free countries, working together in a friendly, civilized society.

This nation has placed its destiny in the hands and heads and hearts of its millions of free men and women; and its faith in freedom under the guidance of God. Freedom means the supremacy of human rights everywhere. Our support goes to those who struggle to gain those rights and keep them. Our strength is our unity of purpose.

To that high concept there can be no end save victory.

34

A DATE WHICH WILL LIVE IN INFAMY

Franklin Roosevelt

Washington, D.C., U.S.A.

8 December 1941

Roosevelt delivered the following speech to the joint session of the U.S. Congress the day after the naval and air forces of Japan attacked Pearl Harbor. The speech urged the Congress to formally declare war on Japan.

It was noted by Paul M. Sparrow, one of the president's confidante, that Roosevelt delivered this speech with a solemn and determined tone, showing a fierce determination that justice would be served. Less than an hour after the speech, the Senate and the House voted for war.

Mr. Vice President, Mr. Speaker, members of the Senate and the House of Representatives:

Yesterday, December 7th, 1941—a date which will live in infamy—the United States of America was suddenly and deliberately attacked by naval and air forces of the Empire of Japan.

The United States was at peace with that nation, and, at the solicitation of Japan, was still in conversation with its government and its Emperor looking toward the maintenance of peace in the Pacific.

Indeed, one hour after Japanese air squadrons had commenced bombing in the American island of Oahu, the Japanese Ambassador to the United States and his colleague delivered to our Secretary of State a formal reply to a recent American message. And, while this reply stated that it seemed useless to continue the existing diplomatic negotiations, it contained no threat or hint of war or of armed attack.

It will be recorded that the distance of Hawaii from Japan makes it obvious that the attack was deliberately planned many days or even weeks ago. During the intervening time the Japanese Government has deliberately sought to deceive the United States by false statements and expressions of hope for continued peace.

The attack yesterday on the Hawaiian Islands has caused severe damage to American naval and military forces, I regret to tell you that very many American lives have been lost. In addition, American ships have been reported torpedoed on the high seas between San Francisco and Honolulu.

Yesterday the Japanese Government also launched an attack against Malaya.

Last night Japanese forces attacked Hong Kong.

Last night Japanese forces attacked Guam.

Last night Japanese forces attacked the Philippine Islands.

Last night the Japanese attacked Wake Island.

And this morning the Japanese attacked Midway Island.

Japan has, therefore, undertaken a surprise offensive extending throughout the Pacific area. The facts of yesterday and today speak for themselves. The people of the United States have already formed their opinions and well understand the implications to the very life and safety of our nation.

As Commander-in-Chief of the Army and Navy, I have directed that all measures be taken for our defence, that always will our whole nation remember the character of the onslaught against us.

No matter how long it may take us to overcome this premeditated invasion, the American people, in their righteous might, will win through to absolute victory.

I believe that I interpret the will of the Congress and of the people when I assert that we will not only defend ourselves to the uttermost but will make it very certain that this form of treachery shall never again endanger us.

Hostilities exist. There is no blinking at the fact that our people, our territory and our interests are in grave danger.

With confidence in our armed forces, with the unbounding determination of our people, we will gain the inevitable triumph—so help us God.

I ask that the Congress declare that since the unprovoked and dastardly attack by Japan on Sunday, December 7th, 1941, a state of war has existed between the United States and the Japanese Empire.

Note: In the first draft of this speech, Roosevelt wrote the famous first line as 'a date that will live in world history' but later changed it to 'a date which will live in infamy.'

35

I AM STILL ALIVE

Subhash Chandra Bose

Germany

25 March 1942

Subhash Chandra Bose escaped from house arrest in Kolkata in January 1941. He disguised himself as a Pathan before coming to Kabul, and then proceeded to go to Moscow and Berlin. The British assumed that Bose died in a plane crash in Tokyo in 1942. Their assumptions were proven false when the following speech was broadcasted over the radio.

The truth regarding Bose's death is still wrapped in mystery. He is said to have died in a plane crash in Taipei on 18th August 1945, but people wonder if this report might have been false, like the one given in 1942. G. D. Bakshi in his book claims this 'was a theory to facilitate his escape to the Soviet Union.'

This is Subhas Chandra Bose, who is still alive, speaking to you over the Azad Hind radio. British news agencies have spread all over the world the report that I died in an aeroplane crash on my way to Tokyo to attend and important conference there. Ever since I left India, last year, British propaganda agencies have, from time to time, given contradictory reports of my whereabouts, while newspapers in England have not hesitated to use uncomplimentary language about me. The latest report about my death is perhaps an instance of wishful thinking. I can imagine that the British Government would, at this critical hour in India's history; like to see me dead since they are now trying their level best to win India over to their side for the purpose of their imperialistic war. I do not have before me the full particulars of the aeroplane disaster referred to above. I cannot, therefore, say if it was the result of sabotage on the part of our enemy. In any case, I beg to offer my respectful homage to the memory of those who lost their lives in that tragic event. Their names will be written in letters of gold in the history of our struggle for independence.

I have considered very carefully the offer of the British Government to India and the radio speech of Sir Stafford Cripps in that connection. I feel perfectly convinced that it is now quite clear that Sir Stafford has gone to India to try the age-long policy of British imperialism—'divide and rule.' Many people in India did not expect Sir Stafford Cripps to play a role which might very well have been reserved for a conservative politician like Mr Amery. Sir Stafford has himself assured us that the terms offered to India are, in his opinion, the soundest and the best, and that the members of the British Cabinet were all unanimous over these proposals. This affords one further proof that, in Britain, all party differences disappear when the question of India comes up. Sir Stafford has told us that India is a subcontinent inhabited by many races and peoples. I would like to remind him that India was unified under the empire of Ashoka the Great, several centuries before the Christian era—more than a thousand years before England was unified. Britain has, in other parts of her Empire, for instance in

Ireland and Palestine, used the religious issue in order to divide the people. She has been utilizing in India for that same purpose not only this issue but other imperial weapons like the Indian princes, depressed classes, etc. Now Sir Stafford is in India to use the same instruments for imperialistic ends. It is no less striking that he is applying the old imperialist policy for working out a compromise with one section of the people while simultaneously suppressing the other. This is why on one side Sir Stafford is conferring with one set of politicians, while on the other the fearless and uncompromising fighters for independence are safely lodged behind prison. The Indian people are fully aware of this nefarious policy of British politicians.

I have no doubt that the spirit of our freedom fighters will hurl down the prison walls and inspire the people of India to know that this is an insult to India's self-respect and honour.

As the London paper, *The Daily Telegraph*, has remarked, Sir Stafford's proposals contain nothing that is fundamentally new. The essence is dominion status within the Empire, which will be realized only when the war is over. But according to the terms of the offer, the speech of Sir Stafford Cripps, and the comments of English papers like *The Manchester Guardian*, it is quite clear that the real intention of the British Government is to split India into a number of states, just as Ireland was split up at the end of the last war. I am doubtful whether India will even look at such an offer. Indians by nature are hospitable, and Sir Stafford will be committing a grievous mistake if he interpreted such hospitality to mean the acceptance of his offer.

Sir Stafford reached the height of imperialist hypocrisy when, at a press conference at Delhi, he remarked that the Indians have not been able to produce an agreed constitution. But the Indian people know from their bitter experience that only the British Government is responsible for the corruption and bribery in

India. The Indian people are, therefore, convinced that they can no longer hope to win their freedom by discussion or argument, propaganda and passive resistance, but must now resort to other methods which are more effective and powerful.

Sir Stafford also mentioned that while the war is going on, a new constitution cannot be framed for India, and hence the inauguration of dominion status will begin on the termination of the war. I may remind Sir Stafford Cripps that, as early as October 1939, I replied to the British Government by suggesting that a provisional national government, commanding the confidence of the majority of the people, should be set up at once. This provisional national government could be made responsible to the present Indian Legislative Assembly. This suggestion was first of all put forward by me on behalf of the Forward Bloc of the Congress, and being practicable and reasonable, the official Congress Committee also adopted it as their own demand. The fact, however, is that the British Government is not ready to part with power at the present moment. By raising the issue of the minorities, princes or of the so-called depressed classes, they can at any time find a plea that the Indians are not united. Sir Stafford must be living in a fool's paradise if he thinks that by making such hopeless offers, he can satisfy India's hunger for freedom. In the last World War, with the help of India, the war was won by England, but India's reward war further suppression and massacre. India has not forgotten those episodes, and she will see that the present golden opportunity is not lost.

Since the beginning of this century, the British Government has been using another organization as a counter-blast to the Congress in order to reject its demands. It has been using the Muslim League for this purpose, because that party is regarded as pro-British in its outlook. In fact, British propaganda has tried to create the impression that the Muslim League is almost as influential a body as the Congress, and that it represents the majority of India's Muslims. This, however, is far from the truth. In reality, there are several influential and important Muslims organizations which are thoroughly nationalist. Moreover, of the eleven provinces in British India, out of which only four have a majority of Muslims, only one, the Punjab, has a cabinet which may be regarded as a Muslim League Cabinet. But even the Punjab premier is strongly opposed to the main program of the Muslim League, namely the division of India. But even then it is said that the majority of the Muslims will not stand for Indian independence.

As far as the defence of India is concerned, it is stated in the British proposals that, so long as the war lasts, the full military control of India will be directly in the hands of Britain, not even in the hands of the viceroy or the commander-in-chief in India. By this policy, Britain wants to achieve a twofold purpose. She desires, on the one hand, to utilize to the fullest extent India's resources for the whole Empire, and on the other, to force thereby, the enemies of Britain to attack Britain's military base in India, so that the Indian people may be provoked into voluntarily entering the war as Britain's ally. I would like to affirm, with all the emphasis at my command, that all the pro-British Indians who are participating in Britain's war will alone be responsible if the war comes ultimately to India. Further, I would like to warn my countrymen that Britain's sole object flow is to drag the Indian people into the war. It has been a successful game of the British people to get other nations involved in the war. Up to the present time, they have been carrying out glorious retreats and successful evacuations. Recently they have adopted a novel policy of burning and destroying everything before taking to their heels. If the British Government apply these scorched earth tactics to their own county—that is no concern of ours. But I have every reason to believe that they have decided to apply these scorched earth tactics in Ceylon and India, should the war come there. Therefore, participation in Britain's war will not only hinder Britain's defeat and overthrow but will also delay the attainment of independence of Indians.

36

QUIT INDIA SPEECH

Mahatma Gandhi

Mumbai, India

8 August 1942

Gandhi launched the Quit India Movement as he gave his speech at the All India Congress Committee in Gowalia Tank Maidan. The Quit India resolution demanded complete independence from the British.

In this speech, Gandhi asserted that he still practised non-violence, and the Quit India Movement will strive to gain independence through civil disobedience. However, after this speech, Gandhi, with other nationalist leaders, was arrested and the movement turned violent.

Before you discuss the resolution, let me place before you one or two things, I want you to understand two things very clearly and to consider them from the same point of view from which I am placing them before you. I ask you to consider it from my point of view, because if you approve of it, you will be enjoined to carry out all I say. It will be a great responsibility. There are people who ask me whether I am the same man that I was in 1920, or whether there has been any change in me. You are right in asking that question.

Let me, however, hasten to assure that I am the same Gandhi as I was in 1920. I have not changed in any fundamental respect. I attach the same importance to non-violence that I did then. If at all, my emphasis on it has grown stronger. There is no real contradiction between the present resolution and my previous writings and utterances.

Occasions like the present do not occur in everybody's and but rarely in anybody's life. I want you to know and feel that there is nothing but purest Ahimsa in all that I am saying and doing today. The draft resolution of the Working Committee is based on Ahimsa, the contemplated struggle similarly has its roots in Ahimsa. If, therefore, there is any among you who has lost faith in Ahimsa or is wearied of it, let him not vote for this resolution. Let me explain my position clearly. God has vouchsafed to me a priceless gift in the weapon of Ahimsa. I and my Ahimsa are on our trail today. If in the present crisis, when the earth is being scorched by the flames of Himsa and crying for deliverance, I failed to make use of the God given talent, God will not forgive me and I shall be judged unworthy of the great gift. I must act now. I may not hesitate and merely look on, when Russia and China are threatened.

Ours is not a drive for power, but purely a non-violent fight for India's independence. In a violent struggle, a successful general has been often known to effect a military coup and to set up a dictatorship. But under the Congress scheme of things, essentially non-violent as it is, there can be no room for dictatorship. A non-violent soldier of freedom will covet nothing for himself, he fights only for the freedom of his country. The Congress is unconcerned as to who will rule, when freedom is attained. The power, when it comes, will belong to the people of India, and it will be for them to decide to whom it placed in the entrusted. May be that the reins will be placed in the hands of the Parsis, for instance—as I would love to see happen—or they may be handed to some others whose names are not heard in the Congress today. It will not be for you then to object saying, 'This community is microscopic. That party did not play its due part in the freedom's struggle; why should it have all the power?' Ever since its inception the Congress has kept itself meticulously free of the communal taint. It has thought always in terms of the whole nation and has acted accordingly . . . I know how imperfect our Ahimsa is and how far away we are still from the ideal, but in Ahimsa there is no final failure or defeat. I have faith, therefore, that if, in spite of our shortcomings, the big thing does happen, it will be because God wanted to help us by crowning with success our silent, unremitting Sadhana for the last twenty-two years.

I believe that in the history of the world, there has not been a more genuinely democratic struggle for freedom than ours. I read Carlyle's *The French Revolution* while I was in prison, and Pandit Jawaharlal has told me something about the Russian revolution. But it is my conviction that inasmuch as these struggles were fought with the weapon of violence they failed to realize the democratic ideal. In the democracy which I have envisaged, a democracy established by non-violence, there will be equal freedom for all. Everybody will be his own master. It is to join a struggle for such democracy that I invite you today. Once you realize this you will forget the differences between the Hindus and Muslims, and think of yourselves as Indians only, engaged in the common struggle for independence.

Then, there is the question of your attitude towards the British. I have noticed that there is hatred towards the British among the people. The people say they are disgusted with their behaviour. The people make no distinction between British imperialism and the British people. To them, the two are one. This hatred would even make them welcome the Japanese. It is most dangerous. It means that they will exchange one slavery for another. We must get rid of this feeling. Our quarrel is not with the British people, we fight their imperialism. The proposal for the withdrawal of British power did not come out of anger. It came to enable India to play its due part at the present critical juncture It is not a happy position for a big country like India to be merely helping with money and material obtained willy-nilly from her while the United Nations are conducting the war. We cannot evoke the true spirit of sacrifice and valour, so long as we are not free. I know the British Government will not be able to withhold freedom from us, when we have made enough self-sacrifice. We must, therefore, purge ourselves of hatred. Speaking for myself, I can say that I have never felt any hatred. As a matter of fact, I feel myself to be a greater friend of the British now than ever before. One reason is that they are today in distress. My very friendship, therefore, demands that I should try to save them from their mistakes. As I view the situation, they are on the brink of an abyss. It, therefore, becomes my duty to warn them of their danger even though it may, for the time being, anger them to the point of cutting off the friendly hand that is stretched out to help them. People may laugh, nevertheless that is my claim. At a time when I may have to launch the biggest struggle of my life, I may not harbour hatred against anybody.

37

GIVE ME BLOOD AND I SHALL GIVE YOU FREEDOM

Subhash Chandra Bose

Burma, Myanmar

July 1944

Subhash Chandra Bose addressed this speech to the Indian National Army. The I.N.A. was first formed under the leadership of Mohan Singh in 1942. It collapsed in December of that year and was then revived by Subhash Chandra Bose. Led by Bose, the Army consisted of ex-convicts and civilians from the Indian expatriate population from Malaya and Burma.

Friends! Twelve months ago a new programme of total mobilization or maximum sacrifice was placed before Indians in East Asia. Today I shall give you an account of our achievements during the past year and shall place before you our demands for the coming year. But, before I do so, I want you to realize once again what a golden opportunity we have for winning freedom. The British are engaged in a worldwide struggle and in the course of this struggle they have suffered defeat after defeat on so many fronts. The enemy having been thus considerably weakened, our fight for liberty has become very much easier than it was five years ago. Such a rare and God-given opportunity comes once in a century. That is why we have sworn to fully utilize this opportunity for liberating our motherland from the British yoke.

I am so very hopeful and optimistic about the outcome of our struggle, because I do not rely merely on the efforts of three million Indians in East Asia. There is a gigantic movement going on inside India and millions of our countrymen are prepared for maximum suffering and sacrifice in order to achieve liberty. Unfortunately, ever since the great fight of 1857, our countrymen are disarmed, whereas the enemy is armed to the teeth. Without arms and without a modern army, it is impossible for a disarmed people to win freedom in this modern age. Through the grace of Providence and through the help of generous Nippon, it has become possible for Indians in East Asia to get arms to build up a modern army. Moreover, Indians in East Asia are united to a man in the endeavour to win freedom and all the religious and other differences that the British tried to engineer inside India, simply do not exist in East Asia. Consequently, we have now an ideal combination of circumstances favouring the success of our struggle—and all that is wanted is that Indians should themselves come forward to pay the price of liberty. According to the programme of 'total mobilization,' I demanded of you men, money, and materials. Regarding men, I am glad to tell you that I have obtained sufficient recruits already. Recruits have come to us from every corner of east Asia—from China, Japan, Indo-China, Philippines, Java, Borneo, Celebes, Sumatra, Malaya, Thailand, and Burma . . .

You must continue the mobilization of men, money and materials with greater vigour and energy, in particular, the problem of supplies and transport has to be solved satisfactorily.

We require more men and women of all categories for administration and reconstruction in liberated areas. We must be prepared for a situation in which the enemy will ruthlessly apply the scorched earth policy, before withdrawing from a particular area and will also force the civilian population to evacuate as was attempted in Burma.

The most important of all is the problem of sending reinforcement in men and in supplies to the fighting fronts. If we do not do so, we cannot hope to maintain our success at he fronts. Nor can we hope to penetrate depper into India.

Those of you who will continue to work on the Home Front should never forget that East Asia—and particularly Burma—from our base for the war of liberation. If this base is not strong, our fighting forces can never be victorious. Remember that this is a 'total war' and not merely a war between two armies. That is why for a full one year I have been laying so much stress on 'total mobilization' in the East.

There is another reason why I want you to look after the Home Front properly. During the coming months I and my colleagues on the War Committee of the Cabinet desire to devote our whole attention to the fighting front—and also to the task of working up the revolution inside India. Consequently, we want to be fully assured that the work at the base will go on smoothly and uninterruptedly even in our absence.

Friends, one year ago, when I made certain demands of you, I told you that if you give me 'total mobilization,' I would give you a 'second front.' I have redeemed that pledge. The first phase of our campaign is over. Our victorious troops, fighting side by side with Nipponese troops, have pushed back the enemy and are now fighting bravely on the sacred soil of our dear motherland.

Gird up your loins for the task that now lies ahead. I had asked you for men, money and materials. I have got them in generous measure. Now I demand more of you. Men, money and materials cannot by themselves bring victory or freedom. We must have the motive-power that will inspire us to brave deeds and heroic exploits.

It will be a fatal mistake for you to wish to live and see India free simply because victory is now within reach. No one here should have the desire to live to enjoy freedom. A long fight is still in front of us. We should have but one desire today—the desire to die so that India may live, the desire to face a martyr's death so that the path to freedom may be paved with the martyr's blood.

Friends! My comrades in the War of Liberation! Today I demand of you one thing, above all. I demand of you blood. It is blood alone that can avenge the blood that the enemy has spilt. It is blood alone that can pay the price of freedom. Give me blood and I promise you freedom!

38

IRON CURTAIN

Winston Churchill

Fulton, Missouri, U.S.A.

5 March 1946

Churchill, now former Prime Minister of U.K., delivered the following speech at Westminster College. Along with the students, Harry Truman, President of the United States, also sat in the audience.

A special relationship between the United States and Britain called for, Churchill termed the two countries as the great powers of the 'English-speaking world.'

Many people believe that this speech started the animosity that later developed into the Cold War. Russian leader, Joseph Stalin, expressed his outrage at this speech by calling it 'war-mongering' with hints of imperialistic racism.

I am very glad indeed to come to Westminster College this afternoon, and I am complimented that you should give me a degree from an institution whose reputation has been so solidly established.

The name 'Westminster' is somehow familiar to me. I seem to have heard of it before. Indeed, it was at Westminster that I received a very large part of my education in politics, dialectic, rhetoric, and one or two other things. In fact we have both been educated at the same, or similar, or, at any rate, kindred establishments.

It is also an honour, perhaps almost unique, for a private visitor to be introduced to an academic audience by the President of the United States. Amid his heavy burdens, duties, and responsibilities—unsought but not recoiled from—the president has travelled a thousand miles to dignify and magnify our meeting here today and to give me an opportunity of addressing this kindred nation, as well as my own countrymen across the ocean, and perhaps some other countries too. The president has told you that it is his wish, as I am sure it is yours, that I should have full liberty to give my true and faithful counsel in these anxious and baffling times. I shall certainly avail myself of this freedom, and feel the more right to do so because any private ambitions I may have cherished in my younger days have been satisfied beyond my wildest dreams. Let me, however, make it clear that I have no official mission or status of any kind, and that I speak only for myself. There is nothing here but what you see.

I can therefore allow my mind, with the experience of a lifetime, to play over the problems which beset us on the morrow of our absolute victory in arms, and to try to make sure with what strength I have that what has been gained with so much sacrifice and suffering shall be preserved for the future glory and safety of mankind.

The United States stands at this time at the pinnacle of world power. It is a solemn moment for the American Democracy. For with primacy in power is also joined an awe inspiring accountability to the future. If you look around you, you must feel not only the sense of duty done but also you must feel anxiety lest you fall below the level of achievement. Opportunity is here now, clear and shining for both our countries. To reject it or ignore it or fritter it away will bring upon us all the long reproaches of the after-time. It is necessary that constancy of mind, persistency of purpose, and the grand simplicity of decision shall rule and guide the conduct of the English-speaking peoples in peace as they did in war. We must, and I believe we shall, prove ourselves equal to this severe requirement.

When American military men approach some serious situation they are wont to write at the head of their directive the words 'overall strategic concept.' There is wisdom in this, as it leads to clarity of thought. What then is the overall strategic concept which we should inscribe today? It is nothing less than the safety and welfare, the freedom and progress, of all the homes and families of all the men and women in all the lands. And here I speak particularly of the myriad cottage or apartment homes where the wage-earner strives amid the accidents and difficulties of life to guard his wife and children from privation and bring the family up in the fear of the Lord, or upon ethical conceptions which often play their potent part.

To give security to these countless homes, they must be shielded from the two giant marauders, war and tyranny. We all know the frightful disturbances in which the ordinary family is plunged when the curse of war swoops down upon the bread-winner and those for whom he works and contrives. The awful ruin of Europe, with all its vanished glories, and of large parts of Asia glares us in the eyes. When the designs of wicked men or the aggressive urge of mighty States dissolve over large areas the frame of civilized society, humble folk are confronted with difficulties with which they cannot cope. For them all is distorted, all is broken, even ground to pulp.

When I stand here this quiet afternoon I shudder to visualize what is actually happening to millions now and what is going to happen in this period when famine stalks the earth. None can compute what has been called 'the unestimated sum of human pain.' Our supreme task and duty is to guard the homes of the common people from the horrors and miseries of another war. We are all agreed on that.

Our American military colleagues, after having proclaimed their 'overall strategic concept' and computed available resources, always proceed to the next step—namely, the method. Here again there is widespread agreement. A world organization has already been erected for the prime purpose of preventing war, UNO, the successor of the League of Nations, with the decisive addition of the United States and all that that means, is already at work. We must make sure that its work is fruitful, that it is a reality and not a sham, that it is a force for action, and not merely a frothing of words, that it is a true temple of peace in which the shields of many nations can someday be hung up, and not merely a cockpit in a Tower of Babel. Before we cast away the solid assurances of national armaments for self-preservation we must be certain that our temple is built, not upon shifting sands or quagmires, but upon the rock. Anyone can see with his eyes open that our path will be difficult and also long, but if we persevere together as we did in the two world wars—though not, alas, in the interval between them—I cannot doubt that we shall achieve our common purpose in the end.

I have, however, a definite and practical proposal to make for action. Courts and magistrates may be set up but they cannot function without sheriffs and constables. The United Nations Organization must immediately begin to be equipped with an international armed force. In such a matter we can only go step by step, but we must begin now. I propose that each of the Powers and States should be invited to delegate a certain number of air squadrons to the service of the world organization. These squadrons would be trained and prepared in their own countries, but would move around in rotation from one country to another. They would wear the uniform of their own countries but with different badges. They would not be required to act against their own nation, but in other respects they would be directed by the world organization. This might be started on a modest scale and would grow as confidence grew. I wished to see this done after the First World War, and I devoutly trust it may be done forthwith.

It would nevertheless be wrong and imprudent to entrust the secret knowledge or experience of the atomic bomb, which the United States, Great Britain, and Canada now share, to the world organization, while it is still in its infancy. It would be criminal madness to cast it adrift in this still agitated and un-united world. No one in any country has slept less well in their beds because this knowledge and the method and the raw materials to apply it, are at present largely retained in American hands. I do not believe we should all have slept so soundly had the positions been reversed and if some Communist or neo-fascist State monopolized for the time being these dread agencies. The fear of them alone might easily have been used to enforce totalitarian systems upon the free democratic world, with consequences appalling to human imagination. God has willed that this shall not be and we have at least a breathing space to set our house in order before this peril has to be encountered: and even then, if no effort is spared, we should still possess so formidable a superiority as to impose effective deterrents upon its employment, or threat of employment, by others. Ultimately, when the essential brotherhood of man is truly embodied and expressed in a world organization with all the necessary practical safeguards to make it effective, these powers would naturally be confided to that world organization.

Now I come to the second danger of these two marauders

which threatens the cottage, the home, and the ordinary people—namely, tyranny. We cannot be blind to the fact that the liberties enjoyed by individual citizens throughout the British Empire are not valid in a considerable number of countries, some of which are very powerful. In these States control is enforced upon the common people by various kinds of all-embracing police governments. The power of the State is exercised without restraint, either by dictators or by compact oligarchies operating through a privileged party and a political police. It is not our duty at this time when difficulties are so numerous to interfere forcibly in the internal affairs of countries which we have not conquered in war. But we must never cease to proclaim in fearless tones the great principles of freedom and the rights of man which are the joint inheritance of the English-speaking world and which through Magna Carta, the Bill of Rights, the Habeas Corpus, trial by jury, and the English common law find their most famous expression in the American Declaration of Independence.

All this means that the people of any country have the right, and should have the power by constitutional action, by free unfettered elections, with secret ballot, to choose or change the character or form of government under which they dwell; that freedom of speech and thought should reign; that courts of justice, independent of the executive, unbiased by any party, should administer laws which have received the broad assent of large majorities or are consecrated by time and custom. Here are the title deeds of freedom which should lie in every cottage home. Here is the message of the British and American peoples to mankind. Let us preach what we practice—let us practice what we preach.

I have now stated the two great dangers which menace the homes of the people: War and Tyranny. I have not yet spoken of poverty and privation which are in many cases the prevailing anxiety. But if the dangers of war and tyranny are removed, there is no doubt that science and cooperation can bring in the next few years to the world, certainly in the next few decades newly taught in the sharpening school of war, an expansion of material well-being beyond anything that has yet occurred in human experience. Now, at this sad and breathless moment, we are plunged in the hunger and distress which are the aftermath of our stupendous struggle; but this will pass and may pass quickly, and there is no reason except human folly or sub-human crime which should deny to all the nations the inauguration and enjoyment of an age of plenty. I have often used words which I learned fifty years ago from a great Irish-American orator, a friend of mine, Mr. Bourke Cockran. 'There is enough for all. The earth is a generous mother; she will provide in plentiful abundance food for all her children if they will but cultivate her soil in justice and in peace.' So far I feel that we are in full agreement.

Now, while still pursuing the method of realizing our overall strategic concept, I come to the crux of what I have traveled here to say. Neither the sure prevention of war, nor the continuous rise of world organization will be gained without what I have called the fraternal association of the English-speaking peoples. This means a special relationship between the British Commonwealth and Empire and the United States. This is no time for generalities, and I will venture to be precise. Fraternal association requires not only the growing friendship and mutual understanding between our two vast but kindred systems of society, but the continuance of the intimate relationship between our military advisers, leading to common study of potential dangers, the similarity of weapons and manuals of instructions, and to the interchange of officers and cadets at technical colleges. It should carry with it the continuance of the present facilities for mutual security by the joint use of all Naval and Air Force bases in the possession of either country all over the world. This would perhaps double the mobility of the

American Navy and Air Force. It would greatly expand that of the British Empire Forces and it might well lead, if and as the world calms down, to important financial savings. Already we use together a large number of islands; more may well be entrusted to our joint care in the near future.

The United States has already a Permanent Defence Agreement with the Dominion of Canada, which is so devotedly attached to the British Commonwealth and Empire. This Agreement is more effective than many of those which have often been made under formal alliances. This principle should be extended to all British Commonwealths with full reciprocity. Thus, whatever happens, and thus only, shall we be secure ourselves and able to work together for the high and simple causes that are dear to us and bode no ill to any. Eventually there may come—I feel eventually there will come—the principle of common citizenship, but that we may be content to leave to destiny, whose outstretched arm many of us can already clearly see.

There is however an important question we must ask ourselves. Would a special relationship between the United States and the British Commonwealth be inconsistent with our over-riding loyalties to the World Organization? I reply that, on the contrary, it is probably the only means by which that organization will achieve its full stature and strength. There are already the special United States relations with Canada which I have just mentioned, and there are the special relations between the United States and the South American Republics. We British have our twenty years Treaty of Collaboration and Mutual Assistance with Soviet Russia. I agree with Mr. Bevin, the Foreign Secretary of Great Britain, that it might well be a fifty years Treaty so far as we are concerned. We aim at nothing but mutual assistance and collaboration. The British have an alliance with Portugal unbroken since 1384, and which produced fruitful results at critical moments in the late war. None of these clash with the general interest of a world agreement, or a world organization; on the contrary they help it. 'In my father's house are many mansions.' Special associations between members of the United Nations which have no aggressive point against any other country, which harbour no design incompatible with the Charter of the United Nations, far from being harmful, are beneficial and, as I believe, indispensable.

I spoke earlier of the Temple of Peace. Workmen from all countries must build that temple. If two of the workmen know each other particularly well and are old friends, if their families are intermingled, and if they have 'faith in each other's purpose, hope in each other's future and charity towards each other's shortcomings'—to quote some good words I read here the other day—why cannot they work together at the common task as friends and partners? Why cannot they share their tools and thus increase each other's working powers? Indeed they must do so or else the temple may not be built, or, being built, it may collapse, and we shall all be proved again unteachable and have to go and try to learn again for a third time in a school of war, incomparably more rigorous than that from which we have just been released. The Dark Ages may return, the Stone Age may return on the gleaming wings of science, and what might now shower immeasurable material blessings upon mankind, may even bring about its total destruction. Beware, I say; time may be short. Do not let us take the course of allowing events to drift along until it is too late. If there is to be a fraternal association of the kind I have described, with all the extra strength and security which both our countries can derive from it, let us make sure that that great fact is known to the world, and that it plays its part in steadying and stabilizing the foundations of peace. There is the path of wisdom. Prevention is better than cure.

A shadow has fallen upon the scenes so lately lighted by the

Allied victory. Nobody knows what Soviet Russia and its Communist international organization intends to do in the immediate future, or what are the limits, if any, to their expansive and proselytizing tendencies. I have a strong admiration and regard for the valiant Russian people and for my wartime comrade, Marshal Stalin. There is deep sympathy and goodwill in Britain—and I doubt not here also—towards the peoples of all the Russians and a resolve to persevere through many differences and rebuffs in establishing lasting friendships. We understand the Russian need to be secure on her western frontiers by the removal of all possibility of German aggression. We welcome Russia to her rightful place among the leading nations of the world. We welcome her flag upon the seas. Above all, we welcome constant, frequent and growing contacts between the Russian people and our own people on both sides of the Atlantic. It is my duty however, for I am sure you would wish me to state the facts as I see them to you, to place before you certain facts about the present position in Europe.

From Stettin in the Baltic to Trieste in the Adriatic, an iron curtain has descended across the continent. Behind that line lie all the capitals of the ancient states of Central and Eastern Europe. Warsaw, Berlin, Prague, Vienna, Budapest, Belgrade, Bucharest and Sofia, all these famous cities and the populations around them lie in what I must call the Soviet sphere, and all are subject in one form or another, not only to Soviet influence but to a very high and, in some cases, increasing measure of control from Moscow. Athens alone—Greece with its immortal glories—is free to decide its future at an election under British, American and French observation. The Russian-dominated Polish Government has been encouraged to make enormous and wrongful inroads upon Germany, and mass expulsions of millions of Germans on a scale grievous and undreamed-of are now taking place. The Communist parties, which were very small in all these Eastern States of Europe, have been raised to pre-eminence and power far beyond their numbers and are seeking everywhere to obtain totalitarian control. Police Governments are prevailing in nearly every case, and so far, except in Czechoslovakia, there is no true democracy.

Turkey and Persia are both profoundly alarmed and disturbed at the claims which are being made upon them and at the pressure being exerted by the Moscow Government. An attempt is being made by the Russians in Berlin to build up a quasi-Communist party in their zone of Occupied Germany by showing special favours to groups of left-wing German leaders. At the end of the fighting last June, the American and British Armies withdrew westwards, in accordance with an earlier agreement, to a depth at some points of one hundred and fifty miles upon a front of nearly four hundred miles, in order to allow our Russian allies to occupy this vast expanse of territory which the Western Democracies had conquered.

If now the Soviet Government tries, by separate action, to build up a pro-Communist Germany in their areas, this will cause new serious difficulties in the American and British zones, and will give the defeated Germans the power of putting themselves up to auction between the Soviets and the Western Democracies. Whatever conclusions may be drawn from these facts—and facts they are—this is certainly not the Liberated Europe we fought to build up. Nor is it one which contains the essentials of permanent peace.

The safety of the world requires a new unity in Europe, from which no nation should be permanently outcast. It is from the quarrels of the strong parent races in Europe that the world wars we have witnessed, or which occurred in former times, have sprung. Twice in our own lifetime we have seen the United States, against their wishes and their traditions, against arguments, the force of which it is impossible not to comprehend, drawn by irresistible forces, into these wars in time to secure the victory of the good cause, but only after frightful slaughter and devastation had occurred. Twice the United States has had to send several millions of its young men across the Atlantic to find the war; but now war can find any nation, wherever it may dwell between dusk and dawn. Surely we should work with conscious purpose for a grand pacification of Europe, within the structure of the United Nations and in accordance with our Charter. That I feel is an open cause of policy of very great importance.

In front of the iron curtain which lies across Europe are other causes for anxiety. In Italy the Communist Party is seriously hampered by having to support the Communist-trained Marshal Tito's claims to former Italian territory at the head of the Adriatic. Nevertheless the future of Italy hangs in the balance. Again one cannot imagine a regenerated Europe without a strong France. All my public life I have worked for a strong France and I never lost faith in her destiny, even in the darkest hours. I will not lose faith now. However, in a great number of countries, far from the Russian frontiers and throughout the world, Communist fifth columns are established and work in complete unity and absolute obedience to the directions they receive from the Communist centre. Except in the British Commonwealth and in the United States where Communism is in its infancy, the Communist parties or fifth columns constitute a growing challenge and peril to Christian civilization. These are sombre facts for anyone to have to recite on the morrow of a victory gained by so much splendid comradeship in arms and in the cause of freedom and democracy; but we should be most unwise not to face them squarely while time remains.

The outlook is also anxious in the Far East and especially in Manchuria. The Agreement which was made at Yalta, to which I was a party, was extremely favourable to Soviet Russia, but it was made at a time when no one could say that the German war might not extend all through the summer and autumn of 1945 and when the Japanese war was expected by the best judges to last for a further eighteen months from the end of the German war. In this country you are all so well-informed about the Far East, and such devoted friends of China, that I do not need to expatiate on the situation there.

I have, however, felt bound to portray the shadow which, alike in the west and in the east, falls upon the world. I was a minister at the time of the Versailles Treaty and a close friend of Mr. Lloyd George, who was the head of the British delegation at Versailles. I did not myself agree with many things that were done, but I have a very strong impression in my mind of that situation, and I find it painful to contrast it with that which prevails now. In those days there were high hopes and unbounded confidence that the wars were over, and that the League of Nations would become all-powerful. I do not see or feel that same confidence or even the same hopes in the haggard world at the present time.

On the other hand I repulse the idea that a new war is inevitable; still more that it is imminent. It is because I am sure that our fortunes are still in our own hands and that we hold the power to save the future, that I feel the duty to speak out now that I have the occasion and the opportunity to do so. I do not believe that Soviet Russia desires war. What they desire is the fruits of war and the indefinite expansion of their power and doctrines. But what we have to consider here today while time remains, is the permanent prevention of war and the establishment of conditions of freedom and democracy as rapidly as possible in all countries. Our difficulties and dangers will not be removed by closing our eyes to them. They will not be removed by mere waiting to see what happens; nor will they be removed by a policy of appeasement. What is needed is a settlement, and the longer this is delayed, the more difficult it will be and the greater our dangers will become.

From what I have seen of our Russian friends and Allies during the war, I am convinced that there is nothing they admire so much as strength, and there is nothing for which they have less respect than for weakness, especially military weakness. For that reason the old doctrine of a balance of power is unsound. We cannot afford, if we can help it, to work on narrow margins, offering temptations to a trial of strength. If the Western Democracies stand together in strict adherence to the principles of the United Nations Charter, their influence for furthering those principles will be immense and no one is likely to molest them. If however they become divided or falter in their duty and if these all-important years are allowed to slip away then indeed catastrophe may overwhelm us all.

Last time I saw it all coming and I cried aloud to my own fellow countrymen and to the world, but no one paid any attention. Up till the year 1933 or even 1935, Germany might have been saved from the awful fate which has overtaken her and we might all have been spared the miseries Hitler let loose upon mankind. There never was a war in history easier to prevent by timely action than the one which has just desolated such great areas of the globe. It could have been prevented in my belief without the firing of a single shot, and Germany might be powerful, prosperous and honoured today; but no one would listen and one by one we were all sucked into the awful whirlpool. We surely must not let that happen again. This can only be achieved by reaching now, in 1946, a good understanding on all points with Russia under the general authority of the United Nations Organization and by the maintenance of that good understanding through many peaceful years, by the world instrument, supported by the whole strength of the English-speaking world and all its connections. There is the solution which I respectfully offer to you in this address to which I have given the title 'The Sinews of Peace.'

Let no man underrate the abiding power of the British Empire and Commonwealth. Because you see the forty-six millions in our island harassed about their food supply, of which they only grow one half, even in war-time, or because we have difficulty in restarting our industries and export trade after six years of passionate war effort, do not suppose that we shall not come through these dark years of privation as we have come through the glorious years of agony. Do not suppose that half a century from now, you will not see seventy or eighty millions of Britons spread about the world united in defence of our traditions, and our way of life, and of the world causes which you and we espouse. If the population of the English-speaking Commonwealths be added to that of the United States with all that such cooperation implies in the air, on the sea, all over the globe and in science and in industry, and in moral force, there will be no quivering, precarious balance of power to offer its temptation to ambition or adventure. On the contrary, there will be an overwhelming assurance of security. If we adhere faithfully to the Charter of the United Nations and walk forward in sedate and sober strength seeking no one's land or treasure, seeking to lay no arbitrary control upon the thoughts of men; if all British moral and material forces and convictions are joined with your own in fraternal association, the high-roads of the future will be clear, not only for us but for all, not only for our time, but for a century to come.

39

A TRYST WITH DESTINY

Jawaharlal Nehru

New Delhi, India

14 August 1947

Before the members of the Constituent Assembly took the pledge, Nehru gave the following speech on the day India gained independence from the British, envisioning a bright future for the nation.

Long years ago we made a tryst with destiny, and now the time comes when we shall redeem our pledge, not wholly or in full measure, but very substantially. At the stroke of the midnight hour, when the world sleeps, India will awake to life and freedom. A moment comes, which comes but rarely in history, when we step out from the old to the new, when an age ends, and when the soul of a nation, long suppressed, finds utterance. It is fitting that at this solemn moment we take the pledge of dedication to the service of India and her people and to the still larger cause of humanity.

At the dawn of history India started on her unending quest, and trackless centuries are filled with her striving and the grandeur of her success and her failures. Through good and ill fortune alike she has never lost sight of that quest or forgotten the ideals which gave her strength. We end today a period of ill fortune and India discovers herself again. The achievement we celebrate today is but a step, an opening of opportunity, to the greater triumphs and achievements that await us. Are we brave enough and wise enough to grasp this opportunity and accept the challenge of the future?

Freedom and power bring responsibility. The responsibility rests upon this Assembly, a sovereign body representing the sovereign people of India. Before the birth of freedom we have endured all the pains of labour and our hearts are heavy with the memory of this sorrow. Some of those pains continue even now. Nevertheless, the past is over and it is the future that beckons to us now.

That future is not one of ease or resting but of incessant striving so that we may fulfil the pledges we have so often taken and the one we shall take today. The service of India means the service of the millions who suffer. It means the ending of poverty, ignorance, disease and inequality of opportunity. The ambition of the greatest man of our generation has been to wipe every tear from every eye. That may be beyond us, but as long as there are tears and suffering, so long our work will not be over.

And so we have to labour and to work, and work hard, to give reality to our dreams. Those dreams are for India, but they are also for the world, for all the nations and peoples are too closely knit together today for any one of them to imagine that it can live apart Peace has been said to be indivisible; so is freedom, so is prosperity now, and so also is disaster in this one world that can no longer be split into isolated fragments.

To the people of India, whose representatives we are, we make an appeal to join us with faith and confidence in this great adventure. This is no time for petty and destructive criticism, no time for ill will or blaming others. We have to build the noble mansion of free India where all her children may dwell.

The appointed day has come—the day appointed by destiny—and India stands forth again, after long slumber and struggle, awake, vital, free and independent. The past clings on to us still in some measure and we have to do much before we redeem the pledges we have so often taken. Yet the turning point is past, and history begins anew for us, the history which we shall live and act and others will write about.

It is a fateful moment for us in India, for all Asia and for the world. A new star rises, the star of freedom in the East, a new hope comes into being, a vision long cherished materializes. May the star never set and that hope never be betrayed!

We rejoice in that freedom, even though clouds surround us, and many of our people are sorrow-stricken and difficult problems encompass us. But freedom brings responsibilities and burdens and we have to face them in the spirit of a free and disciplined people.

On this day our first thoughts go to the architect of this freedom, the Father of our Nation, who, embodying the old spirit of India, held aloft the torch of freedom and lighted up the darkness that surrounded us. We have often been unworthy followers of his and have strayed from his message, but not only we but succeeding generations will remember this message and bear the imprint in their hearts of this great son of India, magnificent in his faith and strength and courage and humility. We shall never allow that torch of freedom to be blown out, however high the wind or stormy the tempest.

Our next thoughts must be of the unknown volunteers and soldiers of freedom who, without praise or reward, have served India even unto death.

We think also of our brothers and sisters who have been cut off from us by political boundaries and who unhappily cannot share at present in the freedom that has come. They are of us and will remain of us whatever may happen, and we shall be sharers in their good [or] ill fortune alike.

The future beckons to us. Whither do we go and what shall be our endeavour? To bring freedom and opportunity to the common man, to the peasants and workers of India; to fight and end poverty and ignorance and disease; to build up a prosperous, democratic and progressive nation, and to create social, economic and political institutions which will ensure justice and fullness of life to every man and woman.

We have hard work ahead. There is no resting for any one of us till we redeem our pledge in full, till we make all the people of India what destiny intended them to be. We are citizens of a great country on the verge of bold advance, and we have to live up to that high standard. All of us, to whatever religion we may belong, are equally the children of India with equal rights, privileges and obligations. We cannot encourage communalism or narrow-mindedness, for no nation can be great whose people are narrow in thought or in action.

To the nations and peoples of the world we send greetings and pledge ourselves to cooperate with them in furthering peace, freedom and democracy.

And to India, our much-loved motherland, the ancient, the eternal and the ever-new, we pay our reverent homage and we bind ourselves afresh to her service.

Jai Hind.

40

THE WRITER'S DUTY

William Faulkner

Stockholm, Sweden

10 December 1950

William Faulkner was awarded the Nobel Prize for his powerful and artistically unique contribution to the American novel.

In the beginning of his acceptance speech, Faulkner wonders when he will be blown up. His audience knew exactly what he was talking about. The tension between the United States and the Soviet Union, during the Cold War, had reached its peak. An atomic war seemed imminent.

As people feared nuclear annihilation, Faulkner outlined the duty of a writer—to forget fear and think of the good things. If despair is the only thing on our minds, that is what we write about, instilling distress instead of inspiration.

I feel that this award was not made to me as a man, but to my work—life's work in the agony and sweat of the human spirit, not for glory and least of all for profit, but to create out of the materials of the human spirit something which did not exist before. So this award is only mine in trust. It will not be difficult to find a dedication for the money part of it commensurate with the purpose and significance of its origin. But I would like to do the same with the acclaim too, by using this moment as a pinnacle from which I might be listened to by the young men and women already dedicated to the same anguish and travail, among whom is already that one who will some day stand where I am standing.

Our tragedy today is a general and universal physical fear so long sustained by now that we can even bear it. There are no longer problems of the spirit. There is only the question: When will I be blown up? Because of this, the young man or woman writing today has forgotten the problems of the human heart in conflict with itself which alone can make good writing because only that is worth writing about, worth the agony and the sweat.

He must learn them again. He must teach himself that the basest of all things is to be afraid; and, teaching himself that, forget it forever, leaving no room in his workshop for anything but the old verities and truths of the heart, the universal truths lacking which any story is ephemeral and doomed—love and honour and pity and pride and compassion and sacrifice. Until he does so, he labours under a curse. He writes not of love but of lust, of defeats in which nobody loses anything of value, of victories without hope and, worst of all, without pity or compassion. His griefs grieve on no universal bones, leaving no scars. He writes not of the heart but of the glands.

Until he relearns these things, he will write as though he stood among and watched the end of man. I decline to accept the end of man. It is easy enough to say that man is immortal simply because he will endure: that when the last ding-dong of doom has clanged and faded from the last worthless rock hanging tideless in the last red and dying evening, that even then there will still be one more sound: that of his puny inexhaustible voice, still talking. I refuse to accept this. I believe that man will not merely endure: he will prevail. He is immortal, not because he alone among creatures has an inexhaustible voice, but because he has a soul, a spirit capable of compassion and sacrifice and endurance. The poet's, the writer's, duty is to write about these things. It is his privilege to help man endure by lifting his heart, by reminding him of the courage and honour and hope and pride and compassion and pity and sacrifice which have been the glory of his past. The poet's voice need not merely be the record of man, it can be one of the props, the pillars to help him endure and prevail.

41

DUTY, HONOUR, COUNTRY

General Douglas MacArthur

West Point, New York, U.S.A.

12 May 1962

The Sylvanus Thayer Award is given by the United States Military Academy each year. MacArthur addressed the cadets at the West Point Military Academy and gave this speech while accepting this award for his service to the nation. He was a U.S. general who commanded the Allied Forces in Southwest Pacific Theatre in World War II and led United Nations forces during the first nine months of the Korean War.

MacArthur instils the importance of three words in his speech—duty, honour, country—which was the motto of the West Point Military Academy.

General Westmoreland, General Groves, distinguished guests, and gentlemen of the Corps:

As I was leaving the hotel this morning, a doorman asked me, 'Where are you bound for, General?' and when I replied, 'West Point,' he remarked, 'Beautiful place, have you ever been there before?'

No human being could fail to be deeply moved by such a tribute as this, coming from a profession I have served so long and a people I have loved so well. It fills me with an emotion I cannot express. But this award is not intended primarily to honour a personality, but to symbolize a great moral code—the code of conduct and chivalry of those who guard this beloved land of culture and ancient descent. That is the meaning of this medallion. For all eyes and for all time, it is an expression of the ethics of the American soldier. That I should be integrated in this way with so noble an ideal arouses a sense of pride and yet of humility which will be with me always.

'Duty,' 'Honour,' 'Country'—those three hallowed words reverently dictate what you ought to be, what you can be, what you will be. They are your rallying points to build courage when courage seems to fail, to regain faith when there seems to be little cause for faith, to create hope when hope becomes forlorn.

Unhappily, I possess neither that eloquence of diction, that poetry of imagination, nor that brilliance of metaphor to tell you all that they mean.

The unbelievers will say they are but words, but a slogan, but a flamboyant phrase. Every pedant, every demagogue, every cynic, every hypocrite, every troublemaker, and, I am sorry to say, some others of an entirely different character, will try to downgrade them even to the extent of mockery and ridicule.

But these are some of the things they do. They build your basic character. They mould you for your future roles as the custodians of the nation's defence. They make you strong enough to know when you are weak, and brave enough to face yourself when you are afraid.

They teach you to be proud and unbending in honest failure, but humble and gentle in success; not to substitute words for action; not to seek the path of comfort, but to face the stress and spur of difficulty and challenge; to learn to stand up in the storm, but to have compassion on those who fall; to master yourself before you seek to master others; to have a heart that is clean, a goal that is high; to learn to laugh, yet never forget how to weep; to reach into the future, yet never neglect the past; to be serious, yet never take yourself too seriously; to be modest so that you will remember the simplicity of true greatness; the open mind of true wisdom, the meekness of true strength.

They give you a temper of the will, a quality of the imagination, a vigour of the emotions, a freshness of the deep springs of life, a temperamental predominance of courage over timidity, an appetite for adventure over love of ease. They create in your heart the sense of wonder, the unfailing hope of what next, and the joy and inspiration of life. They teach you in this way to be an officer and a gentleman.

And what sort of soldiers are those you are to lead? Are they reliable? Are they brave? Are they capable of victory?

Their story is known to all of you. It is the story of the American man at arms. My estimate of him was formed on the battlefields many, many years ago, and has never changed. I regarded him then, as I regard him now, as one of the world's noblest figures; not only as one of the finest military characters, but also as one of the most stainless.

His name and fame are the birthright of every American citizen. In his youth and strength, his love and loyalty, he gave all that mortality can give. He needs no eulogy from me, or from any other man. He has written his own history and written it in red on his enemy's breast.

But when I think of his patience under adversity, of his courage under fire, and of his modesty in victory, I am filled with an emotion of admiration I cannot put into words. He belongs to history as furnishing one of the greatest examples of successful patriotism.

He belongs to posterity as the instructor of future generations in the principles of liberty and freedom. He belongs to the present, to us, by his virtues and by his achievements.

In twenty campaigns, on a hundred battlefields, around a thousand campfires, I have witnessed that enduring fortitude, that patriotic self-abnegation, and that invincible determination which have carved his statue in the hearts of his people.

From one end of the world to the other, he has drained deep the chalice of courage. As I listened to those songs of the glee club, in memory's eye I could see those staggering columns of the First World War, bending under soggy packs on many a weary march, from dripping dusk to drizzling dawn, slogging ankle deep through mire of shell-pocked roads; to form grimly for the attack, blue-lipped, covered with sludge and mud, chilled by the wind and rain, driving home to their objective, and for many, to the judgment seat of God.

I do not know the dignity of their birth, but I do know the glory of their death. They died unquestioning, uncomplaining, with faith in their hearts, and on their lips the hope that we would go on to victory. Always for them: Duty, Honour, Country; always their blood, and sweat, and tears, as we sought the way and the light and the truth.

And twenty years after, on the other side of the globe, against the filth of dirty foxholes, the stench of ghostly trenches, the slime of dripping dugouts, those boiling suns of the relentless heat, those torrential rains of devastating storms, the loneliness and utter desolation of jungle trails, the bitterness of long separation of those they loved and cherished, the deadly pestilence of tropic disease, the horror of stricken areas of war.

Their resolute and determined defence, their swift and sure attack, their indomitable purpose, their complete and decisive victory—always victory, always through the bloody haze of their last reverberating shot, the vision of gaunt, ghastly men, reverently following your password of Duty, Honour, Country.

The code which those words perpetuate embraces the highest moral laws and will stand the test of any ethics or philosophies ever promulgated for the uplift of mankind. Its requirements are for the things that are right, and its restraints are from the things that are wrong. The soldier, above all other men, is required to practice the greatest act of religious training—sacrifice. In battle and in the face of danger and death, he discloses those divine attributes which his Maker gave when he created man in his own image. No physical courage and no brute instinct can take the place of the Divine help which alone can sustain him. However horrible the incidents of war may be, the soldier who is called upon to offer and to give his life for his country, is the noblest development of mankind.

You now face a new world—a world of change. The thrust into outer space of the satellite, spheres, and missiles marked the beginning of another epoch in the long story of mankind—the chapter of the space age. In the five or more billions of years the scientists tell us it has taken to form the earth, in the three or more billion years of development of the human race, there has never been a greater, a more abrupt or staggering evolution. We deal now not with things of this world alone, but with the illimitable distances and as yet unfathomed mysteries of the universe. We are reaching out for a new and boundless frontier. We speak in strange terms: of harnessing the cosmic energy; of making winds and tides work for us; of creating unheard synthetic materials to supplement or even replace our old standard basics; of purifying sea water for our drink; of mining ocean floors for new fields of wealth and food; of disease preventatives to expand life into the hundreds of years; of controlling the weather for a more equitable distribution of heat and cold, of rain and shine; of space ships to the moon; of the primary target in war, no longer limited to the armed forces of an enemy, but instead to include his civil populations; of ultimate conflict between a united human race and the sinister forces of some other planetary galaxy; of such dreams and fantasies as to make life the most exciting of all time.

And through all this welter of change and development your mission remains fixed, determined, inviolable. It is to win our wars. Everything else in your professional career is but corollary to this vital dedication. All other public purpose, all other public projects, all other public needs, great or small, will find others for their accomplishments; but you are the ones who are trained to fight.

Yours is the profession of arms, the will to win, the sure knowledge that in war there is no substitute for victory, that if you lose, the Nation will be destroyed, that the very obsession of your public service must be Duty, Honour, Country.

Others will debate the controversial issues, national and international, which divide men's minds. But serene, calm, aloof, you stand as the Nation's war guardians, as its lifeguards from the raging tides of international conflict, as its gladiators in the arena of battle. For a century and a half you have defended, guarded, and protected its hallowed traditions of liberty and freedom, of right and justice.

Let civilian voices argue the merits or demerits of our processes of government. Whether our strength is being sapped by deficit financing indulged in too long, by federal paternalism grown too mighty, by power groups grown too arrogant, by politics grown too corrupt, by crime grown too rampant, by morals grown too low, by taxes grown too high, by extremists grown too violent; whether our personal liberties are as firm and complete as they should be.

These great national problems are not for your professional participation or military solution. Your guidepost stands out like a tenfold beacon in the night: Duty, Honour, Country.

You are the leaven which binds together the entire fabric of our national system of defence. From your ranks come the great captains who hold the Nation's destiny in their hands the moment the war tocsin sounds.

The long grey line has never failed us. Were you to do so, a million ghosts in olive drab, in brown khaki, in blue and grey, would rise from their white crosses, thundering those magic words: Duty, Honour, Country.

This does not mean that you are warmongers. On the contrary, the soldier above all other people prays for peace, for he must suffer and bear the deepest wounds and scars of war. But always in our ears ring the ominous words of Plato, that wisest of all philosophers: Only the dead have seen the end of war.

The shadows are lengthening for me. The twilight is here. My days of old have vanished, tone and tint. They have gone glimmering through the dreams of things that were. Their memory is one of wondrous beauty, watered by tears and coaxed and caressed by the smiles of yesterday. I listen then, but with thirsty ear, for the witching melody of faint bugles blowing reveille, of far drums beating the long roll.

In my dreams I hear again the crash of guns, the rattle of musketry, the strange, mournful mutter of the battlefield. But in the evening of my memory I come back to West Point. Always there echoes and re-echoes: Duty, Honour, Country.

Today marks my final roll call with you. But I want you to know that when I cross the river, my last conscious thoughts will be of the Corps, and the Corps, and the Corps.

I bid you farewell.

42

WE CHOOSE TO GO TO THE MOON

John F. Kennedy

Houston, Texas, U.S.A.

12 September 1962

The space race was on between the Cold War rivals, United States of America and the Soviet Union.

A year before Kennedy gave the following speech, Soviet cosmonaut, Yuri Gagarin became the first person to ever go into space.

In the following speech, the president dramatically announced his ambitious goal to land a person on the moon within a decade. This goal was realized seven years later, when Apollo 11's commander, Neil Armstrong, became the first man to go to the moon.

President Pitzer, Mr. Vice President, Governor, Congressman Thomas, Senator Wiley, and Congressman Miller, Mr. Webb, Mr. Bell, scientists, distinguished guests, and ladies and gentlemen:

I appreciate your president having made me an honorary visiting professor, and I will assure you that my first lecture will be very brief.

I am delighted to be here and I'm particularly delighted to be here on this occasion.

We meet at a college noted for knowledge, in a city noted for progress, in a state noted for strength, and we stand in need of all three, for we meet in an hour of change and challenge, in a decade of hope and fear, in an age of both knowledge and ignorance. The greater our knowledge increases, the greater our ignorance unfolds.

Despite the striking fact that most of the scientists that the world has ever known are alive and working today, despite the fact that this Nation's own scientific manpower is doubling every twelve years in a rate of growth more than three times that of our population as a whole, despite that, the vast stretches of the unknown and the unanswered and the unfinished still far outstrip our collective comprehension.

No man can fully grasp how far and how fast we have come, but condense, if you will, the fifty thousand years of man's recorded history in a time span of but a half-century. Stated in these terms, we know very little about the first forty years, except at the end of them advanced man had learned to use the skins of animals to cover them. Then about ten years ago, under this standard, man emerged from his caves to construct other kinds of shelter. Only five years ago man learned to write and use a cart with wheels. Christianity began less than two years ago. The printing press came this year, and then less than two months ago, during this whole fifty-year span of human history, the steam engine provided a new source of power. Newton explored the meaning of gravity. Last month electric lights and telephones and automobiles and airplanes became available. Only last week did we develop penicillin and television and nuclear power, and now if America's new spacecraft succeeds in reaching Venus, we will have literally reached the stars before midnight tonight.

This is a breathtaking pace, and such a pace cannot help but create new ills as it dispels old, new ignorance, new problems, new dangers. Surely the opening vistas of space promise high costs and hardships, as well as high reward.

So it is not surprising that some would have us stay where we are a little longer to rest, to wait. But this city of Houston, this state of Texas, this country of the United States was not built by those who waited and rested and wished to look behind them. This country was conquered by those who moved forward—and so will space.

William Bradford, speaking in 1630 of the founding of the Plymouth Bay Colony, said that all great and honourable actions are accompanied with great difficulties, and both must be enterprised and overcome with answerable courage.

If this capsule history of our progress teaches us anything, it is that man, in his quest for knowledge and progress, is determined and cannot be deterred. The exploration of space will go ahead, whether we join in it or not, and it is one of the great adventures of all time, and no nation which expects to be the leader of other nations can expect to stay behind in this race for space.

Those who came before us made certain that this country rode the first waves of the industrial revolution, the first waves of modern invention, and the first wave of nuclear power, and this generation does not intend to founder in the backwash of the coming age of space. We mean to be a part of it—we mean to lead it. For the eyes of the world now look into space, to the moon and to the planets beyond, and we have vowed that we shall not see it governed by a hostile flag of conquest, but by a banner of freedom and peace. We have vowed that we shall not see space filled with weapons of mass destruction, but with instruments of knowledge and understanding.

Yet the vows of this Nation can only be fulfilled if we in this Nation are first, and, therefore, we intend to be first. In short, our leadership in science and industry, our hopes for peace and security, our obligations to ourselves as well as others, all require us to make this effort, to solve these mysteries, to solve them for the good of all men, and to become the world's leading space-faring nation.

We set sail on this new sea because there is new knowledge to be gained, and new rights to be won, and they must be won and used for the progress of all people. For space science, like nuclear science and all technology, has no conscience of its own. Whether it will become a force for good or ill depends on man, and only if the United States occupies a position of pre-eminence can we help decide whether this new ocean will be a sea of peace or a new terrifying theatre of war. I do not say that we should or will go unprotected against the hostile misuse of space any more than we go unprotected against the hostile use of land or sea, but I do say that space can be explored and mastered without feeding the fires of war, without repeating the mistakes that man has made in extending his writ around this globe of ours.

There is no strife, no prejudice, no national conflict in outer space as yet. Its hazards are hostile to us all. Its conquest deserves the best of all mankind, and its opportunity for peaceful cooperation many never come again. But why, some say, the moon? Why choose this as our goal? And they may well ask why climb the highest mountain? Why, thirty-five years ago, fly the Atlantic? Why does Rice play Texas?

We choose to go to the moon. We choose to go to the moon in this decade and do the other things, not because they are easy, but because they are hard, because that goal will serve to organize and measure the best of our energies and skills, because that challenge is one that we are willing to accept, one we are unwilling to postpone, and one which we intend to win, and the others, too.

It is for these reasons that I regard the decision last year to shift our efforts in space from low to high gear as among the most important decisions that will be made during my incumbency in the office of the Presidency.

In the last twenty-four hours we have seen facilities now being created for the greatest and most complex exploration in man's history. We have felt the ground shake and the air shattered by the testing of a Saturn C-1 booster rocket, many times as powerful as the Atlas which launched John Glenn, generating power equivalent to ten thousand automobiles with their accelerators on the floor. We have seen the site where five F-1 rocket engines, each one as powerful as all eight engines of the Saturn combined, will be clustered together to make the advanced Saturn missile, assembled in a new building to be built at Cape Canaveral as tall as a forty-eight story structure, as wide as a city block, and as long as two lengths of this field.

Within these last nineteen months at least forty-five satellites have circled the earth. Some forty of them were made in the United States of America and they were far more sophisticated and supplied far more knowledge to the people of the world than those of the Soviet Union.

The Mariner spacecraft now on its way to Venus is the most intricate instrument in the history of space science. The accuracy of that shot is comparable to firing a missile from Cape Canaveral and dropping it in this stadium between the forty-yard lines.

Transit satellites are helping our ships at sea to steer a safer course. Tiros satellites have given us unprecedented warnings of hurricanes and storms, and will do the same for forest fires and icebergs.

We have had our failures, but so have others, even if they do not admit them. And they may be less public.

To be sure, we are behind, and will be behind for some time

in manned flight. But we do not intend to stay behind, and in this decade, we shall make up and move ahead.

The growth of our science and education will be enriched by new knowledge of our universe and environment, by new techniques of learning and mapping and observation, by new tools and computers for industry, medicine, the home as well as the school. Technical institutions, such as Rice, will reap the harvest of these gains.

And finally, the space effort itself, while still in its infancy, has already created a great number of new companies, and tens of thousands of new jobs. Space and related industries are generating new demands in investment and skilled personnel, and this city and this state, and this region, will share greatly in this growth. What was once the furthest outpost on the old frontier of the West will be the furthest outpost on the new frontier of science and space. Houston, your city of Houston, with its Manned Spacecraft Centre, will become the heart of a large scientific and engineering community. During the next five years the National Aeronautics and Space Administration expects to double the number of scientists and engineers in this area, to increase its outlays for salaries and expenses to $60 million a year; to invest some $200 million in plant and laboratory facilities; and to direct or contract for new space efforts over $1 billion from this centre in this city.

To be sure, all this costs us all a good deal of money. This year's space budget is three times what it was in January 1961, and it is greater than the space budget of the previous eight years combined. That budget now stands at $5,400 million a year—a staggering sum, though somewhat less than we pay for cigarettes and cigars every year. Space expenditures will soon rise some more, from forty cents per person per week to more than fifty cents a week for every man, woman and child in the United States, for we have given this program a high national priority—

even though I realize that this is in some measure an act of faith and vision, for we do not now know what benefits await us. But if I were to say, my fellow citizens, that we shall send to the moon, 240,000 miles away from the control station in Houston, a giant rocket more than three hundred feet tall, the length of this football field, made of new metal alloys, some of which have not yet been invented, capable of standing heat and stresses several times more than have ever been experienced, fitted together with a precision better than the finest watch, carrying all the equipment needed for propulsion, guidance, control, communications, food and survival, on an untried mission, to an unknown celestial body, and then return it safely to earth, re-entering the atmosphere at speeds of over twenty-five thousand miles per hour, causing heat about half that of the temperature of the sun—almost as hot as it is here today—and do all this, and do it right, and do it first before this decade is out—then we must be bold.

I'm the one who is doing all the work, so we just want you to stay cool for a minute.

However, I think we're going to do it, and I think that we must pay what needs to be paid. I don't think we ought to waste any money, but I think we ought to do the job. And this will be done in the decade of the Sixties. It may be done while some of you are still here at school at this college and university. It will be done during the terms of office of some of the people who sit here on this platform. But it will be done. And it will be done before the end of this decade.

And I am delighted that this university is playing a part in putting a man on the moon as part of a great national effort of the United States of America.

Many years ago the great British explorer George Mallory, who was to die on Mount Everest, was asked why did he want to climb it. He said, 'Because it is there.'

Well, space is there, and we're going to climb it, and the moon and the planets are there, and new hopes for knowledge and peace are there. And, therefore, as we set sail we ask God's blessing on the most hazardous and dangerous and greatest adventure on which man has ever embarked.

Thank you.

43

ICH BIN EIN BERLINER

John F. Kennedy

Berlin, Germany

26 June 1963

The title of the speech translates to 'I am a Berliner.'

In 1961, millions of people migrated from East Germany to West Germany. The people of East Germany were suffering under the repressions of the Communist Party while democracy flourished in West. Life in West Germany seemed promising. It had managed to rope in financial help through the Marshall Plan of the U.S.A.

The Eastern government did what they could to prevent further migration to their western counterpart—they closed the border by erecting the Berlin Wall. This move separated families and robbed the citizens of their freedom.

Kennedy delivered the following speech to the citizens of West Berlin, making it clear that the Wall was a mark of failure of the communist system.

I am proud to come to this city as the guest of your distinguished Mayor, who has symbolized throughout the world the fighting spirit of West Berlin. And I am proud to visit the Federal Republic with your distinguished Chancellor who for so many years has committed Germany to democracy and freedom and progress, and to come here in the company of my fellow American, General Clay, who has been in this city during its great moments of crisis and will come again if ever needed.

Two thousand years ago the proudest boast was *civis Romanus sum*. Today, in the world of freedom, the proudest boast is *Ich bin ein Berliner*.

I appreciate my interpreter translating my German!

There are many people in the world who really don't understand, or say they don't, what is the great issue between the free world and the Communist world. Let them come to Berlin. There are some who say that communism is the wave of the future. Let them come to Berlin. And there are some who say in Europe and elsewhere we can work with the Communists. Let them come to Berlin. And there are even a few who say that it is true that communism is an evil system, but it permits us to make economic progress. *Lass' sie nach Berlin kommen*. Let them come to Berlin.

Freedom has many difficulties and democracy is not perfect, but we have never had to put a wall up to keep our people in, to prevent them from leaving us. I want to say, on behalf of my countrymen, who live many miles away on the other side of the Atlantic, who are far distant from you, that they take the greatest pride that they have been able to share with you, even from a distance, the story of the last eighteen years. I know of no town, no city, that has been besieged for eighteen years that still lives with the vitality and the force, and the hope and the determination of the city of West Berlin. While the wall is the most obvious and vivid demonstration of the failures of the Communist system, for all the world to see, we take no satisfaction in it, for it is, as your Mayor has said, an offense not only against history but an offense against humanity, separating families, dividing husbands and wives and brothers and sisters, and dividing a people who wish to be joined together.

What is true of this city is true of Germany—real, lasting peace in Europe can never be assured as long as one German out of four is denied the elementary right of free men, and that is to make a free choice. In eighteen years of peace and good faith, this generation of Germans has earned the right to be free, including the right to unite their families and their nation in lasting peace, with goodwill to all people. You live in a defended island of freedom, but your life is part of the main. So let me ask you as I close, to lift your eyes beyond the dangers of today, to the hopes of tomorrow, beyond the freedom merely of this city of Berlin, or your country of Germany, to the advance of freedom everywhere, beyond the wall to the day of peace with justice, beyond yourselves and ourselves to all mankind.

Freedom is indivisible, and when one man is enslaved, all are not free. When all are free, then we can look forward to that day when this city will be joined as one and this country and this great Continent of Europe in a peaceful and hopeful globe. When that day finally comes, as it will, the people of West Berlin can take sober satisfaction in the fact that they were in the front lines for almost two decades.

All free men, wherever they may live, are citizens of Berlin, and, therefore, as a free man, I take pride in the words *Ich bin ein Berliner.*

44

I HAVE A DREAM

Martin Luther King Jr.

Washington, D.C., U.S.A.

28 August 1963

Slavery had been abolished, voting rights had been gained, and still African-Americans faced a struggle of their own in the white society of America. The following speech was delivered at such a time, in front a crowd gathered to demand equal civil and political rights for blacks.

The greatest, the most iconic, the profoundly inspirational speech given by Martin Luther King Jr, on the steps of the Lincoln Memorial, poignantly paints his vision, his dream of living in a world of racial harmony.

I am happy to join with you today in what will go down in history as the greatest demonstration for freedom in the history of our nation.

Five score years ago, a great American, in whose symbolic shadow we stand today, signed the Emancipation Proclamation. This momentous decree came as a great beacon light of hope to millions of Negro slaves who had been seared in the flames of withering injustice. It came as a joyous daybreak to end the long night of their captivity.

But one hundred years later, the Negro still is not free. One hundred years later, the life of the Negro is still sadly crippled by the manacles of segregation and the chains of discrimination. One hundred years later, the Negro lives on a lonely island of poverty in the midst of a vast ocean of material prosperity. One hundred years later, the Negro is still languishing in the corners of American society and finds himself an exile in his own land. So we have come here today to dramatize a shameful condition.

In a sense we have come to our nation's capital to cash a check. When the architects of our republic wrote the magnificent words of the Constitution and the Declaration of Independence, they were signing a promissory note to which every American was to fall heir. This note was a promise that all men, yes, black men as well as white men, would be guaranteed the unalienable rights of life, liberty, and the pursuit of happiness.

It is obvious today that America has defaulted on this promissory note insofar as her citizens of color are concerned. Instead of honoring this sacred obligation, America has given the Negro people a bad check, a check which has come back marked "insufficient funds." But we refuse to believe that the bank of justice is bankrupt. We refuse to believe that there are insufficient funds in the great vaults of opportunity of this nation. So we have come to cash this check—a check that will give us upon demand the riches of freedom and the security of justice. We have also come to this hallowed spot to remind America of the fierce urgency of now. This is no time to engage in the luxury of cooling off or to take the tranquilizing drug of gradualism. Now is the time to make real the promises of democracy. Now is the time to rise from the dark and desolate valley of segregation to the sunlit path of racial justice. Now is the time to lift our nation from the quick sands of racial injustice to the solid rock of brotherhood. Now is the time to make justice a reality for all of God's children.

It would be fatal for the nation to overlook the urgency of the moment. This sweltering summer of the Negro's legitimate discontent will not pass until there is an invigorating autumn of freedom and equality. Nineteen sixty-three is not an end, but a beginning. Those who hope that the Negro needed to blow off steam and will now be content will have a rude awakening if the nation returns to business as usual. There will be neither rest nor tranquility in America until the Negro is granted his citizenship rights. The whirlwinds of revolt will continue to shake the foundations of our nation until the bright day of justice emerges.

But there is something that I must say to my people who stand on the warm threshold which leads into the palace of justice. In the process of gaining our rightful place we must not be guilty of wrongful deeds. Let us not seek to satisfy our thirst for freedom by drinking from the cup of bitterness and hatred.

We must forever conduct our struggle on the high plane of dignity and discipline. We must not allow our creative protest to degenerate into physical violence. Again and again we must rise to the majestic heights of meeting physical force with soul force. The marvelous new militancy which has engulfed the Negro community must not lead us to a distrust of all white people, for many of our white brothers, as evidenced by their presence here today, have come to realize that their destiny is tied up with our destiny. They have come to realize that their freedom is inextricably bound to our freedom. We cannot walk alone.

As we walk, we must make the pledge that we shall always march ahead. We cannot turn back. There are those who are asking the devotees of civil rights, "When will you be satisfied?" We can never be satisfied as long as the Negro is the victim of the unspeakable horrors of police brutality. We can never be satisfied, as long as our bodies, heavy with the fatigue of travel, cannot gain lodging in the motels of the highways and the hotels of the cities. We cannot be satisfied as long as the Negro's basic mobility is from a smaller ghetto to a larger one. We can never be satisfied as long as our children are stripped of their selfhood and robbed of their dignity by signs stating "For Whites Only". We cannot be satisfied as long as a Negro in Mississippi cannot vote and a Negro in New York believes he has nothing for which to vote. No, no, we are not satisfied, and we will not be satisfied until justice rolls down like waters and righteousness like a mighty stream.

I am not unmindful that some of you have come here out of great trials and tribulations. Some of you have come fresh from narrow jail cells. Some of you have come from areas where your quest for freedom left you battered by the storms of persecution and staggered by the winds of police brutality. You have been the veterans of creative suffering. Continue to work with the faith that unearned suffering is redemptive.

Go back to Mississippi, go back to Alabama, go back to South Carolina, go back to Georgia, go back to Louisiana, go back to the slums and ghettos of our northern cities, knowing that somehow this situation can and will be changed. Let us not wallow in the valley of despair.

I say to you today, my friends, so even though we face the difficulties of today and tomorrow, I still have a dream. It is a dream deeply rooted in the American dream.

I have a dream that one day this nation will rise up and live out the true meaning of its creed: "We hold these truths to be self-evident: that all men are created equal."

I have a dream that one day on the red hills of Georgia the sons of former slaves and the sons of former slave owners will be able to sit down together at the table of brotherhood.

I have a dream that one day even the state of Mississippi, a state sweltering with the heat of injustice, sweltering with the heat of oppression, will be transformed into an oasis of freedom and justice.

I have a dream that my four little children will one day live in a nation where they will not be judged by the color of their skin but by the content of their character.

I have a dream today.

I have a dream that one day, down in Alabama, with its vicious racists, with its governor having his lips dripping with the words of interposition and nullification; one day right there in Alabama, little black boys and black girls will be able to join hands with little white boys and white girls as sisters and brothers.

I have a dream today.

I have a dream that one day every valley shall be exalted, every hill and mountain shall be made low, the rough places will be made plain, and the crooked places will be made straight, and the glory of the Lord shall be revealed, and all flesh shall see it together.

This is our hope. This is the faith that I go back to the South with. With this faith we will be able to hew out of the mountain of despair a stone of hope. With this faith we will be able to transform the jangling discords of our nation into a beautiful symphony of brotherhood. With this faith we will be able to work together, to pray together, to struggle together, to go to jail together, to stand up for freedom together, knowing that we will be free one day.

This will be the day when all of God's children will be able to sing with a new meaning, "My country, 'tis of thee, sweet land of liberty, of thee I sing. Land where my fathers died, land of the pilgrim's pride, from every mountainside, let freedom ring."

And if America is to be a great nation this must become true. So let freedom ring from the prodigious hilltops of New Hampshire.

Let freedom ring from the mighty mountains of New York. Let freedom ring from the heightening Alleghenies of Pennsylvania!

Let freedom ring from the snowcapped Rockies of Colorado!

Let freedom ring from the curvaceous slopes of California!

But not only that; let freedom ring from Stone Mountain of Georgia!

Let freedom ring from Lookout Mountain of Tennessee!

Let freedom ring from every hill and molehill of Mississippi. From every mountainside, let freedom ring.

And when this happens, when we allow freedom to ring, when we let it ring from every village and every hamlet, from every state and every city, we will be able to speed up that day when all of God's children, black men and white men, Jews and Gentiles, Protestants and Catholics, will be able to join hands and sing in the words of the old Negro spiritual, "Free at last! free at last! thank God Almighty, we are free at last!"

Note: This speech was given during the March on Washington for Jobs and Freedom organized by A. Philip Randolph and Bayard Rustin, both of whom were civil rights activists. The crowd at this march was estimated to be 250,000 people.

45

I AM PREPARED TO DIE

Nelson Mandela

Johannesburg, U.S.A.

20 April 1964

The philosophy of apartheid was introduced in South Africa in 1948. The government openly discriminated based on people's skin colour—inter-racial marriage was prohibited and an act was passed which stated that people belonging to different racial groups could not cohabit.

Nelson Mandela was sentenced to life imprisonment for trying to overthrow the South African apartheid government. After spending two years in jail, he delivered the following speech at the dock of the Pretoria courtroom, critiquing the racial discrimination that the apartheid brought about.

I am the First Accused.

I hold a Bachelor's Degree in Arts and practised as an attorney in Johannesburg for a number of years in partnership with Oliver Tambo. I am a convicted prisoner serving five years for leaving the country without a permit and for inciting people to go on strike at the end of May 1961.

At the outset, I want to say that the suggestion made by the State in its opening that the struggle in South Africa is under the influence of foreigners or communists is wholly incorrect. I have done whatever I did, both as an individual and as a leader of my people, because of my experience in South Africa and my own proudly felt African background, and not because of what any outsider might have said.

In my youth in the Transkei I listened to the elders of my tribe telling stories of the old days. Amongst the tales they related to me were those of wars fought by our ancestors in defence of the fatherland. The names of Dingane and Bambata, Hintsa and Makana, Squngthi and Dalasile, Moshoeshoe and Sekhukhuni, were praised as the glory of the entire African nation. I hoped then that life might offer me the opportunity to serve my people and make my own humble contribution to their freedom struggle. This is what has motivated me in all that I have done in relation to the charges made against me in this case.

Having said this, I must deal immediately and at some length with the question of violence. Some of the things so far told to the Court are true and some are untrue. I do not, however, deny that I planned sabotage. I did not plan it in a spirit of recklessness, nor because I have any love of violence. I planned it as a result of a calm and sober assessment of the political situation that had arisen after many years of tyranny, exploitation, and oppression of my people by the Whites.

I admit immediately that I was one of the persons who helped to form Umkhonto we Sizwe, and that I played a prominent role in its affairs until I was arrested in August 1962.

In the statement which I am about to make I shall correct certain false impressions which have been created by State witnesses. Amongst other things, I will demonstrate that certain of the acts referred to in the evidence were not and could not have been committed by Umkhonto. I will also deal with the relationship between the African National Congress and Umkhonto, and with the part which I personally have played in the affairs of both organizations. I shall deal also with the part played by the Communist Party. In order to explain these matters properly, I will have to explain what Umkhonto set out to achieve; what methods it prescribed for the achievement of these objects, and why these methods were chosen. I will also have to explain how I became involved in the activities of these organizations.

I deny that Umkhonto was responsible for a number of acts which clearly fell outside the policy of the organization, and which have been charged in the indictment against us. I do not know what justification there was for these acts, but to demonstrate that they could not have been authorized by Umkhonto, I want to refer briefly to the roots and policy of the organization.

I have already mentioned that I was one of the persons who helped to form Umkhonto. I, and the others who started the organization, did so for two reasons. Firstly, we believed that as a result of government policy, violence by the African people had become inevitable, and that unless responsible leadership was given to canalize and control the feelings of our people, there would be outbreaks of terrorism which would produce an intensity of bitterness and hostility between the various races of this country which is not produced even by war. Secondly, we felt that without violence there would be no way open to the African people to succeed in their struggle against the principle of white supremacy. All lawful modes of expressing opposition to this principle had been closed by legislation, and we were placed in a position in which we had either to accept a permanent state of inferiority, or to defy the government. We chose to defy the law. We first broke the law in a way which avoided any recourse to violence; when this form was legislated against, and then the government resorted to a show of force to crush opposition to its policies, only then did we decide to answer violence with violence.

But the violence which we chose to adopt was not terrorism. We who formed Umkhonto were all members of the African National Congress, and had behind us the A.N.C. tradition of non-violence and negotiation as a means of solving political disputes. We believe that South Africa belongs to all the people who live in it, and not to one group, be it black or white. We did not want an interracial war, and tried to avoid it to the last minute. If the Court is in doubt about this, it will be seen that the whole history of our organization bears out what I have said, and what I will subsequently say, when I describe the tactics which Umkhonto decided to adopt. I want, therefore, to say something about the African National Congress.

The African National Congress was formed in 1912 to defend the rights of the African people which had been seriously curtailed by the South Africa Act, and which were then being threatened by the Native Land Act. For thirty-seven years—that is until 1949—it adhered strictly to a constitutional struggle. It put forward demands and resolutions; it sent delegations to the government in the belief that African grievances could be settled through peaceful discussion and that Africans could advance gradually to full political rights. But White Governments remained unmoved, and the rights of Africans became less instead of becoming greater. In the words of my leader, Chief Lutuli, who became President of the A.N.C. in 1952, and who was later awarded the Nobel Peace Prize:

'Who will deny that thirty years of my life have been spent knocking in vain, patiently, moderately, and modestly at a closed and barred door? What have been the fruits of moderation? The past thirty years have seen the greatest number of laws restricting our rights and progress, until today we have reached a stage where we have almost no rights at all.'

Even after 1949, the A.N.C. remained determined to avoid violence. At this time, however, there was a change from the strictly constitutional means of protest which had been employed in the past. The change was embodied in a decision which was taken to protest against apartheid legislation by peaceful, but unlawful, demonstrations against certain laws. Pursuant to this policy the A.N.C. launched the Defiance Campaign, in which I was placed in charge of volunteers. This campaign was based on the principles of passive resistance. More than eight thousand and five hundred people defied apartheid laws and went to jail. Yet there was not a single instance of violence in the course of this campaign on the part of any defier. I and nineteen colleagues were convicted for the role which we played in organizing the campaign, but our sentences were suspended mainly because the Judge found that discipline and non-violence had been stressed throughout. This was the time when the volunteer section of the A.N.C. was established, and when the word 'Amadelakufa' was first used: this was the time when the volunteers were asked to take a pledge to uphold certain principles. Evidence dealing with volunteers and their pledges has been introduced into this case, but completely out of context. The volunteers were not, and are not, the soldiers of a black army pledged to fight a civil war against the whites. They were, and are, dedicated workers who are prepared to lead campaigns initiated by the A.N.C. to distribute leaflets, to organize strikes, or do whatever the particular campaign required. They are called volunteers because they volunteer to face the penalties of imprisonment and whipping which are now prescribed by the legislature for such acts.

During the Defiance Campaign, the Public Safety Act and the Criminal Law Amendment Act were passed. These Statutes provided harsher penalties for offences committed by way of protests against laws. Despite this, the protests continued and the A.N.C. adhered to its policy of non-violence. In 1956, one hundred and fifty-six leading members of the Congress Alliance, including myself, were arrested on a charge of high treason and charges under the Suppression of Communism Act. The non-violent policy of the A.N.C. was put in issue by the State, but when the Court gave judgement some five years later, it found that the A.N.C. did not have a policy of violence. We were acquitted on all counts, which included a count that the A.N.C. sought to set up a communist state in place of the existing regime. The government has always sought to label all its opponents as communists. This allegation has been repeated in the present case, but as I will show, the A.N.C. is not, and never has been, a communist organization.

In 1960 there was the shooting at Sharpeville, which resulted in the proclamation of a state of emergency and the declaration of the A.N.C. as an unlawful organization. My colleagues and I, after careful consideration, decided that we would not obey this decree. The African people were not part of the government and did not make the laws by which they were governed. We believed in the words of the Universal Declaration of Human Rights, that 'the will of the people shall be the basis of authority of the government,' and for us to accept the banning was equivalent to accepting the silencing of the Africans for all time. The A.N.C. refused to dissolve, but instead went underground. We believed it was our duty to preserve this organization which had been built up with almost fifty years of unremitting toil. I have no doubt that no self-respecting White political organization would disband itself if declared illegal by a government in which it had no say.

In 1960 the government held a referendum which led to the establishment of the Republic. Africans, who constituted approximately seventy per cent of the population of South Africa, were not entitled to vote, and were not even consulted about the proposed constitutional change. All of us were apprehensive of our future under the proposed White Republic, and a resolution was taken to hold an All-In African Conference to call for a National Convention, and to organize mass demonstrations on the eve of the unwanted Republic, if the government failed to call the Convention. The conference was attended by Africans of various political persuasions. I was the secretary of the conference and undertook to be responsible for organizing the national stay-at-home which was subsequently called to coincide with the declaration of the Republic. As all strikes by Africans are illegal, the person organizing such a strike must avoid arrest. I was chosen to be this person, and consequently I had to leave my home and family and my practice and go into hiding to avoid arrest.

The stay-at-home, in accordance with A.N.C. policy, was to be a peaceful demonstration. Careful instructions were given to organizers and members to avoid any recourse to violence. The government's answer was to introduce new and harsher laws, to mobilize its armed forces, and to send Saracens, armed vehicles, and soldiers into the townships in a massive show of force designed to intimidate the people. This was an indication that the government had decided to rule by force alone, and this decision was a milestone on the road to Umkhonto.

Some of this may appear irrelevant to this trial. In fact, I believe none of it is irrelevant because it will, I hope, enable the Court to appreciate the attitude eventually adopted by the various persons and bodies concerned in the National Liberation Movement. When I went to jail in 1962, the dominant idea was that loss of life should be avoided. I now know that this was still so in 1963.

I must return to June 1961. What were we, the leaders of our people, to do? Were we to give in to the show of force and the implied threat against future action, or were we to fight it and, if so, how?

We had no doubt that we had to continue the fight. Anything else would have been abject surrender. Our problem was not whether to fight, but was how to continue the fight. We of the A.N.C. had always stood for a non-racial democracy, and we shrank from any action which might drive the races further apart than they already were. But the hard facts were that fifty years of non-violence had brought the African people nothing but more and more repressive legislation, and fewer and fewer rights. It may not be easy for this Court to understand, but it is a fact that for a long time the people had been talking of violence—of the day when they would fight the White man and win back their country—and we, the leaders of the A.N.C., had nevertheless always prevailed upon them to avoid violence and to pursue peaceful methods. When some of us discussed this in May and June of 1961, it could not be denied that our policy to achieve a non-racial state by non-violence had achieved nothing, and that our followers were beginning to lose confidence in this policy and were developing disturbing ideas of terrorism.

It must not be forgotten that by this time violence had, in fact, become a feature of the South African political scene. There had been violence in 1957 when the women of Zeerust were ordered to carry passes; there was violence in 1958 with the enforcement of cattle culling in Sekhukhuniland; there was violence in 1959 when the people of Cato Manor protested against pass raids; there was violence in 1960 when the government attempted to impose Bantu Authorities in Pondoland. Thirty-nine Africans died in these disturbances. In 1961 there had been riots in Warmbaths, and all this time the Transkei had been a seething mass of unrest. Each disturbance pointed clearly to the inevitable growth among Africans of the belief that violence was the only way out—it showed that a government which uses force to maintain its rule teaches the oppressed to use force to oppose it. Already small groups had arisen in the urban areas and were spontaneously making plans for violent forms of political struggle. There now arose a danger that these groups would adopt terrorism against Africans, as well as Whites, if not properly directed. Particularly disturbing was the type of violence engendered in places such as Zeerust, Sekhukhuniland, and Pondoland amongst Africans. It was increasingly taking the form, not of struggle against the government—though this is what prompted it—but of civil strife amongst themselves, conducted in such a way that it could not hope to achieve anything other than a loss of life and bitterness.

At the beginning of June 1961, after a long and anxious assessment of the South African situation, I, and some colleagues, came to the conclusion that as violence in this country was inevitable, it would be unrealistic and wrong for African leaders to continue preaching peace and non-violence at a time when the government met our peaceful demands with force.

This conclusion was not easily arrived at. It was only when all else had failed, when all channels of peaceful protest had been barred to us, that the decision was made to embark on violent forms of political struggle, and to form Umkhonto we Sizwe. We did so not because we desired such a course, but solely because the government had left us with no other choice. In the Manifesto of Umkhonto published on 16th December 1961, which is Exhibit AD, we said:

'The time comes in the life of any nation when there remain only two choices—submit or fight. That time has now come to South Africa. We shall not submit and we have no choice but to hit back by all means in our power in defence of our people, our future, and our freedom.'

This was our feeling in June of 1961 when we decided to press for a change in the policy of the National Liberation Movement. I can only say that I felt morally obliged to do what I did.

We who had taken this decision started to consult leaders of various organizations, including the A.N.C. I will not say whom we spoke to, or what they said, but I wish to deal with the role of the African National Congress in this phase of the struggle, and with the policy and objectives of Umkhonto we Sizwe.

As far as the A.N.C. was concerned, it formed a clear view which can be summarized as follows:

It was a mass political organization with a political function to fulfil. Its members had joined on the express policy of non-violence.

Because of all this, it could not and would not undertake violence. This must be stressed. One cannot turn such a body into the small, closely knit organization required for sabotage. Nor would this be politically correct, because it would result in members ceasing to carry out this essential activity: political propaganda and organization. Nor was it permissible to change the whole nature of the organization.

On the other hand, in view of this situation I have described, the A.N.C. was prepared to depart from its fifty-year-old policy of non-violence to this extent that it would no longer disapprove of properly controlled violence. Hence members who undertook such activity would not be subject to disciplinary action by the A.N.C.

I say 'properly controlled violence' because I made it clear that if I formed the organization I would at all times subject it to the political guidance of the A.N.C. and would not undertake any different form of activity from that contemplated without the consent of the A.N.C. And I shall now tell the Court how that form of violence came to be determined.

As a result of this decision, Umkhonto was formed in November 1961. When we took this decision, and subsequently formulated our plans, the A.N.C. heritage of non-violence and racial harmony was very much with us. We felt that the country was drifting towards a civil war in which Blacks and Whites would fight each other. We viewed the situation with alarm. Civil war could mean the destruction of what the A.N.C. stood for; with civil war, racial peace would be more difficult than ever to achieve. We already have examples in South African history of the results of war. It has taken more than fifty years for the scars of the South African War to disappear. How much longer would it take to eradicate the scars of inter-racial civil war, which could not be fought without a great loss of life on both sides?

The avoidance of civil war had dominated our thinking for many years, but when we decided to adopt violence as part of our policy, we realized that we might one day have to face the prospect of such a war. This had to be taken into account in formulating our plans. We required a plan which was flexible and which permitted us to act in accordance with the needs of the times; above all, the plan had to be one which recognized civil war as the last resort, and left the decision on this question to the future. We did not want to be committed to civil war, but we wanted to be ready if it became inevitable.

Four forms of violence were possible. There is sabotage, there is guerrilla warfare, there is terrorism, and there is open revolution. We chose to adopt the first method and to exhaust it before taking any other decision.

In the light of our political background the choice was a logical one. Sabotage did not involve loss of life, and it offered the best hope for future race relations. Bitterness would be kept to a minimum and, if the policy bore fruit, democratic government could become a reality. This is what we felt at the time, and this is what we said in our Manifesto (Exhibit AD):

'We of Umkhonto we Sizwe have always sought to achieve liberation without bloodshed and civil clash. We hope, even at this late hour, that our first actions will awaken everyone to a realization of the disastrous situation to which the Nationalist policy is leading. We hope that we will bring the government and its supporters to their senses before it is too late, so that both the government and its policies can be changed before matters reach the desperate state of civil war.'

The initial plan was based on a careful analysis of the political and economic situation of our country. We believed that South Africa depended to a large extent on foreign capital and foreign trade. We felt that planned destruction of power plants, and interference with rail and telephone communications, would tend to scare away capital from the country, make it more difficult for goods from the industrial areas to reach the seaports on schedule, and would in the long run be a heavy drain on the economic life of the country, thus compelling the voters of the country to reconsider their position.

Attacks on the economic lifelines of the country were to be linked with sabotage on government buildings and other symbols of apartheid. These attacks would serve as a source of inspiration to our people. In addition, they would provide an outlet for those people who were urging the adoption of violent methods and would enable us to give concrete proof to our followers that we had adopted a stronger line and were fighting back against government violence.

In addition, if mass action were successfully organized, and mass reprisals taken, we felt that sympathy for our cause would be roused in other countries, and that greater pressure would be brought to bear on the South African Government.

This then was the plan. Umkhonto was to perform sabotage, and strict instructions were given to its members right from the start, that on no account were they to injure or kill people in planning or carrying out operations. These instructions have been referred to in the evidence of 'Mr. X' and 'Mr. Z.'

The affairs of the Umkhonto were controlled and directed by

a National High Command, which had powers of co-option and which could, and did, appoint Regional Commands. The High Command was the body which determined tactics and targets and was in charge of training and finance. Under the High Command there were Regional Commands which were responsible for the direction of the local sabotage groups. Within the framework of the policy laid down by the National High Command, the Regional Commands had authority to select the targets to be attacked. They had no authority to go beyond the prescribed framework and thus had no authority to embark upon acts which endangered life, or which did not fit into the overall plan of sabotage. For instance, Umkhonto members were forbidden ever to go armed into operation. Incidentally, the terms High Command and Regional Command were an importation from the Jewish national underground organization Irgun Zvai Leumi, which operated in Israel between 1944 and 1948.

Umkhonto had its first operation on 16th December 1961, when government buildings in Johannesburg, Port Elizabeth and Durban were attacked. The selection of targets is proof of the policy to which I have referred. Had we intended to attack life we would have selected targets where people congregated and not empty buildings and power stations. The sabotage which was committed before 16th December 1961 was the work of isolated groups and had no connection whatever with Umkhonto. In fact, some of these and a number of later acts were claimed by other organizations.

The Manifesto of Umkhonto was issued on the day that operations commenced. The response to our actions and Manifesto among the white population was characteristically violent. The government threatened to take strong action, and called upon its supporters to stand firm and to ignore the demands of the Africans. The Whites failed to respond by suggesting change; they responded to our call by suggesting the laager.

In contrast, the response of the Africans was one of encouragement. Suddenly there was hope again. Things were happening. People in the townships became eager for political news. A great deal of enthusiasm was generated by the initial successes, and people began to speculate on how soon freedom would be obtained.

But we in Umkhonto weighed up the white response with anxiety. The lines were being drawn. The whites and blacks were moving into separate camps, and the prospects of avoiding a civil war were made less. The white newspapers carried reports that sabotage would be punished by death. If this was so, how could we continue to keep Africans away from terrorism?

Already scores of Africans had died as a result of racial friction. In 1920 when the famous leader, Masabala, was held in Port Elizabeth jail, twenty-four of a group of Africans who had gathered to demand his release were killed by the police and white civilians. In 1921 more than one hundred Africans died in the Bulhoek affair. In 1924 over two hundred Africans were killed when the Administrator of South-West Africa led a force against a group which had rebelled against the imposition of dog tax. On 1st May 1950, eighteen Africans died as a result of police shootings during the strike. On 21st March 1960, sixty-nine unarmed Africans died at Sharpeville.

How many more Sharpevilles would there be in the history of our country? And how many more Sharpevilles could the country stand without violence and terror becoming the order of the day? And what would happen to our people when that stage was reached? In the long run we felt certain we must succeed, but at what cost to ourselves and the rest of the country? And if this happened, how could black and white ever live together again in peace and harmony? These were the problems that faced us, and these were our decisions.

Experience convinced us that rebellion would offer the government limitless opportunities for the indiscriminate slaughter of our people. But it was precisely because the soil of South Africa is already drenched with the blood of innocent Africans that we felt it our duty to make preparations as a long-term undertaking to use force in order to defend ourselves against force. If war were inevitable, we wanted the fight to be conducted on terms most favorable to our people. The fight which held out prospects best for us and the least risk of life to both sides was guerrilla warfare. We decided, therefore, in our preparations for the future, to make provision for the possibility of guerrilla warfare.

All whites undergo compulsory military training, but no such training was given to Africans. It was in our view essential to build up a nucleus of trained men who would be able to provide the leadership which would be required if guerrilla warfare started. We had to prepare for such a situation before it became too late to make proper preparations. It was also necessary to build up a nucleus of men trained in civil administration and other professions, so that Africans would be equipped to participate in the government of this country as soon as they were allowed to do so.

At this stage it was decided that I should attend the Conference of the Pan-African Freedom Movement for Central, East, and Southern Africa, which was to be held early in 1962 in Addis Ababa, and, because of our need for preparation, it was also decided that, after the conference, I would undertake a tour of the African States with a view to obtaining facilities for the training of soldiers, and that I would also solicit scholarships for the higher education of matriculated Africans. Training in both fields would be necessary, even if changes came about by peaceful means. Administrators would be necessary who would be willing and able to administer a non-racial State and so would men be necessary to control the army and police force of such a State.

It was on this note that I left South Africa to proceed to Addis Ababa as a delegate of the A.N.C. My tour was a success. Wherever I went I met sympathy for our cause and promises of help. All Africa was united against the stand of White South Africa, and even in London I was received with great sympathy by political leaders, such as Mr. Gaitskell and Mr. Grimond. In Africa I was promised support by such men as Julius Nyerere, now President of Tanganyika; Mr. Kawawa, then Prime Minister of Tanganyika; Emperor Haile Selassie of Ethiopia; General Abboud, President of the Sudan; Habib Bourguiba, President of Tunisia; Ben Bella, now President of Algeria; Modibo Keita, President of Mali; Leopold Senghor, President of Senegal; Sekou Toure, President of Guinea; President Tubman of Liberia; and Milton Obote, Prime Minister of Uganda. It was Ben Bella who invited me to visit Oujda, the Headquarters of the Algerian Army of National Liberation, the visit which is described in my diary, one of the Exhibits.

I started to make a study of the art of war and revolution and, whilst abroad, underwent a course in military training. If there was to be guerrilla warfare, I wanted to be able to stand and fight with my people and to share the hazards of war with them. Notes of lectures which I received in Algeria are contained in Exhibit 16, produced in evidence. Summaries of books on guerrilla warfare and military strategy have also been produced. I have already admitted that these documents are in my writing, and I acknowledge that I made these studies to equip myself for the role which I might have to play if the struggle drifted into guerrilla warfare. I approached this question as every African Nationalist should do. I was completely objective. The Court will see that I attempted to examine all types of authority on the subject—from the East and from the West, going back to the classic work of Clausewitz, and covering such a variety as Mao Tse Tung and Che Guevara on the one hand, and the writings on the Anglo-Boer War on the other. Of course, these notes are merely summaries of the books I read and do not contain my personal views.

I also made arrangements for our recruits to undergo military training. But here it was impossible to organize any scheme without the cooperation of the A.N.C. offices in Africa. I consequently obtained the permission of the A.N.C. in South Africa to do this. To this extent then there was a departure from the original decision of the A.N.C., but it applied outside South Africa only. The first batch of recruits actually arrived in Tanganyika when I was passing through that country on my way back to South Africa.

I returned to South Africa and reported to my colleagues on the results of my trip. On my return I found that there had been little alteration in the political scene save that the threat of a death penalty for sabotage had now become a fact. The attitude of my colleagues in Umkhonto was much the same as it had been before I left. They were feeling their way cautiously and felt that it would be a long time before the possibilities of sabotage were exhausted. In fact, the view was expressed by some that the training of recruits was premature. This is recorded by me in the document which is Exhibit R.14. After a full discussion, however, it was decided to go ahead with the plans for military training because of the fact that it would take many years to build up a sufficient nucleus of trained soldiers to start a guerrilla campaign, and whatever happened, the training would be of value.

I wish to turn now to certain general allegations made in this case by the State. But before doing so, I wish to revert to certain occurrences said by witnesses to have happened in Port Elizabeth and East London. I am referring to the bombing of private houses of pro-government persons during September, October and November 1962. I do not know what justification there was for these acts, nor what provocation had been given. But if what I have said already is accepted, then it is clear that these acts had nothing to do with the carrying out of the policy of Umkhonto.

One of the chief allegations in the indictment is that the A.N.C. was a party to a general conspiracy to commit sabotage. I have already explained why this is incorrect but how, externally, there was a departure from the original principle laid down by the A.N.C. There has, of course, been overlapping of functions internally as well, because there is a difference between a resolution adopted in the atmosphere of a committee room and the concrete difficulties that arise in the field of practical activity. At a later stage the position was further affected by bannings and house arrests, and by persons leaving the country to take up political work abroad. This led to individuals having to do work in different capacities. But though this may have blurred the distinction between Umkhonto and the A.N.C., it by no means abolished that distinction. Great care was taken to keep the activities of the two organizations in South Africa distinct. The A.N.C. remained a mass political body of Africans only carrying on the type of political work they had conducted prior to 1961. Umkhonto remained a small organization recruiting its members from different races and organizations and trying to achieve its own particular object. The fact that members of Umkhonto were recruited from the A.N.C., and the fact that persons served both organizations, like Solomon Mbanjwa, did not, in our view, change the nature of the A.N.C. or give it a policy of violence. This overlapping of officers, however, was more the exception than the rule. This is why persons such as 'Mr. X' and 'Mr. Z,' who were on the Regional Command of their respective areas, did not participate in any of the A.N.C. committees or activities, and why people such as Mr. Bennett Mashiyana and Mr. Reginald Ndubi did not hear of sabotage at their A.N.C. meetings.

Another of the allegations in the indictment is that Rivonia was the headquarters of Umkhonto. This is not true of the time when

I was there. I was told, of course, and knew that certain of the activities of the Communist Party were carried on there. But this is no reason why I should not use the place.

I came there in the following manner:

As already indicated, early in April 1961 I went underground to organize the May general strike. My work entailed travelling throughout the country, living now in African townships, then in country villages and again in cities.

During the second half of the year I started visiting the Parktown home of Arthur Goldreich, where I used to meet my family privately. Although I had no direct political association with him, I had known Arthur Goldreich socially since 1958.

In October, Arthur Goldreich informed me that he was moving out of town and offered me a hiding place there. A few days thereafter, he arranged for Michael Harmel to take me to Rivonia. I naturally found Rivonia an ideal place for the man who lived the life of an outlaw. Up to that time I had been compelled to live indoors during the daytime and could only venture out under cover of darkness. But at Liliesleaf [farm, Rivonia,] I could live differently and work far more efficiently.

For obvious reasons, I had to disguise myself and I assumed the fictitious name of David. In December, Arthur Goldreich and his family moved in. I stayed there until I went abroad on 11th January 1962. As already indicated, I returned in July 1962 and was arrested in Natal on 5th August.

Up to the time of my arrest, Liliesleaf farm was the headquarters of neither the African National Congress nor Umkhonto. With the exception of myself, none of the officials or members of these bodies lived there, no meetings of the governing bodies were ever held there, and no activities connected with them were either organized or directed from there. On numerous occasions during my stay at Liliesleaf farm I met both the Executive Committee of the A.N.C., as well as the NHC, but such meetings were held elsewhere and not on the farm.

Whilst staying at Liliesleaf farm, I frequently visited Arthur Goldreich in the main house and he also paid me visits in my room. We had numerous political discussions covering a variety of subjects. We discussed ideological and practical questions, the Congress Alliance, Umkhonto and its activities generally, and his experiences as a soldier in the Palmach, the military wing of the Haganah. Haganah was the political authority of the Jewish National Movement in Palestine.

Because of what I had got to know of Goldreich, I recommended on my return to South Africa that he should be recruited to Umkhonto. I do not know of my personal knowledge whether this was done.

Another of the allegations made by the State is that the aims and objects of the A.N.C. and the Communist Party arc the same. I wish to deal with this and with my own political position, because I must assume that the State may try to argue from certain Exhibits that I tried to introduce Marxism into the A.N.C. The allegation as to the A.N.C. is false. This is an old allegation which was disproved at the Treason Trial and which has again reared its head. But since the allegation has been made again, I shall deal with it as well as with the relationship between the A.N.C. and the Communist Party and Umkhonto and that party.

The ideological creed of the A.N.C. is, and always has been, the creed of African Nationalism. It is not the concept of African Nationalism expressed in the cry, 'Drive the White man into the sea.' The African Nationalism for which the A.N.C. stands is the concept of freedom and fulfilment for the African people in their own land. The most important political document ever adopted by the A.N.C. is the 'Freedom Charter.' It is by no means a blueprint for a socialist state. It calls for redistribution, but not nationalization, of land; it provides for nationalization of mines, banks, and monopoly industry, because big monopolies are owned by one race only, and without such nationalization racial domination would be perpetuated despite the spread of political power. It would be a hollow gesture to repeal the Gold Law prohibitions against Africans when all gold mines are owned by European companies. In this respect the A.N.C.'s policy corresponds with the old policy of the present Nationalist Party which, for many years, had as part of its programme the nationalization of the gold mines which, at that time, were controlled by foreign capital. Under the Freedom Charter, nationalization would take place in an economy based on private enterprise. The realization of the Freedom Charter would open up fresh fields for a prosperous African population of all classes, including the middle class. The A.N.C. has never at any period of its history advocated a revolutionary change in the economic structure of the country, nor has it, to the best of my recollection, ever condemned capitalist society.

As far as the Communist Party is concerned, and if I understand its policy correctly, it stands for the establishment of a State based on the principles of Marxism. Although it is prepared to work for the Freedom Charter, as a short term solution to the problems created by white supremacy, it regards the Freedom Charter as the beginning, and not the end, of its program.

The A.N.C., unlike the Communist Party, admitted Africans only as members. Its chief goal was, and is, for the African people to win unity and full political rights. The Communist Party's main aim, on the other hand, was to remove the capitalists and to replace them with a working-class government. The Communist Party sought to emphasize class distinctions whilst the A.N.C. seeks to harmonize them. This is a vital distinction.

It is true that there has often been close cooperation between the A.N.C. and the Communist Party. But cooperation is merely proof of a common goal—in this case the removal of white supremacy—and is not proof of a complete community of interests.

The history of the world is full of similar examples. Perhaps the most striking illustration is to be found in the cooperation between Great Britain, the United States of America, and the Soviet Union in the fight against Hitler. Nobody but Hitler would have dared to suggest that such cooperation turned Churchill or Roosevelt into communists or communist tools, or that Britain and America were working to bring about a communist world.

Another instance of such cooperation is to be found precisely in Umkhonto. Shortly after Umkhonto was constituted, I was informed by some of its members that the Communist Party would support Umkhonto, and this then occurred. At a later stage the support was made openly.

I believe that communists have always played an active role in the fight by colonial countries for their freedom, because the short-term objects of communism would always correspond with the long-term objects of freedom movements. Thus communists have played an important role in the freedom struggles fought in countries such as Malaya, Algeria, and Indonesia, yet none of these States today are communist countries. Similarly in the underground resistance movements which sprung up in Europe during the last World War, communists played an important role. Even General Chiang Kai-Shek, today one of the bitterest enemies of communism, fought together with the communists against the ruling class in the struggle which led to his assumption of power in China in the 1930s.

This pattern of cooperation between communists and non-communists has been repeated in the National Liberation Movement of South Africa. Prior to the banning of the Communist Party, joint campaigns involving the Communist Party and the Congress movements were accepted practice. African communists could, and did, become members of the A.N.C., and some served on the National, Provincial, and local committees. Amongst those who served on the National Executive are Albert Nzula, a former Secretary of the Communist Party, Moses Kotane, another former Secretary, and J. B. Marks, a former member of the Central Committee.

I joined the A.N.C. in 1944, and in my younger days I held the view that the policy of admitting communists to the A.N.C., and the close cooperation which existed at times on specific issues between the A.N.C. and the Communist Party, would lead to a watering down of the concept of African Nationalism. At that stage I was a member of the African National Congress Youth League, and was one of a group which moved for the expulsion of communists from the A.N.C. This proposal was heavily defeated. Amongst those who voted against the proposal were some of the most conservative sections of African political opinion. They defended the policy on the ground that from its inception the A.N.C. was formed and built up, not as a political party with one school of political thought, but as a Parliament of the African people, accommodating people of various political convictions, all united by the common goal of national liberation. I was eventually won over to this point of view and I have upheld it ever since.

It is perhaps difficult for white South Africans, with an ingrained prejudice against communism, to understand why experienced African politicians so readily accept communists as their friends. But to us the reason is obvious. Theoretical differences amongst those fighting against oppression is a luxury we cannot afford at this stage. What is more, for many decades communists were the only political group in South Africa who were prepared to treat Africans as human beings and their equals; who were prepared to eat with us; talk with us, live with us, and work with us. They were the only political group which was prepared to work with the

Africans for the attainment of political rights and a stake in society. Because of this, there are many Africans who, today, tend to equate freedom with communism. They are supported in this belief by a legislature which brands all exponents of democratic government and African freedom as communists and bans many of them (who are not communists) under the Suppression of Communism Act. Although I have never been a member of the Communist Party, I myself have been named under that pernicious Act because of the role I played in the Defiance Campaign. I have also been banned and imprisoned under that Act.

It is not only in internal politics that we count communists as amongst those who support our cause. In the international field, communist countries have always come to our aid. In the United Nations and other Councils of the world the communist bloc has supported the Afro-Asian struggle against colonialism and often seems to be more sympathetic to our plight than some of the Western powers. Although there is a universal condemnation of apartheid, the communist bloc speaks out against it with a louder voice than most of the white world. In these circumstances, it would take a brash young politician, such as I was in 1949, to proclaim that the Communists are our enemies.

I turn now to my own position. I have denied that I am a communist, and I think that in the circumstances I am obliged to state exactly what my political beliefs are.

I have always regarded myself, in the first place, as an African patriot. After all, I was born in Umtata, forty-six years ago. My guardian was my cousin, who was the acting paramount chief of Tembuland, and I am related both to the present paramount chief of Tembuland, Sabata Dalindyebo, and to Kaizer Matanzima, the Chief Minister of the Transkei.

Today I am attracted by the idea of a classless society, an attraction which springs in part from Marxist reading and, in part, from my admiration of the structure and organization of early African societies in this country. The land, then the main means of production, belonged to the tribe. There were no rich or poor and there was no exploitation.

It is true, as I have already stated, that I have been influenced by Marxist thought. But this is also true of many of the leaders of the new independent States. Such widely different persons as Gandhi, Nehru, Nkrumah, and Nasser all acknowledge this fact. We all accept the need for some form of socialism to enable our people to catch up with the advanced countries of this world and to overcome their legacy of extreme poverty. But this does not mean we are Marxists.

Indeed, for my own part, I believe that it is open to debate whether the Communist Party has any specific role to play at this particular stage of our political struggle. The basic task at the present moment is the removal of race discrimination and the attainment of democratic rights on the basis of the Freedom Charter. In so far as that Party furthers this task, I welcome its assistance. I realize that it is one of the means by which people of all races can be drawn into our struggle.

From my reading of Marxist literature and from conversations with Marxists, I have gained the impression that communists regard the parliamentary system of the West as undemocratic and reactionary. But, on the contrary, I am an admirer of such a system.

The Magna Carta, the Petition of Rights, and the Bill of Rights are documents which are held in veneration by democrats throughout the world.

I have great respect for British political institutions, and for the country's system of justice. I regard the British Parliament as the most democratic institution in the world, and the independence and impartiality of its judiciary never fails to arouse my admiration.

The American Congress, that country's doctrine of separation of powers, as well as the independence of its judiciary, arouses in me similar sentiments.

I have been influenced in my thinking by both West and East. All this has led me to feel that in my search for a political formula, I should be absolutely impartial and objective. I should tie myself to no particular system of society other than of socialism. I must leave myself free to borrow the best from the West and from the East . . .

There are certain Exhibits which suggest that we received financial support from abroad, and I wish to deal with this question.

Our political struggle has always been financed from internal sources—from funds raised by our own people and by our own supporters. Whenever we had a special campaign or an important political case—for example, the Treason Trial—we received financial assistance from sympathetic individuals and organizations in the Western countries. We had never felt it necessary to go beyond these sources.

But when in 1961 the Umkhonto was formed, and a new phase of struggle introduced, we realized that these events would make a heavy call on our slender resources, and that the scale of our activities would be hampered by the lack of funds. One of my instructions, as I went abroad in January 1962, was to raise funds from the African states.

I must add that, whilst abroad, I had discussions with leaders of political movements in Africa and discovered that almost every single one of them, in areas which had still not attained independence, had received all forms of assistance from the socialist countries, as well as from the West, including that of financial support. I also discovered that some well-known African states, all of them non-communists, and even anti-communists, had received similar assistance.

On my return to the Republic, I made a strong recommendation to the A.N.C. that we should not confine ourselves to Africa and the Western countries, but that we should also send a mission to the socialist countries to raise the funds which we so urgently needed.

I have been told that after I was convicted such a mission was sent, but I am not prepared to name any countries to which it went, nor am I at liberty to disclose the names of the organizations and countries which gave us support or promised to do so.

As I understand the State case, and in particular the evidence of 'Mr. X,' the suggestion is that Umkhonto was the inspiration of the Communist Party which sought by playing upon imaginary grievances to enrol the African people into an army which ostensibly was to fight for African freedom, but in reality was fighting for a communist state. Nothing could be further from the truth. In fact the suggestion is preposterous. Umkhonto was formed by Africans to further their struggle for freedom in their own land. Communists and others supported the movement, and we only wish that more sections of the community would join us.

Our fight is against real, and not imaginary, hardships or, to use the language of the State Prosecutor, 'so-called hardships.' Basically, we fight against two features which are the hallmarks of African life in South Africa and which are entrenched by legislation which we seek to have repealed. These features are poverty and lack of human dignity, and we do not need communists or so-called 'agitators' to teach us about these things.

South Africa is the richest country in Africa, and could be one of the richest countries in the world. But it is a land of extremes and remarkable contrasts. The whites enjoy what may well be the highest standard of living in the world, whilst Africans live in poverty and misery. Forty per cent of the Africans live in hopelessly overcrowded and, in some cases, drought-stricken Reserves, where soil erosion and the overworking of the soil makes it impossible for them to live properly off the land. Thirty per cent are labourers, labour tenants, and squatters on white farms and work and live under conditions similar to those of the serfs of the Middle Ages. The other thirty per cent live in towns where they have developed economic and social habits which bring them closer in many respects to white standards. Yet most Africans, even in this group, are impoverished by low incomes and high cost of living.

The highest-paid and the most prosperous section of urban African life is in Johannesburg. Yet their actual position is desperate. The latest figures were given on 25th March 1964 by Mr. Carr, Manager of the Johannesburg Non-European Affairs Department. The poverty datum line for the average African family in Johannesburg (according to Mr. Carr's department) is R42.84 per month. He showed that the average monthly wage is R32.24 and that forty-six per cent of all African families in Johannesburg do not earn enough to keep them going.

Poverty goes hand in hand with malnutrition and disease. The incidence of malnutrition and deficiency diseases is very high amongst Africans. Tuberculosis, pellagra, kwashiorkor, gastroenteritis, and scurvy bring death and destruction of health. The incidence of infant mortality is one of the highest in the world. According to the Medical Officer of Health for Pretoria, tuberculosis kills forty people a day (almost all Africans), and in 1961 there were 58,491 new cases reported. These diseases not only destroy the vital organs of the body, but they result in retarded mental conditions and lack of initiative, and reduce powers of concentration. The secondary results of such conditions affect the whole community and the standard of work performed by African labourers.

The complaint of Africans, however, is not only that they are poor and the whites are rich, but that the laws which are made by the whites are designed to preserve this situation. There are two ways to break out of poverty. The first is by formal education, and the second is by the worker acquiring a greater skill at his work and thus higher wages. As far as Africans are concerned, both these avenues of advancement are deliberately curtailed by legislation.

The present government has always sought to hamper Africans in their search for education. One of their early acts, after coming into power, was to stop subsidies for African school feeding. Many African children who attended schools depended on this supplement to their diet. This was a cruel act.

There is compulsory education for all white children at virtually no cost to their parents, be they rich or poor. Similar facilities are not provided for the African children, though there are some who receive such assistance. African children, however, generally have to pay more for their schooling than whites. According to figures quoted by the South African Institute of Race Relations in its 1963 journal, approximately forty per cent of African children in the age group between seven to fourteen do not attend school. For those who do attend school, the standards are vastly different from those afforded to white children. In 1960-61 the per capita government spending on African students at State-aided schools was estimated at R12.46. In the same years, the per capita spending on white children in the Cape Province (which are the only figures available to me) was R144.57. Although there are no figures available to me, it can be stated, without doubt, that the white children on whom R144.57 per head was being spent all came from wealthier homes than African children on whom R12.46 per head was being spent.

The quality of education is also different. According to the Bantu Educational Journal, only five thousand six hundred and sixty African children in the whole of South Africa passed their Junior Certificate in 1962, and in that year only three hundred and sixty-two passed matric. This is presumably consistent with the policy of Bantu education about which the present prime minister said, during the debate on the Bantu Education Bill in 1953:

'When I have control of Native education I will reform it so that Natives will be taught from childhood to realize that equality with Europeans is not for them . . . People who believe in equality are not desirable teachers for Natives. When my Department controls Native education it will know for what class of higher education a Native is fitted, and whether he will have a chance in life to use his knowledge.'

The other main obstacle to the economic advancement of the African is the industrial colour-bar under which all the better jobs of industry are reserved for Whites only. Moreover, Africans who do obtain employment in the unskilled and semi-skilled occupations which are open to them are not allowed to form trade unions which have recognition under the Industrial Conciliation Act. This means that strikes of African workers are illegal, and that they are denied the right of collective bargaining which is permitted to the better-paid White workers. The discrimination in the policy of successive South African Governments towards African workers is demonstrated by the so-called 'civilized labour policy' under which sheltered, unskilled government jobs are found for those white workers who cannot make the grade in industry, at wages which far exceed the earnings of the average African employee in industry.

The government often answers its critics by saying that Africans in South Africa are economically better off than the inhabitants of the other countries in Africa. I do not know whether this statement is true and doubt whether any comparison can be made without having regard to the cost-of-living index in such countries. But even if it is true, as far as the African people are concerned it is irrelevant. Our complaint is not that we are poor by comparison with people in other countries, but that we are poor by comparison with the white people in our own country, and that we are prevented by legislation from altering this imbalance.

The lack of human dignity experienced by Africans is the direct result of the policy of white supremacy. White supremacy implies black inferiority. Legislation designed to preserve white supremacy entrenches this notion. Menial tasks in South Africa are invariably performed by Africans. When anything has to be carried or cleaned the white man will look around for an African to do it for him, whether the African is employed by him or not. Because of this sort of attitude, whites tend to regard Africans as a separate breed. They do not look upon them as people with families of their own; they do not realize that they have emotions—that they fall in love like white people do; that they want to be with their wives and children like white people want to be with theirs; that they want to earn enough money to support their families properly, to feed and clothe them and send them to school. And what 'house-boy' or 'garden-boy' or labourer can ever hope to do this?

Pass laws, which to the Africans are among the most hated bits of legislation in South Africa, render any African liable to police surveillance at any time. I doubt whether there is a single African male in South Africa who has not at some stage had a brush with the police over his pass. Hundreds and thousands of Africans are thrown into jail each year under pass laws. Even worse than this is the fact that pass laws keep husband and wife apart and lead to the breakdown of family life.

Poverty and the breakdown of family life have secondary effects. Children wander about the streets of the townships because they have no schools to go to, or no money to enable them to go to school, or no parents at home to see that they go to school, because both parents (if there be two) have to work to keep the family alive. This leads to a breakdown in moral standards, to an alarming rise in illegitimacy, and to growing violence which erupts not only politically, but everywhere. Life in the townships is dangerous. There is not a day that goes by without somebody being stabbed or assaulted. And violence is carried out of the townships in the white living areas. People are afraid to walk alone in the streets after dark.

Housebreakings and robberies are increasing, despite the fact that the death sentence can now be imposed for such offences. Death sentences cannot cure the festering sore.

Africans want to be paid a living wage. Africans want to perform work which they are capable of doing, and not work which the government declares them to be capable of. Africans want to be allowed to live where they obtain work, and not be endorsed out of an area because they were not born there. Africans want to be allowed to own land in places where they work, and not to be obliged to live in rented houses which they can never call their own. Africans want to be part of the general population, and not confined to living in their own ghettoes. African men want to have their wives and children to live with them where they work, and not be forced into an unnatural existence in men's hostels. African women want to be with their menfolk and not be left permanently widowed in the Reserves. Africans want to be allowed out after eleven o'clock at night and not to be confined to their rooms like little children. Africans want to be allowed to travel in their own country and to seek work where they want to and not where the Labour Bureau tells them to. Africans want a just share in the whole of South Africa; they want security and a stake in society.

Above all, we want equal political rights, because without them our disabilities will be permanent. I know this sounds revolutionary to the whites in this country, because the majority of voters will be Africans. This makes the white man fear democracy.

But this fear cannot be allowed to stand in the way of the only solution which will guarantee racial harmony and freedom for all. It is not true that the enfranchisement of all will result in racial domination. Political division, based on colour, is entirely artificial and, when it disappears, so will the domination of one colour group by another. The A.N.C. has spent half a century fighting against racialism. When it triumphs it will not change that policy.

This then is what the A.N.C. is fighting. Their struggle is a truly national one. It is a struggle of the African people, inspired by their own suffering and their own experience. It is a struggle for the right to live.

During my lifetime I have dedicated myself to this struggle of the African people. I have fought against white domination, and I have fought against black domination. I have cherished the ideal of a democratic and free society in which all persons live together in harmony and with equal opportunities. It is an ideal which I hope to live for and to achieve. But if needs be, it is an ideal for which I am prepared to die.

46

ON THE DEATH OF MARTIN LUTHER KING

Robert F. Kennedy

Indianapolis, Indiana, U.S.A.

4 April 1968

Martin Luther King was a social activist who fought for equal rights for African-Americans. He was shot to death in Memphis, Tennessee.

Knowing the uproar Luther's death had the potential to create, Kennedy appealed to all the people to turn from revenge to prayer. He believed that there would come a day when the people will witness the eradication of racial discrimination—the vision Luther fought for all his life.

Ladies and Gentlemen:

I'm only going to talk to you just for a minute or so this evening. Because . . .

I have some very sad news for all of you, and I think sad news for all of our fellow citizens, and people who love peace all over the world, and that is that Martin Luther King was shot and was killed tonight in Memphis, Tennessee.

Martin Luther King dedicated his life to love and to justice between fellow human beings. He died in the cause of that effort. In this difficult day, in this difficult time for the United States, it's perhaps well to ask what kind of a nation we are and what direction we want to move in.

For those of you who are black—considering the evidence evidently is that there were white people who were responsible—you can be filled with bitterness, and with hatred, and a desire for revenge.

We can move in that direction as a country, in greater polarization—black people amongst blacks, and white amongst whites, filled with hatred toward one another. Or we can make an effort, as Martin Luther King did, to understand and to comprehend, and replace that violence, that stain of bloodshed that has spread across our land, with an effort to understand, compassion and love.

For those of you who are black and are tempted to be filled with hatred and mistrust of the injustice of such an act, against all white people, I would only say that I can also feel in my own heart the same kind of feeling. I had a member of my family killed, but he was killed by a white man.

But we have to make an effort in the United States, we have to make an effort to understand, to get beyond these rather difficult times.

My favourite poet was Aeschylus. He once wrote: Even in our sleep, pain which cannot forget falls drop by drop upon the heart, until, in our own despair, against our will, comes wisdom through the awful grace of God.

What we need in the United States is not division; what we need in the United States is not hatred; what we need in the United States is not violence and lawlessness, but is love and wisdom, and compassion toward one another, and a feeling of justice toward those who still suffer within our country, whether they be white or whether they be black.

So I ask you tonight to return home, to say a prayer for the family of Martin Luther King, yeah that's true, but more importantly to say a prayer for our own country, which all of us love—a prayer for understanding and that compassion of which I spoke. We can do well in this country. We will have difficult times. We've had difficult times in the past. And we will have difficult times in the future. It is not the end of violence; it is not the end of lawlessness; and it's not the end of disorder.

But the vast majority of white people and the vast majority of black people in this country want to live together, want to improve the quality of our life, and want justice for all human beings that abide in our land.

Let us dedicate ourselves to what the Greeks wrote so many years ago: to tame the savageness of man and make gentle the life of this world.

Let us dedicate ourselves to that, and say a prayer for our country and for our people. Thank you very much.

47

TEAR DOWN THIS WALL

Ronald Reagan

Berlin, Germany

12 June 1987

The Berlin Wall, built in 1961, had become a powerful symbol of the Cold War. During this war, communism in East Germany propelled 2.5 million people to flee to West Germany. To curb this migration, the Eastern government decided to seal the free passage from East to West, and set up a wall.

Twenty-six years later, Ronald Reagan stood at the Brandenburg Gate and delivered the following speech, clearly conveying America's backing to Germany's efforts to unify their country.

Thank you. Thank you very much. Chancellor Kohl, Governing Mayor Diepgen, ladies and gentlemen: Twenty-four years ago, President John F. Kennedy visited Berlin, speaking to the people of this city and the world at the City Hall. Well, since then two other presidents have come, each in his turn, to Berlin. And today I, myself, make my second visit to your city.

We come to Berlin, we American presidents, because it's our duty to speak, in this place, of freedom. But I must confess, we're drawn here by other things as well: by the feeling of history in this city, more than five hundred years older than our own nation; by the beauty of the Grunewald and the Tiergarten; most of all, by your courage and determination. Perhaps the composer Paul Lincke understood something about American presidents. You see, like so many presidents before me, I come here today because wherever I go, whatever I do: *Ich hab noch einen Koffer* in Berlin. [I still have a suitcase in Berlin.] Our gathering today is being broadcast throughout Western Europe and North America. I understand that it is being seen and heard as well in the East. To those listening throughout Eastern Europe, I extend my warmest greeting and the goodwill of the American people. To those listening in Eastern Berlin, a special word: Although I cannot be with you, I address my remarks to you just as surely as to those standing here before me. For I join you, as I join your fellow countrymen in the West, in this firm, this unalterable belief: *Es gibt nur ein Berlin.* [There is only one Berlin.]

Behind me stands a wall that encircles the free sectors of this city, part of a vast system of barriers that divides the entire continent of Europe. From the Baltic, south, those barriers cut across Germany in a gash of barbed wire, concrete, dog runs, and guard towers. Farther south, there may be no visible, no obvious wall. But there remain armed guards and checkpoints all the same—still a restriction on the right to travel, still an instrument to impose upon ordinary men and women the will of a totalitarian state. Yet it is here in Berlin where the wall emerges most clearly; here, cutting across your city, where the news photo and the television screen have imprinted this brutal division of a continent upon the mind of the world. Standing before the Brandenburg Gate, every man is a German, separated from his fellow men. Every man is a Berliner, forced to look upon a scar. President Von Weizsacker has said, 'The German question is open as long as the Brandenburg Gate is closed.' Today I say: As long as the gate is closed, as long as this scar of a wall is permitted to stand, it is not the German question alone that remains open, but the question of freedom for all mankind. Yet I do not come here to lament. For I find in Berlin a message of hope, even in the shadow of this wall, a message of triumph.

In this season of spring in 1945, the people of Berlin emerged from their air-raid shelters to find devastation. Thousands of miles away, the people of the United States reached out to help. And in 1947, Secretary of State—as you've been told—George Marshall announced the creation of what would become known as the Marshall Plan. Speaking precisely forty years ago this month, he said: 'Our policy is directed not against any country or doctrine, but against hunger, poverty, desperation, and chaos.' In the Reichstag a few moments ago, I saw a display commemorating this fortieth anniversary of the Marshall Plan. I was struck by the sign on a burnt out, gutted structure that was being rebuilt. I understand that Berliners of my own generation can remember seeing signs like it dotted throughout the western sectors of the city. The sign read simply: 'The Marshall Plan is helping here to strengthen the free world.' A strong, free world in the West, that dream became real. Japan rose from ruin to become an economic giant. Italy, France, Belgium—virtually every nation in Western Europe saw political and economic rebirth; the European Community was founded. In West Germany and here in Berlin, there took place an economic miracle, the Wirtschaftswunder. Adenauer, Erhard, Reuter, and other leaders understood the practical importance of liberty—that just as truth can flourish only when the journalist is given freedom of speech, so prosperity can come about only when the farmer and businessman enjoy economic freedom. The German leaders reduced tariffs, expanded free trade, lowered taxes. From 1950 to

1960 alone, the standard of living in West Germany and Berlin doubled.

Where four decades ago there was rubble, today in West Berlin there is the greatest industrial output of any city in Germany—busy office blocks, fine homes and apartments, proud avenues, and the spreading lawns of parkland. Where a city's culture seemed to have been destroyed, today there are two great universities, orchestras and an opera, countless theaters, and museums. Where there was want, today there's abundance—food, clothing, automobiles—the wonderful goods of the Ku'damm. From devastation, from utter ruin, you Berliners have, in freedom, rebuilt a city that once again ranks as one of the greatest on earth. The Soviets may have had other plans. But my friends, there were a few things the Soviets didn't count on—*Berliner Herz, Berliner Humor, ja, und Berliner Schnauze.* [Berliner heart, Berliner humor, yes, and a Berliner Schnauze.]

In the 1950s, Khrushchev predicted: 'We will bury you.' But in the West today, we see a free world that has achieved a level of prosperity and well-being unprecedented in all human history. In the Communist world, we see failure, technological backwardness, declining standards of health, even want of the most basic kind—too little food. Even today, the Soviet Union still cannot feed itself. After these four decades, then, there stands before the entire world one great and inescapable conclusion: Freedom leads to prosperity. Freedom replaces the ancient hatreds among the nations with comity and peace. Freedom is the victor.

And now the Soviets themselves may, in a limited way, be coming to understand the importance of freedom. We hear much from Moscow about a new policy of reform and openness. Some political prisoners have been released. Certain foreign news broadcasts are no longer being jammed. Some economic enterprises have been permitted to operate with greater freedom from state control. Are these the beginnings of profound changes in the Soviet state? Or are they token gestures, intended to raise false hopes in the West, or to strengthen the Soviet system without changing it? We welcome change and openness; for we believe that freedom and security go together, that the advance of human liberty can only strengthen the cause of world peace. There is one sign the Soviets can make that would be unmistakable, that would advance dramatically the cause of freedom and peace.

General Secretary Gorbachev, if you seek peace, if you seek prosperity for the Soviet Union and Eastern Europe, if you seek liberalization: Come here to this gate! Mr. Gorbachev, open this gate! Mr. Gorbachev, tear down this wall!

I understand the fear of war and the pain of division that afflict this continent—and I pledge to you my country's efforts to help overcome these burdens. To be sure, we in the West must resist Soviet expansion. So we must maintain defenses of unassailable strength. Yet we seek peace; so we must strive to reduce arms on both sides. Beginning ten years ago, the Soviets challenged the Western alliance with a grave new threat, hundreds of new and more deadly SS-20 nuclear missiles, capable of striking every capital in Europe. The Western alliance responded by committing itself to a counter-deployment unless the Soviets agreed to negotiate a better solution; namely, the elimination of such weapons on both sides. For many months, the Soviets refused to bargain in earnestness. As the alliance, in turn, prepared to go forward with its counter-deployment, there were difficult days—days of protests like those during my 1982 visit to this city—and the Soviets later walked away from the table.

But through it all, the alliance held firm. And I invite those who protested then—I invite those who protest today—to mark this fact: Because we remained strong, the Soviets came back to the table. And because we remain strong today, we have within reach the possibility, not merely of limiting the growth of arms, but of eliminating, for the first time, an entire class of nuclear weapons from the face of the earth.

As I speak, NATO ministers are meeting in Iceland to review the progress of our proposals for eliminating these weapons. At the talks in Geneva, we have also proposed deep cuts in strategic offensive weapons. And the Western allies have likewise made far-reaching proposals to reduce the danger of conventional war and to place a total ban on chemical weapons.

While we pursue these arms reductions, I pledge to you that we will maintain the capacity to deter Soviet aggression at any level at which it might occur. And in cooperation with many of our allies, the United States is pursuing the Strategic Defense Initiative—research to base deterrence not on the threat of offensive retaliation, but on defenses that truly defend; on systems, in short, that will not target populations, but shield them. By these means we seek to increase the safety of Europe and all the world. But we must remember a crucial fact: East and West do not mistrust each other because we are armed; we are armed because we mistrust each other. And our differences are not about weapons but about liberty. When President Kennedy spoke at the City Hall those twenty-four years ago, freedom was encircled, Berlin was under siege. And today, despite all the pressures upon this city, Berlin stands secure in its liberty. And freedom itself is transforming the globe.

In the Philippines, in South and Central America, democracy has been given a rebirth. Throughout the Pacific, free markets are working miracle after miracle of economic growth. In the industrialized nations, a technological revolution is taking place—a revolution marked by rapid, dramatic advances in computers and telecommunications.

In Europe, only one nation and those it controls refuse to join the community of freedom. Yet in this age of redoubled economic growth, of information and innovation, the Soviet Union faces a choice: It must make fundamental changes, or it will become obsolete. Today, thus, represents a moment of hope. We in the West stand ready to cooperate with the East to promote true openness, to break down barriers that separate people, to create a safe, freer world. And surely there is no better place than Berlin, the meeting place of East and West, to make a start. Free people of Berlin: Today, as in the past, the United States stands for the strict observance and full implementation of all parts of the Four Power Agreement of 1971. Let us use this occasion, the seven hundred and fiftieth anniversary of this city, to usher in a new era, to seek a still fuller, richer life for the Berlin of the future. Together, let us maintain and develop the ties between the Federal Republic and the Western sectors of Berlin, which is permitted by the 1971 agreement.

And I invite Mr. Gorbachev: Let us work to bring the Eastern and Western parts of the city closer together, so that all the inhabitants of all Berlin can enjoy the benefits that come with life in one of the great cities of the world. To open Berlin still further to all Europe, East and West, let us expand the vital air access to this city, finding ways of making commercial air service to Berlin more convenient, more comfortable, and more economical. We look to the day when West Berlin can become one of the chief aviation hubs in all central Europe.

With our French and British partners, the United States is prepared to help bring international meetings to Berlin. It would be only fitting for Berlin to serve as the site of United Nations meetings, or world conferences on human rights and arms control or other issues that call for international cooperation.

There is no better way to establish hope for the future than to enlighten young minds, and we would be honoured to sponsor summer youth exchanges, cultural events, and other programs for young Berliners from the East. Our French and British friends, I'm certain, will do the same. And it's my hope that an authority can be found in East Berlin to sponsor visits from young people of the Western sectors.

One final proposal, one close to my heart: Sport represents a source of enjoyment and ennoblement, and you may have noted that the Republic of Korea—South Korea—has offered to permit certain events of the 1988 Olympics to take place in the North. International sports competitions of all kinds could take place in both parts of this city. And what better way to demonstrate to the world the openness of this city than to offer in some future year to hold the Olympic games here in Berlin, East and West? In these four decades, as I have said, you Berliners have built a great city. You've done so in spite of threats—the Soviet attempts to impose the East-mark, the blockade. Today the city thrives in spite of the challenges implicit in the very presence of this wall. What keeps you here? Certainly there's a great deal to be said for your fortitude, for your defiant courage. But I believe there's something deeper, something that involves Berlin's whole look and feel and way of life—not mere sentiment. No one could live long in Berlin without being completely disabused of illusions. Something instead, that has seen the difficulties of life in Berlin but chose to accept them, that continues to build this good and proud city in contrast to a surrounding totalitarian presence that refuses to release human energies or aspirations. Something that speaks with a powerful voice of affirmation, that says yes to this city, yes to the future, yes to freedom. In a word, I would submit that what keeps you in Berlin is love—love both profound and abiding.

Perhaps this gets to the root of the matter, to the most fundamental distinction of all between East and West. The totalitarian world produces backwardness because it does such violence to the spirit, thwarting the human impulse to create, to enjoy, to worship. The totalitarian world finds even symbols of love and of worship an affront. Years ago, before the East Germans began rebuilding their churches, they erected a secular structure: the television tower at Alexander Platz. Virtually ever since, the authorities have been working to correct what they view as the tower's one major flaw, treating the glass sphere at the top with paints and chemicals of every kind. Yet even today when the sun strikes that sphere—that sphere that towers over all Berlin—the light makes the sign of the cross. There in Berlin, like the city itself, symbols of love, symbols of worship, cannot be suppressed.

As I looked out a moment ago from the Reichstag, that embodiment of German unity, I noticed words crudely spray-painted upon the wall, perhaps by a young Berliner: 'This wall will fall. Beliefs become reality.' Yes, across Europe, this wall will fall. For it cannot withstand faith; it cannot withstand truth. The wall cannot withstand freedom.

And I would like, before I close, to say one word. I have read, and I have been questioned since I've been here about certain demonstrations against my coming. And I would like to say just one thing, and to those who demonstrate so. I wonder if they have ever asked themselves that if they should have the kind of government they apparently seek, no one would ever be able to do what they're doing again.

Thank you and God bless you all.

48

ADDRESS ON HIS RELEASE FROM PRISON

Nelson Mandela

Cape Town, South Africa

11 February 1990

The wait was finally over. The leader of the African National Congress, Nelson Mandela, walked out the gates of Victor Verster Prison after nearly three decades, hand-in-hand with his wife. He had been jailed for trying to overthrow the apartheid system from the South African Government.

Mandela, through this speech, assured the people that he was the same person as he was when he was imprisoned in 1964. The following speech encompasses his political goals as he strived to end white supremacy on political power.

He was appointed as the President of South Africa four years later.

Friends, comrades and fellow South Africans:

I greet you all in the name of peace, democracy and freedom for all.

I stand here before you not as a prophet but as a humble servant of you, the people. Your tireless and heroic sacrifices have made it possible for me to be here today. I therefore place the remaining years of my life in your hands.

On this day of my release, I extend my sincere and warmest gratitude to the millions of my compatriots and those in every corner of the globe who have campaigned tirelessly for my release.

I send special greetings to the people of Cape Town, this city which has been my home for three decades. Your mass marches and other forms of struggle have served as a constant source of strength to all political prisoners.

I salute the African National Congress. It has fulfilled our every expectation in its role as leader of the great march to freedom.

I salute our president, Comrade Oliver Tambo, for leading the A.N.C. even under the most difficult circumstances.

I salute the rank and file members of the A.N.C. You have sacrificed life and limb in the pursuit of the noble cause of our struggle.

I salute combatants of Umkhonto we Sizwe, like Solomon Mahlangu and Ashley Kriel who have paid the ultimate price for the freedom of all South Africans.

I salute the South African Communist Party for its sterling contribution to the struggle for democracy. You have survived forty years of unrelenting persecution. The memory of great communists like Moses Kotane, Yusuf Dadoo, Bram Fischer and Moses Mabhida will be cherished for generations to come.

I salute General Secretary Joe Slovo, one of our finest patriots. We are heartened by the fact that the alliance between ourselves and the Party remains as strong as it always was.

I salute the United Democratic Front, the National Education Crisis Committee, the South African Youth Congress, the Transvaal and Natal Indian Congresses and COSATU and the many other formations of the Mass Democratic Movement.

I also salute the Black Sash and the National Union of South

African Students. We note with pride that you have acted as the conscience of white South Africa. Even during the darkest days in the history of our struggle you held the flag of liberty high. The large-scale mass mobilisation of the past few years is one of the key factors which led to the opening of the final chapter of our struggle.

I extend my greetings to the working class of our country. Your organised strength is the pride of our movement. You remain the most dependable force in the struggle to end exploitation and oppression.

I pay tribute to the many religious communities who carried the campaign for justice forward when the organisations for our people were silenced.

I greet the traditional leaders of our country—many of you continue to walk in the footsteps of great heroes like Hintsa and Sekhukune.

I pay tribute to the endless heroism of youth, you, the young lions. You, the young lions, have energised our entire struggle.

I pay tribute to the mothers and wives and sisters of our nation. You are the rock-hard foundation of our struggle. Apartheid has inflicted more pain on you than on anyone else.

On this occasion, we thank the world community for their great contribution to the anti-apartheid struggle. Without your support our struggle would not have reached this advanced stage. The sacrifice of the frontline states will be remembered by South Africans forever.

My salutations would be incomplete without expressing my deep appreciation for the strength given to me during my long and lonely years in prison by my beloved wife and family. I am convinced that your pain and suffering was far greater than my own.

Before I go any further I wish to make the point that I intend making only a few preliminary comments at this stage. I will make a more complete statement only after I have had the opportunity to consult with my comrades.

Today the majority of South Africans, black and white, recognise that apartheid has no future. It has to be ended by our own decisive mass action in order to build peace and security. The mass campaign of defiance and other actions of our organisation and people can only culminate in the establishment of democracy. The destruction caused by apartheid on our subcontinent is incalculable. The fabric of family life of millions of my people has been shattered. Millions are homeless and unemployed. Our economy lies in ruins and our people are embroiled in political strife. Our resort to the armed struggle in 1960 with the formation of the military wing of the A.N.C., Umkhonto we Sizwe, was a purely defensive action against the violence of apartheid. The factors which necessitated the armed struggle still exist today. We have no option but to continue. We express the hope that a climate conducive to a negotiated settlement will be created soon so that there may no longer be the need for the armed struggle.

I am a loyal and disciplined member of the African National Congress. I am therefore in full agreement with all of its objectives, strategies and tactics.

The need to unite the people of our country is as important a task now as it always has been. No individual leader is able to take on this enormous task on his own. It is our task as leaders to place our views before our organisation and to allow the democratic structures to decide. On the question of democratic practice, I feel duty bound to make the point that a leader of the movement is a person who has been democratically elected at a national conference. This is a principle which must be upheld without any exceptions.

Today, I wish to report to you that my talks with the government have been aimed at normalising the political situation in the country. We have not as yet begun discussing the basic demands of the struggle. I wish to stress that I myself have at no time entered into negotiations about the future of our country except to insist on a meeting between the A.N.C. and the government.

Mr. De Klerk has gone further than any other Nationalist president in taking real steps to normalise the situation. However, there are further steps as outlined in the Harare Declaration that have to be met before negotiations on the basic demands of our people can begin. I reiterate our call for, inter alia, the immediate ending of the State of Emergency and the freeing of all, and not only some, political prisoners. Only such a normalised situation, which allows for free political activity, can allow us to consult our people in order to obtain a mandate.

The people need to be consulted on who will negotiate and on the content of such negotiations. Negotiations cannot take place above the heads or behind the backs of our people. It is our belief that the future of our country can only be determined by a body which is democratically elected on a non-racial basis. Negotiations on the dismantling of apartheid will have to address the overwhelming demand of our people for a democratic, non-racial and unitary South Africa. There must be an end to white monopoly on political power and a fundamental restructuring of our political and economic systems to ensure that the inequalities of apartheid are addressed and our society thoroughly democratised.

It must be added that Mr. De Klerk himself is a man of integrity who is acutely aware of the dangers of a public figure not honouring his undertakings. But as an organisation we base our policy and strategy on the harsh reality we are faced with. And this reality is that we are still suffering under the policy of the Nationalist government.

Our struggle has reached a decisive moment. We call on our people to seize this moment so that the process towards democracy is rapid and uninterrupted. We have waited too long for our freedom. We can no longer wait. Now is the time to intensify the struggle on all fronts. To relax our efforts now would be a mistake which generations to come will not be able to forgive. The sight of freedom looming on the horizon should encourage us to redouble our efforts.

It is only through disciplined mass action that our victory can be assured. We call on our white compatriots to join us in the shaping of a new South Africa. The freedom movement is a political home for you too. We call on the international community to continue the campaign to isolate the apartheid regime. To lift sanctions now would be to run the risk of aborting the process towards the complete eradication of apartheid.

Our march to freedom is irreversible. We must not allow fear to stand in our way. Universal suffrage on a common voters' role in a united democratic and non-racial South Africa is the only way to peace and racial harmony.

In conclusion I wish to quote my own words during my trial in 1964. They are true today as they were then:

'I have fought against white domination and I have fought against black domination. I have cherished the ideal of a democratic and free society in which all persons live together in harmony and with equal opportunities. It is an ideal which I hope to live for and to achieve. But if needs be, it is an ideal for which I am prepared to die.'

49

YES WE CAN

Barack Obama

Chicago, U.S.A.

4 November 2008

After days of anticipation, the verdict was out—Barack Obama emerged victorious in the election and became the first black President of the United States. The public's jubilation was through the roof.

Everyone doubted that a black man would be able to win the presidential election, though most of them hoped he would. Obama delivered the following speech after he won, indicating that his success was proof of social and political emancipation in America's attitude.

Hello, Chicago.

If there is anyone out there who still doubts that America is a place where all things are possible, who still wonders if the dream of our founders is alive in our time, who still questions the power of our democracy, tonight is your answer.

It's the answer told by lines that stretched around schools and churches in numbers this nation has never seen, by people who waited three hours and four hours, many for the first time in their lives, because they believed that this time must be different, that their voices could be that difference.

It's the answer spoken by young and old, rich and poor, Democrat and Republican, black, white, Hispanic, Asian, Native American, gay, straight, disabled and not disabled. Americans who sent a message to the world that we have never been just a collection of individuals or a collection of red states and blue states. We are, and always will be, the United States of America.

It's the answer that led those who've been told for so long by so many to be cynical and fearful and doubtful about what we can achieve to put their hands on the arc of history and bend it once more toward the hope of a better day.

It's been a long time coming, but tonight, because of what we did on this day, in this election, at this defining moment, change has come to America.

A little bit earlier this evening, I received an extraordinarily gracious call from Senator McCain.

Senator McCain fought long and hard in this campaign. And he's fought even longer and harder for the country that he loves. He has endured sacrifices for America that most of us cannot begin to imagine. We are better off for the service rendered by this brave and selfless leader.

I congratulate him; I congratulate Governor Palin for all that they've achieved. And I look forward to working with them to renew this nation's promise in the months ahead.

I want to thank my partner in this journey, a man who campaigned from his heart, and spoke for the men and women he grew up with on the streets of Scranton . . . and rode with on the train home to Delaware, the vice president-elect of the United States, Joe Biden.

And I would not be standing here tonight without the unyielding support of my best friend for the last sixteen years . . . the rock of our family, the love of my life, the nation's next first lady . . . Michelle Obama.

Sasha and Malia . . . I love you both more than you can imagine. And you have earned the new puppy that's coming with us . . . to the White House.

And while she's no longer with us, I know my grandmother's watching, along with the family that made me who I am. I miss them tonight. I know that my debt to them is beyond measure.

To my sister Maya, my sister Auma, all my other brothers and sisters, thank you so much for all the support that you've given me. I am grateful to them.

And to my campaign manager, David Plouffe . . . the unsung hero of this campaign, who built the best—the best political campaign, I think, in the history of the United States of America.

To my chief strategist David Axelrod . . . who's been a partner with me every step of the way.

To the best campaign team ever assembled in the history of politics . . . you made this happen, and I am forever grateful for what you've sacrificed to get it done.

But above all, I will never forget who this victory truly belongs to. It belongs to you. It belongs to you.

I was never the likeliest candidate for this office. We didn't start with much money or many endorsements. Our campaign was not hatched in the halls of Washington. It began in the backyards of Des Moines and the living rooms of Concord and the front porches of Charleston.

It was built by working men and women who dug into what little savings they had to give five dollars and ten dollars and twenty dollars to the cause. It grew strength from the young people who rejected the myth of their generation's apathy; who left their homes and their families for jobs that offered little pay and less sleep. It drew strength from the not-so-young people who braved the bitter cold and scorching heat to knock on doors of perfect strangers, and from the millions of Americans who volunteered and organized and proved that more than two centuries later a government of the people, by the people, and for the people has not perished from the Earth. This is your victory.

And I know you didn't do this just to win an election. And I know you didn't do it for me. You did it because you understand the enormity of the task that lies ahead. For even as we celebrate tonight, we know the challenges that tomorrow will bring are the greatest of our lifetime—two wars, a planet in peril, the worst financial crisis in a century.

Even as we stand here tonight, we know there are brave Americans waking up in the deserts of Iraq and the mountains of Afghanistan to risk their lives for us.

There are mothers and fathers who will lie awake after the children fall asleep and wonder how they'll make the mortgage or pay their doctors' bills or save enough for their child's college education.

There's new energy to harness, new jobs to be created, new schools to build, and threats to meet, alliances to repair.

The road ahead will be long. Our climb will be steep. We may not get there in one year or even in one term. But, America, I have never been more hopeful than I am tonight that we will get there. I promise you, we as a people will get there.

There will be setbacks and false starts. There are many who won't agree with every decision or policy I make as president. And we know the government can't solve every problem.

But I will always be honest with you about the challenges we face. I will listen to you, especially when we disagree. And, above all, I will ask you to join in the work of remaking this nation, the only way it's been done in America for two hundred and twenty-one years—block by block, brick by brick, calloused hand by calloused hand.

What began twenty-one months ago in the depths of winter cannot end on this autumn night.

This victory alone is not the change we seek. It is only the chance for us to make that change. And that cannot happen if we go back to the way things were.

It can't happen without you, without a new spirit of service, a new spirit of sacrifice.

So let us summon a new spirit of patriotism, of responsibility, where each of us resolves to pitch in and work harder and look after not only ourselves but each other.

Let us remember that, if this financial crisis taught us anything, it's that we cannot have a thriving Wall Street while Main Street suffers.

In this country, we rise or fall as one nation, as one people. Let's resist the temptation to fall back on the same partisanship and pettiness and immaturity that has poisoned our politics for so long.

Let's remember that it was a man from this state who first carried the banner of the Republican Party to the White House, a party founded on the values of self-reliance and individual liberty and national unity.

Those are values that we all share. And while the Democratic Party has won a great victory tonight, we do so with a measure of humility and determination to heal the divides that have held back our progress.

As Lincoln said to a nation far more divided than ours, we are not enemies but friends. Though passion may have strained, it must not break our bonds of affection.

And to those Americans whose support I have yet to earn,

I may not have won your vote tonight, but I hear your voices. I need your help. And I will be your president, too. And to all those watching tonight from beyond our shores, from parliaments and palaces, to those who are huddled around radios in the forgotten corners of the world, our stories are singular, but our destiny is shared, and a new dawn of American leadership is at hand.

To those—to those who would tear the world down: We will defeat you. To those who seek peace and security: We support you. And to all those who have wondered if America's beacon still burns as bright: Tonight we proved once more that the true strength of our nation comes not from the might of our arms or the scale of our wealth, but from the enduring power of our ideals: democracy, liberty, opportunity and unyielding hope.

That's the true genius of America: that America can change. Our union can be perfected. What we've already achieved gives us hope for what we can and must achieve tomorrow.

This election had many firsts and many stories that will be told for generations. But one that's on my mind tonight is about a woman who cast her ballot in Atlanta. She's a lot like the millions of others who stood in line to make their voice heard in this election except for one thing: Ann Nixon Cooper is one hundred and six years old.

She was born just a generation past slavery; a time when there were no cars on the road or planes in the sky; when someone like her couldn't vote for two reasons—because she was a woman and because of the colour of her skin.

And tonight, I think about all that she's seen throughout her century in America—the heartache and the hope; the struggle and the progress; the times we were told that we can't, and the people who pressed on with that American creed:

Yes we can.

At a time when women's voices were silenced and their hopes

dismissed, she lived to see them stand up and speak out and reach out for the ballot.

Yes we can.

When there was despair in the dust bowl and depression across the land, she saw a nation conquer fear itself with a New Deal, new jobs, a new sense of common purpose.

Yes we can.

When the bombs fell on our harbour and tyranny threatened the world, she was there to witness a generation rise to greatness and a democracy was saved.

Yes we can.

She was there for the buses in Montgomery, the hoses in Birmingham, a bridge in Selma, and a preacher from Atlanta who told a people that we shall overcome.

Yes we can.

A man touched down on the moon, a wall came down in Berlin, a world was connected by our own science and imagination.

And this year, in this election, she touched her finger to a screen, and cast her vote, because after one hundred and six years in America, through the best of times and the darkest of hours, she knows how America can change.

Yes we can.

America, we have come so far. We have seen so much. But there is so much more to do. So tonight, let us ask ourselves—if our children should live to see the next century; if my daughters should be so lucky to live as long as Ann Nixon Cooper, what change will they see? What progress will we have made?

This is our chance to answer that call. This is our moment.

This is our time, to put our people back to work and open doors of opportunity for our kids; to restore prosperity and promote the cause of peace; to reclaim the American dream and reaffirm that fundamental truth, that, out of many, we are one; that while we breathe, we hope. And where we are met with cynicism and doubts and those who tell us that we can't, we will respond with that timeless creed that sums up the spirit of a people:

Yes, we can.

Thank you; God bless you, and may God bless the United States of America.

50

WHO YOU ARE AND WHAT YOU STAND FOR

Michelle Obama

Columbus, Ohio, U.S.A.

5 May 2012

Six months before presidential election of 2012, Michelle Obama delivered the following speech to the Ohio State University students.

Oh, wow. Thank you guys. Wow. It sounds like you all are already fired up and ready to go. This is amazing. It is truly amazing. And you know what? Being here with all of you today . . . let me tell you: I'm feeling pretty fired up and ready to go myself. I really am. But there is a reason why we're here today. And—

[Man in crowd: We love you!]

And we love you too! And it's not just because we support one extraordinary man. Although I'll admit I'm a little biased, because I think our president is awesome. And it's not just because we want to win an election. We are here because of the values we believe in. We're here because of the vision for this country that we all share. We're here because we want all our children to have a good education, right? Schools that push them, and inspire them; prepare them for good jobs. We want our parents and our grandparents to retire with dignity, because we believe that after a lifetime of hard work, they should enjoy their golden years.

We want to restore that basic middle-class security for our families, because we believe that folks shouldn't go bankrupt because they get sick. They shouldn't lose their home because someone loses a job. We believe that responsibility should be rewarded, and hard work should pay off. And, truly, these are basic American values. They're the same values that so many of us were raised with, including myself. You see, my father was a blue-collar city worker at the city water plant, and my family lived in a little-bitty apartment on the South Side of Chicago. And neither of my parents had the chance to go to college.

But let me tell you what my parents did do. They saved. They sacrificed. I mean, they poured everything they had into me and my brother. They wanted us to have the kind of education they could only dream of. And, while pretty much all of my college tuition came from student loans and grants, my dad still paid a little-bitty portion of that tuition himself. And let me tell you: every semester, my dad was determined to pay that bill right on time, because he was so proud to be sending his kids to college. And he couldn't bear the thought of me or my brother missing that registration deadline because his check was late.

Like so many people in this country, my father took great pride in being able to earn a living that allowed him to handle his responsibility to his family, to pay all of his bills, and to pay them on time. And, truly, more than anything else, that is what's at stake. It's that fundamental promise, that no matter who you are or how you started out, if you work hard, you can build a decent life for yourself and, yes, an even better life for your kids. And it is that promise that binds us together as Americans. It's what makes us who we are. And whether it's equal pay for women, or health care for our kids; whether it's tax cuts for middle-class families, or student loans for our young people; that is what my husband has been fighting for every single day as president. Every single day.

And let me tell you something: as First Lady, I have had the chance to see, up-close and personal, what being president looks like. Right? I have seen how the issues that come across a president's desk are always the hard ones.

[Woman in crowd: You're beautiful, Michelle!]

But in all seriousness. These problems: they're always the hard ones. The problems with no clear solutions. The judgment calls where the stakes are so high and there's no margin for error. And as president, you can get all kinds of advice from all kinds of people, but at the end of the day, when it comes time to make that decision, all you have to guide you are your life experiences. Your values. And your vision for this country. That's all you have. In the end, when you're making those impossible choices, it all boils down to who you are and what you stand for.

And we all know what Barack Obama is. Who he is. We all know what our president stands for, right? He is the son of a single mother who struggled to put herself through school, and pay the bills. That's who he is. He's the grandson of a woman who woke up before dawn every day to catch a bus to her job at the bank. And even though Barack's grandmother worked hard to help support his family—and she was good at her job—like so many women, she hit that glass ceiling, and men no more qualified than she was were promoted up the ladder ahead of her. So believe me: Barack knows what it means when a family struggles. He knows what it means when someone doesn't have a chance to fulfill their potential. And what you need to know, America: those are the experiences that have made him the man and the president he is today.

But I have said this before, and I will say it again and again: Barack cannot do this alone. And fortunately, he never has. We have always moved this country forward together. And today, more than ever before, Barack needs your help. He needs your help. He needs your help. He needs every single one of you. Every single one of you to give just a little part of your life each week to this campaign. He needs you to register those voters, right? And to all of the college students out there, all of you: if you're going to be moving over the summer, remember to register at your new address in the fall, you got that? Get that done!

Barack needs you to join one of our neighbourhood teams, and start organizing in your community. And just let me say: if there have ever been any doubts about the difference that you can make, I just want you to remember that in the end, this all could come down to those few thousand people who register to vote. Think about it. It could all come down to those last few thousand votes who get out to the polls on November the sixth. And when you average that out over this entire state, it might mean registering just one more person in your town. It might mean helping just one more person in your community get out and vote on election day.

So know this—with every door you knock on, with every call you make, with every conversation you have—I want you to remember that this could be the one that makes the difference. This could be the one. Remember that. That is exactly the kind of impact that each of you can have. Now, I am not going to kid you: this journey is going to be long, and it is going to be hard. But know that that is how change always happens in this country. And if we keep showing up, if we keep fighting the good fight, then eventually we get there. We always do. Maybe not in our lifetimes, but maybe in our children's lifetimes. Maybe in our grandchildren's lifetimes.

Because in the end, that's what this is all about. That is what I think about when I tuck my girls in at night. I think about the world I want to leave for them, and for all of our sons and our daughters.

I think about how I want to do for them what my dad did for me. I want to give them a foundation for their dreams. I want to give them opportunities worthy of their promise. I want to give them that sense of limitless possibility, that belief that here in America, there is always something better out there if you're willing to work for it. So we just cannot turn back now, right?

We have come so far, but we have so much more to do. And if we want to keep on moving forward, then we need to work our hearts out for the man that I have the pleasure of introducing here today. Are you ready? It is my privilege to introduce my husband, and our president. President Barack Obama!